THE PEOPLE'S GAME
HOW TO SAVE FOOTBALL

Gary Neville
With Rob Draper

HODDER

First published in Great Britain in 2022 by Hodder & Stoughton
An Hachette UK company

This paperback edition published in 2023

1

A CIP catalogue record for this title is available from the British Library

Paperback ISBN 9781529396010
ebook ISBN 9781529395990

Typeset in Sabon MT by Hewer Text UK Ltd, Edinburgh
Printed and bound in Great Britain by Clays Ltd, Elcograf S.p.A.

Hodder & Stoughton policy is to use papers that are natural, renewable
and recyclable products and made from wood grown in sustainable
forests. The logging and manufacturing processes are expected to
conform to the environmental regulations of the country of origin.

Hodder & Stoughton Ltd
Carmelite House
50 Victoria Embankment
London EC4Y 0DZ

www.hodder.co.uk

THE PEOPLE'S GAME

CONTENTS

PREFACE

When I finally finished *The People's Game* in the summer of 2022, I felt that football was in a good place, with an independent regulator imminent. As I sit down to reflect, almost a year later, that feeling remains and yet it hardly does justice to the political turmoil we've been through since then.

We're on our third Prime Minister since that summer, and it became clear during the short-lived reign of Liz Truss, the 49-day PM, that the hard work that was done to persuade people of the benefits of a regulator had been in vain. Tracey Crouch's report on football was about to be unceremoniously punted into the long grass and you could almost hear the champagne corks popping at the Premier League. Our best hope was that Labour would be elected, as Keir Starmer had made clear they would bring in regulation for football.

To be fair, current Prime Minister Rishi Sunak has done the right thing and recognised that there is cross-party support to help football create a better, more balanced, model and the Government's proposals, known as a White Paper, have many positives.

When I set out in 2020 calling for independent regulation with a group headed by former FA chairman David Bernstein, I don't think we imagined how far we would travel, and how quickly. The government's White Paper, titled "A sustainable future - reforming club football governance" and published in February 2023, covers much of what we asked for in this book.

There will be enhanced financial monitoring of clubs and a stricter licensing system, with clubs having to declare who is the ultimate beneficial owner, with government agencies empowered to investigate and assist inquiries. There will better corporate governance and a requirement for owners to disclose their financial plans. There will be key rules to protect a club's heritage, such as the name, badge and kit, which could only be changed with meaningful consent, which would also apply to a proposed stadium relocation. There will be a minimum standard of engagement from clubs with their fans, though it isn't exactly clear how the regulator will achieve this. It is even considering whether Glazer-style leveraged buy-outs, where the debt is piled on to the club, should be barred. A regulator would even have the power to take over a club in exceptional circumstances, such as when a failed owner is obstructing a sale, as happened at the end with Bury. Crucially, clubs wouldn't be able to breakaway to set up their own Super League without regulator permission.

This would be a radical reshaping of the game and much needed. I won't relax until the legislation is over the line, because as is always the case in football, time waits for no one.

By the time you read this, it's likely Manchester United will be sold, something we anticipated back in 2022 at the end of the chapter on my former club. Having discussed the pros and cons of state ownership in the chapters on Manchester City and Newcastle United, it's possible that United might follow suit.

Manchester City, having escaped UEFA's charges, leapt straight from frying pan and into the fire and have since been charged by what looks like a more-robust Premier League inquiry. Chelsea, meanwhile, have been busy sacking managers, spending £600m on transfers, and giving players eight-year contracts. Let's hope they know what they're doing.

Life comes at you fast in football, so much so that I think there is an argument for some kind of temporary appointment while the new regulator is formulated. My fear now is that by the time we do get a regulator, the game will have changed irrevocably.

The Premier League and the English Football League are still in discussions about a fairer settlement for the game. Let's hope that is completed by the time this edition is published. If it isn't, then it will only go to show that how much a regulator is needed to knock heads together. I can understand why, on this particular issue, the current Government is reluctant to intervene directly and would prefer football to sort its own financial mess out: it would be odd for a free-market party to step in. But the threat that it might have to remains and I welcome that. It's time for the Premier League to rise to the occasion.

Even now, the bigger clubs, like the ones who tried to kill our game with a Super League, are moaning. They're saying they shouldn't bear any more of the burden than their less well-off competitors. When it comes to collecting money from TV deals, they seem to think the free market should prevail and they should always have the lion's share. When it comes to paying out, they declare that all shares should be split equally across the 20 clubs.

As you'll read in this book, what we witnessed with the attempt to set up a Super League was the attempted murder of English football. It won't be good enough if, over the next few years, the Big Six simply walk away from this shameful episode, like a failed murderer, who says: 'Oh well, I didn't actually kill anyone because you grabbed the weapon off me before I could. So, all's well that ends well.' They need to be held to account for what they tried to do and certainly the burden ought to fall proportionately on them when the bill for redistributing money through the game is calculated.

*   *   *

The basic premise of my argument hasn't changed. The Premier League needs to be the best in the business, as it is now, but required to stay within boundaries and fully recognising the role that fans play. A pyramid won't stand with just a shiny top; it needs a strong foundation. The redistribution settlement is vital, as is real-time financial monitoring for EFL clubs and even stronger owner tests.

Football is too important to be left in the hands of the greedy, wealthy elite. The government has recognised the devastation that can be caused by great local institutions, such as football clubs, being allowed to die. It doesn't guarantee success or insulate a club against mistakes, but with better and more joined-up regulation and monitoring, the worst examples of con-men and gamblers playing fast-and-loose with cherished cultural touchstones would be avoided.

It might not all be clear at the start. Like VAR, it will take time to settle and become accepted. I would hope that over five or ten years, the regulator might be able to hand its responsibilities back to a reformed and empowered Football Association. With structural change, the FA can do this job. There are many excellent people there, but it will take time.

I'd still like to believe that football will prove it's bigger than its critics, including me. I still work on the principle, and I think most people do, that if you have more you pay more. If your mate is facing a hard time financially, you make sure you buy him a pint. If someone in your family earns more, they pick up most of the bill when you eat out. I'd love to think Manchester United's new owners, or the new regime at Chelsea, would step up and say: 'You know what? This regulator will be good for the game and we'll fund it. We'll pay our share and a bit more.' The leading clubs of this country should behave like the guardians of the game, not ruthless capitalists.

My mind still goes back to Euro '96 when the England squad flew back from Hong Kong after a pre-tournament break and the plane was badly damaged. The FA were desperate for us to give them a name. They wanted someone to kick out of the squad and take the blame. Tony Adams, the England captain at the time, stood up in a team meeting and said: 'We're not giving them a name. We all take responsibility. We stick together as a team and all of our match fees will cover the cost of the damage and then some.' That's leadership.

What players and fans instinctively understand, and some of the richest clubs don't seem to get, is that when there's trouble, you stick together. Ultimately you're stronger for it. The Big Six should be leading the game through this, not being dragged along kicking, screaming and sulking into the new era.

We have an opportunity now to forge a new deal for English football and that can sustain it for the next 30 years. We can make it a world leader, not just on the pitch but off the pitch in terms of governance. This could consolidate football's role in society for our children and our grandchildren. The time is now. Let's seize the day.

Gary Neville, July 2023

INTRODUCTION

The good news is that we're winning. If you're a football fan and reading this book, I hope that you take heart and realise what English football could become in the next few years, largely thanks to what you helped to achieve.

On Sunday 18 April 2021, there was an attempted coup. John W. Henry, Joel Glazer, Stan Kroenke, Roman Abramovich, Sheikh Mansour and Joe Lewis attempted to steal the game from you. From us. From all of us who love football, who have grown up with it and for whom it is a huge part of our lives. It was a corporate heist, but the people fought back. And thankfully the government did the right thing and presented us with an extraordinary opportunity to reshape football thanks to a Fan-led Review, led by Tracey Crouch.

This is a book that was born out of that proposal to form a European Super League and the subsequent anger it caused. But it goes back further than that. When I was sat watching Manchester United v Burnley on that fateful day and launched into my attack on the European Super League, it was the final straw. Some people might think my interest in the governance of football, and the anger I felt, began that day. But the reality is that it was just a catalyst. I suppose I've always had some concerns about football. You could argue that I was schooled in it as a child, watching my mum and dad trying to hold a great community club like Bury together. Or as a pundit and journalist, watching the malign ownership of the Glazer family unravel after Sir Alex Ferguson retired. Or as an England player and coach watching the FA try to grapple with big issues. Or as a club owner at Salford, seeing football stare into the abyss during the Covid shutdown. No, my anger has been building for a long time.

As the pandemic started in the spring of 2020, former FA Chairman David Bernstein had asked me to be part of a group called Saving Our Beautiful Game, a group that included the Mayor of Manchester Andy Burnham, former Sports Minister Helen Grant, Lord King, the former governor of The Bank of England, former FA executive David Davies, Olympic gold medallist Denise Lewis and lawyer Greg Scott. Over long Zoom calls during the pandemic, we plotted a way to make football better. We had all been involved in the game at different levels. Anyone can see that the Premier League is a world-leading product. Everyone in the group wanted to preserve that. But most people with any involvement in the game can also see that, in terms of governance and regulation, the game is falling apart.

Bury had proved that to me. My hometown club folded in 2019, devastating the community I grew up in. My family ties to that club run deep, as you'll see when you read on. The death of Bury seemed to be a wake-up call. It prompted the government to make their manifesto commitment for a fan-led review of football. Then Covid struck and I spent much of that time on Zoom calls with League Two owners genuinely concerned as to whether their clubs would survive as we shut down that current season and then prepared to start another without fans.

In October 2020, we launched our manifesto. Its key point was that there should be a new independent regulator for football to make radical reforms. It should:

1. Decide on new ways of distributing funds to the wider game based on a funding formula and a fair levy payable by the Premier League.
2. Set up a new and comprehensive licensing system for the professional game.
3. Review the causes of financial stress in the English Football League [EFL] including the levels of the solidarity payments down the football pyramid. It should decide whether parachute payments made to relegated Premier League clubs were fair and investigate the possibility of salary caps and a mandatory reduction in player wages if relegated.
4. Implement governance reforms at the FA which are essential to ensure it is truly independent, diverse and representative of English football today.
5. Liaise with supporters' organisations to progress issues that are of concern to fans and provide a greater voice for supporters.
6. Study lessons from abroad and seek to champion supporter involvement in the running of clubs.

At that point we couldn't have known that a counter plot was brewing, with motives diametrically opposed to ours, to make football a game for the few and not the many.

Within six months of our plan dropping, John W. Henry and Joel Glazer outlined their vision for the future with the European Super League, enabled and supported by Stan Kroenke, Roman Abramovich, Sheikh Mansour and Joe Lewis. Where they saw a chance to make a game for the few – a private club for billionaires hiding away in tax havens or in jurisdictions outside European and UK legislation – we were trying to build a game for the people, to rebalance the direction of travel. We wanted to steer us back to what football was intended to be. They wanted to drive off into the distance with the crown jewels.

The truth is that football in this country has been rusting and rotten beneath its glamorous sheen. We've all just muddled along because the Premier League is such good entertainment content it was easier not to challenge. Pep and Jürgen, José and Rafa; Mohamed Salah, Kevin De Bruyne, Eden Hazard; Manchester United's treble; transfer deadline day; big-money signings: all of this prime content has distracted us from what football really is and what it could be again.

But sometimes there's a breaking point. And a mix of American capitalists, an oligarch about whom evidence before the High Court in 2012 clearly showed had privileged access to Vladimir Putin and a British tax exile sunning himself in the Bahamas managed to find ours. It was stupid of them really. But it seems the tensions around Covid and the pandemic panicked them into making their move. Now they can't take it back. A poorly recorded video with a mealy-mouthed apology from John W. Henry or Joel Glazer turning up to the fans' forum for the first time in twenty years isn't going to win our trust. That's gone for ever now.

In a way they did us a favour. As you'll discover, without the Super League breakaway, the fan-led review promised by the government might only have focussed on EFL finances. Their misjudgement meant the review took in the whole game. That meant the report, Saving Our Beautiful Game, and similar work done by The Football Supporters' Association, who had been researching and planning for this moment, were ready for the fan led review. At the end of it all, when Tracey Crouch published her review, all of our objectives from Our Beautiful Game had been addressed. She recommended an independent regulator, she called for a change to the way TV money is distributed to ensure the pyramid is protected, she called for stricter governance on owner-ship and for fans to have a stake in their club's decision-making. Where reform is hard, like it can be at the FA, with its statutes dating back to 1863, a new regulator can be empowered to break the log jam and enforce change. The government has accepted all these points and by the time this book is published we should have the details of what regulation will look like. When we launched our manifesto in October 2020, we couldn't have imagined how quickly events would turn to see so many our concerns addressed. I must congratulate David Bernstein for bringing this group together and having the foresight and knowledge that the breaking point was on its way and to be ready and waiting to pounce.

But football in this country is in a similar place to the banks in 2008 or in newspapers in 2011, where entire industries had to reform. A crisis always accelerates change and probably Covid and the war in Ukraine are the reason why the creaking structures that previously held the game together now appear so vulnerable. The governance that was set in place thirty years ago when the Premier League was formed wasn't even right then. Since then, globalisation, oligarchs and nation states have overwhelmed the game's authorities. And in the lower leagues, even more conmen and naïve dreamers than ever before have turned up to destroy much-loved clubs, riding roughshod over communities as they do so. It's time for change. Many age-old certainties have been swept aside since 2016. The political divisions in our country have made us more sharply attuned than ever to liars who promise the world with no intent to deliver and only for short term gain.

The challenge for those of us who opposed the Super League is how do we shape football for the future, maintaining a world-class Premier League but with a strengthened and protected pyramid below it. The pyramid is our unique selling point and I believe the reason why English football is more valuable than the closed American franchise systems. How do we ensure the recommendations of the fan-led review are implemented and how do we plot the way forward?

I've been extremely fortunate to earn a very good living from football, specifically the Premier League. I do believe the Premier League is the best in the world. I don't believe it's ever been better in terms of the quality of the teams – notably Manchester City and Liverpool (it hurts to write that) – and the coaches, with the likes of Pep Guardiola, Jürgen Klopp, Antonio Conte and Thomas Tuchel all plying their trade there. I've also been fortunate to see football from all sides. When I was growing up, as you will see in this book, football governed my house long before I was playing for Manchester United, with Bury's financial difficulties dominating my childhood as my mum and dad battled to save the club. As a fan, I watched Manchester United. I played, I coached and managed – albeit not very successfully – and am a journalist working in the media. I've been a representative of the players' union, the Professional Footballers' Association, and I'm now a co-owner of Salford City in League Two and previously was a co-owner of Salford City in non-league for five years. We had to navigate that Covid season where all these issues came to a head, and spent most weeks on Zoom calls with fellow owners.

I spoke to a lot of people for this book. I could have spoken to a lot more. I wish there was even more time and space to address the issues we haven't dealt with here. UEFA and FIFA would take a whole new book of their own. So I'm not pretending this is exhaustive, nor that I have all the answers, but I felt it was the right time to put some principles and beliefs down on paper. Rather than just sounding off on Twitter, I have tried to research, listen and pull together as many themes as possible that are relevant to our game in England and plot a way forward. Most of that is about the money: how we earn it and what to do with it. To understand that, you have to understand why a club like Bury is important and how they became symbolic of the inability of English football to come together when that club collapsed. I wanted to know more about how the women's game developed in this country and why it's lagged behind men's football. The inspirational performance of the England women's team this summer, winning Euro 2022, gripped the nation. It demonstrated the vast potential of the game. Let's seize the moment. We must talk about racism, as I'm sick of hashtags and campaigns. I would like something to change. And I wanted fans to have a voice. Without the work of the Football Supporters' Association, Spirit of Shankly, the Arsenal, Chelsea, Manchester United and Tottenham Supporters' Trusts and Manchester City Supporters' Club, we would never have convinced the government to move against the Super League in the first place. I want to pay tribute to them and the many other fans' groups that have done so much. If this book moves you to action, I hope the first step will be that you join your club's Supporters' Trust or equivalent organisation. There was a moment of unity there where it didn't matter whether you were Rotherham or Liverpool, Orient or Arsenal. We could all rally around one flag: the importance of the pyramid and access to competition.

The greed of the Big Six clubs has presented us with an opportunity that could lay a foundation for the next fifty years. Hopefully, our grandchildren will be watching and playing football in this country then and it will be just as dynamic, exciting and attractive to outside investors as it is now. Yet maybe it could have some deeper foundational roots, something to tether it to the people who sustain it.

It may seem like a dream but the next two or three years, when an independent regulator is likely to be introduced to football, is the opportunity of a lifetime. But it won't happen without a movement of fans continually pressurising the authorities. The outburst of anger against the Super League was unprecedented. We need to keep the fire burning for now, not allow it to be dampened down by superficial reform. Already the Premier League is on manoeuvres. They are actively fighting the idea of an independent regulator for football. My concern is they will now try to scheme and dilute the idea so that it is so weak it makes no difference to them. The fact that the Premier League have been near silent on the outcome of the Fan Led review should make us even more aware. They have proven on multiple occasions in the last few years that they cannot be trusted, either as a collective or within their various cliques. They seemingly don't trust each other. This is equally worrying. While they might never admit it publicly, privately I suspect some of them think they may benefit hugely from an independent regulator.

We need to maintain and harness the energy that mad weekend in April 2021 created.

These are not impossible problems to fix. We can build more competitive balance into the game. We can have a say in who owns our clubs and how they're run. It need not be necessary for clubs to bankrupt themselves, nor should they live in fear that relegation will ruin them financially. We can build a better game. We can distribute money more equitably. We can make the grassroots of this nation's game thrive. Football, the culture it creates and community that surrounds it, is one of this nation's greatest strengths. We can rebuild and restore that so it isn't just a free-market basket case but rather something to be envied around the world. Not just the Premier League, but the whole of our football pyramid.

When it comes down to it, football people are one people. We might be different races, have different ideas, different sexualities, different politics. But we have a common interest whether we're a Bury fan or a Manchester United fan. That means a movement that has the potential to shape society: the People's Game isn't the property of John W. Henry, Joel Glazer, Stan Kroenke, Sheikh Mansour and Joe Lewis. It's our game, our beautiful game.

1

EUROTRASH

'We don't like it and we hope it doesn't happen.'

On Sunday 18 April, during a routine Sky broadcast of Manchester United v Burnley, news began to leak through of proposals for a breakaway European Super League led by Real Madrid, Juventus, Manchester United, Liverpool and Arsenal, which would also include Barcelona, Atletico Madrid, Chelsea, Manchester City, Tottenham, AC Milan and Internazionale and which was backed by investment bank J.P.Morgan. Bayern Munich, Borussia Dortmund and Paris St Germain had declined to join the breakaway.

When you're a kid on holiday, you'll be sat on the edge of the pool and you know it's time to jump in without your armbands for the first time. You'll have put it off previously, found excuses. But eventually you know it's time to go for it. And that's always a difficult moment. Sometimes you step back, walk to your sun lounger and tell yourself: 'I'll do it tomorrow. Or the day after.' Sometimes you end up putting it off until the week after. Or the holiday after. But there comes a point where you know you have to jump in the deep end. There are those moments in life when your stomach churns and you go for it even though you're not quite sure what's going to happen.

Towards the end of the 2020–21 season, with no fans in the

stadia, every game was a bit depressing. We were all going through the motions. It was Manchester United v Burnley on that particular Sunday and it was a pretty boring match, to be fair. Matt, our producer for the match-day, came on to my headset and said: 'Gary, there's going to be an announcement, later on, that there's a breakaway Super League being formed. You need to be across this.' I had read something in *The Times*, before the game, a story by Martyn Ziegler. But no one had really cottoned on to how big this was and so it wasn't something that had immediately alarmed me.

But as the second half went on, Matt said: 'We're getting more detail now, and we think it's going to be very big. It's essentially a franchise league, twelve clubs, four different countries and they're breaking away to create their own league.' The English teams would stay in the Premier League, but ultimately it wouldn't matter where they finished, because they were breaking clear of the need to qualify for European competition; they would always be in the Super League. Ultimately the aim was to have fifteen permanent clubs and five qualifying each year, but the qualifying criteria for other clubs was so tight that the proposed new league was effectively pulling up the draw-bridge and abandoning European football in the middle of a pandemic.

When I was told that, I went. I just instinctively felt this is not right. I grew angrier minute by minute in the second half. I was drawing on years of frustration: my unhappiness at the Glazer family, my anger at what had happened to my home-town club Bury, my despair at how the Premier League had failed to lead during Covid. This all had come to a head during the pandemic. In that terrible winter of Covid, when the game was under pressure, football had turned in on itself. It seemed structurally incapable of doing the right thing. Instead, it was like cats in a bag fighting themselves. At a time when people were desperate and crying out for help, the Premier League was arguing over whether to scrap relegation for a season to, it seemed to me, keep themselves protected. It was as though they were scrambling for the lifeboats ready to leave the weaker passengers behind. They then took ten months to come up with a rescue package for the English Football League (EFL). Ten months!

Then we had Manchester United and Liverpool's Project Big Picture, which was their first stab at seizing control by reforming the Premier League in October 2020. There were some aspects of that reform of domestic football that I liked, specifically redrawing the TV deal for football so that the EFL became more sustainable. That might have helped save the likes of Bury and ensured that relegation from the Premier League wasn't a financial catastrophe that needed to be addressed with a £44m parachute payment, which completely distorts the Championship. Yet the more you picked away at the details, the more you realised it was a naked land grab by the top six clubs: United, Liverpool, Manchester City, Arsenal, Tottenham and Chelsea. Maybe we could have negotiated something decent out of that. But it was killed by the fourteen clubs outside the Big Six.

Having not got their way with Big Picture, then came Super League. We were facing the biggest global crisis of our generation and some of our leading clubs were stepping up. They led the way in caring for their community, running food banks, providing mental health support. They had actually built up some goodwill. But all the time it appears they were thinking about how they could exploit it to grasp more control and money for themselves. 'Never waste a good crisis' became a phrase we heard throughout the pandemic. For some billionaires that seemingly meant never waste the opportunity to try and grasp a few more pounds, roubles, dollars and dirhams for yourself.

All the while that lower-league clubs and football around the world was desperately trying to keep going, to make ends meet; all that time when we were all sat at home, missing funerals of loved ones, unable to say goodbye to parents and children who were dying; it seemed these lot were scheming and planning their way to financial Utopia. The sheer arrogance of it infuriated me. There would be no Paris St Germain, nor Bayern Munich, the two clubs who stayed well out when invited. Fair play to them for that. Clubs in places like Belgium, Holland and Slovakia would never have been able to qualify for this elite Super League, because only five clubs were to be allowed access each year. There were massive clubs from England and Italy that were going to be cut off and isolated – Roma, Everton, Napoli, Aston Villa. Then you think of Ajax, PSV and Feyenoord, all former European Cup winners. And all the great clubs around Europe that basically wouldn't be a part of this: Celtic, Rangers, Porto, Benfica, Valencia, Seville. And you start thinking about who's going to miss out every year on the elite European competition.

What really made me angry was the realisation that this would have required world-class scheming and planning, world-class secrecy and confidentiality. As a businessman, I get that things have to be confidential sometimes to get a project off the ground. But this was sneaking around during a pandemic and the end result would have been that the super-rich could cut themselves adrift of a sinking ship. I got more wound up in the second half and I thought: 'This is it. I'm going to go. I'm going to go and go big.' And you've got a parrot on one shoulder saying: 'Go for it, Gary!' While a second parrot on the other shoulder whispers: 'Am I getting too wound up here?' And then you go. You jump in without the armbands.

Sky Super Sunday, Manchester United v Burnley, 18 April 2021, transcript of post-match discussion

DAVID JONES [Sky Sports presenter]: Let's bring in Gary Neville, who, as you heard, was reacting to news as it seeped through while he was commentating on the game at Old Trafford this afternoon. Gary, what would you say, now that you've had a little time, this European breakaway league is all about and the reaction to it so far?

GARY NEVILLE: Well, the reaction to it is that it has been damned and rightly so. I'm a Manchester United fan and have been for forty years of my life. But I'm disgusted. Absolutely disgusted. I'm disgusted with Liverpool and Manchester United most. I mean, Liverpool. They pretend 'You'll Never Walk Alone', the people's club, the fans' club. Manchester United, one hundred years, born out of workers out here. And they're breaking away to a league without competition? That they can't be relegated from? It's an absolute disgrace and we have to wrestle back the power in this country from the clubs at the top of this league and that includes my club. I've been calling for twelve months, as part of another group, for an independent regulator to bring checks and balances in place to stop this happening. It's pure greed. They're imposters. They're nothing to do . . . the owners of this club, the owners of Liverpool, the owners of Chelsea, the owners of Manchester City, they're nothing to do with football in this country. There are a hundred-odd years of football in this country from fans that have lived and loved these clubs. And they need protecting, the fans need protecting. I've benefited from football hugely, I've made money out of football, I invest money into a football club. I'm not against money in football. But the principles and ethos of fair competition, the right to play the game so that Leicester win the league and reach the Champions League. Manchester United aren't even in the Champions League! Arsenal aren't even in the Champions League! We watched them earlier on today; they're an absolute shambles of a football club at the moment. Tottenham aren't in the Champions League. And they want a God-given right to be in there?! They're an absolute joke and, honestly, the time has come now, independent regulator, stop these clubs having the power base. Enough is enough!

JONES: There does seem to be the suggestion that they would need permission from the Premier League to take part, and without it, it would be a breakaway from not just UEFA competition but from our domestic competition. With that in mind, let's be clear about this, what is the motivation?

NEVILLE: You know what the motivation is. It's greed, Dave. My reaction earlier on wasn't an emotional reaction. Deduct them all points tomorrow. Put them at the bottom of the league. And take the money off them. Seriously. You have got to stamp on this. This is surely criminal. It's akin to a criminal act against football fans in this country. Make no mistake about it. This is the biggest sport in the world, the biggest sport in this country, and it's the same as a criminal act against the fans. Simple as that. Deduct points. Deduct their money. And punish them.

JONES: Do you think these clubs would have the courage, knowing what widespread condemnation there is, to go through with [this], Gary?

NEVILLE: Dave, they're bottle merchants. You never hear from the owners of these clubs. Absolute bottle merchants. They've got no voice. They'll probably hide for a few weeks and say it was nothing to do with them, they were only talking about it. Seriously, in the midst of a pandemic, an economic crisis, football clubs at National League level going bust nearly, furloughing players, clubs on the edge in Leagues One and Two and these lot are having Zoom calls about breaking away and basically having more greed? Joke.

I love watching football matches. I often still have the same excitement I had as a seven-year-old sat in the K Stand at Old Trafford. But I've been doing co-commentary and punditry for ten years now and in all honesty it's hard to maintain the intensity. When I first started I was thirty-seven; it seemed a natural route to channel my passion for the game. Back then I was focusing so hard to impress, I would come alive almost every week on co-commentary with comments that would get noticed. Like when I called David Luiz a PlayStation footballer, which wasn't scripted. It was just an instinctive reaction to what I was seeing. But I would be coming up with something flamboyant almost every week, because my thoughts were so fresh. But ten years in, it's harder to create new material and it's the big moments where you really come alive. That might be something unrelated to the game, such as the racism directed at Antonio Rüdiger at Tottenham, when there was some controversy over what I said about Boris Johnson and Jeremy Corbyn being embroiled in accusations of racism and how that enabled racists. In moments like that, you come alive. The Super League response was a moment like that.

It was emotional and instinctive in some ways, because when I find out about something forty-five minutes beforehand and it's a massive proposal, you don't have much time to prepare. I don't mean that it wasn't thought through, because I had been thinking about how football should reform for years and that had intensi- fied during the pandemic. I had the foundation of plans as to what should be done there in my head. But the jolt of the announcement and its confirmation mid-match, the sheer crass- ness and selfishness of it, is what provided the emotion for that battle cry.

That day was a lesson in the oldest rule in journalism. Anything can happen and you have to be prepared to go big if it does. It was a fairly drab end-of-season Premier League game, but the day ended up being a potentially historic one that might have marked the end of English football as we know it. I look back at my reac- tion, and the ability to act emotionally with passion while speak- ing cogently is what I want. I want to be emotional, I want to be passionate because, if I lose that, I'm dead.

I used strong language that day. I said I was disgusted by my football club, Manchester United, and that it was tantamount to a criminal act against the game. As news filtered through, I was struggling to stay calm especially when I heard more details of the proposal. Jamie Carragher and I always laugh about the fact that one of the first things I said to him when he joined me on *Monday Night Football* was: 'Don't go early!' By which I mean, you can go too big too soon: calling for a sacking, saying a team will defi- nitely be relegated. Then you can end up looking a right fool. Let it churn, let it breathe, let it settle.

But David Jones asked me the question and I just went for it. Within five minutes of coming off air, you walk to the car, and you wonder: 'How's that gone down?' It was the type of address that you're not really sure how it's going to be received and you fear looking at your phone. You sometimes look on social media anticipating what you might read. But, actually, it seemed the fans were with me. And that was important because if the fans aren't with you, you have to think again and change direction. I live close to the ground, so on the drive home I knew something big had happened, and by the time I arrived home the adrenaline was still pumping. And then I thought: 'No one's rung me.' My phone was quiet but it had gone viral.

Within half an hour of getting home, I did receive a call. The producer of *Monday Night Football*, Jack Hazzard, rang me. I wasn't due to be on the show the next day, but Jack said: 'Gary, I just had a call from above. We need you on the show tomorrow night with Carra.'

My initial thought was that I didn't think I should be. I had said my piece. There was nothing more to add. And I thought that this lot would bottle it; that's what they do. They would back down overnight. I went to bed at half past ten assuming just that, so I was asleep when the announcement came out at 11pm from the twelve clubs confirming that they were going ahead. When I woke up in the morning and saw that, I literally couldn't get to my train quickly enough.

On the way down to London started to think about all the plotting and scheming that the likes of Manchester United owner Joel Glazer and Liverpool owner John W. Henry must have been involved in over the preceding four- or five-month period, while the game was in desperation, struggling on its knees. Remember, at the start of Covid there were genuine fears that players might catch it playing a game, no one was sure. All that planning for Project Restart; at the time we didn't know whether players might potentially be risking their lives or not. Even though we weren't 100 per cent sure about the risks, they played on so that the likes of John W. Henry and Joel Glazer would be okay. And all the time, these lot were scheming, trying to create a franchise league that could destroy the whole ethos of English football. So I thought: 'We're going to go again and we all agreed we're not talking about anything else all night, even though there's a game on. We'll cover the game at half time, do five minutes before the game, but otherwise we're not going to talk about anything else all night, other than this.' And we never came off track throughout the broadcast.

JAMIE CARRAGHER

Gary wasn't supposed to be on *Monday Night Football*. It was supposed to be Robbie Fowler because the game was Leeds v Liverpool. But my thought process was: can Robbie still do it? Quite quickly Sky said no. We want Gary to come on. It left me in a bit of an awkward position because Robbie's a mate, but he understood the situation. So there was a lot of talking with Sky as the night went on. In some ways, it was a show that we had never done before because the whole point of *Monday Night Football* is to analyse the weekend's games. I just recall that on the way down to London, we all realised how big a show it was and how different it would be for the producers, for Dave Jones (the host) and for me and Gary.

We always have a meeting round about 10.30am at Sky and go through the ideas of the show. But this time it was basically with Gary Hughes, the head of football, and Jonathan Licht, who's the head of Sky Sports. And when they were in the room, we were thinking: 'Oh, this is pretty big.' In some ways it was almost as if me, Gary and Dave were going out to bat for a lot of other people. Sky were really worried about what this would lead to in the future, how it would affect them, would the Premier League still exist? That's when it hit home again that this was massive. And it was almost like being a player when you know you're going into a big game. I've felt like that going into a big show. I was thinking: 'What are you going to say? You have to make sure you deliver it right.'

I recall we were quite emotional about it, but sometimes that can be a good thing. I said I would never work on the

Super League if it was formed. It would obviously be on TV, be a massive money-spinner. And I just felt that we can't come on here and condemn these owners and then twelve months down the line, we'll be pitch-side at the Bernabéu doing Real Madrid v Liverpool in the Super League. I don't think it was that difficult a thing to say because we were that *against* it. I didn't see how we could possibly work on it.

You don't have an autocue on *Monday Night Football*; we always speak from our heart. Listen, in my job I don't think you can go out looking for trouble. I don't think that. But when something needs to be said it needs to be said. And, to be honest, I believe most people at Liverpool felt the same as me. A lot of people at the club didn't even know this was going on. Only the two or three people at the very top were involved, so I think a lot of people at the club felt let down. I was possibly speaking for about 90 per cent of people at Liverpool Football Club in some ways. But I would never worry about upsetting Liverpool's owners anyway, because I think I'm quite respectful of what they've done for the club. They've been really good owners for us. But when you own a football club, you will be held accountable for decisions you make and you have to accept that. And it's our job to call owners out in situations like this. It would have been a dereliction of duty if we hadn't. We would not have been doing our jobs right if we hadn't called them out on the show as we did. They can't complain at that because if you own a football club, you're up there to be scrutinised, you're in the public domain. And they were fair game for that for the decisions they took. They have to accept that.

By the time *Monday Night Football* started that night, it almost felt that, by then, everyone knew what was going on. Gary had made his passionate speech on the Sunday and it got a great reaction, rightly so. But most people probably weren't quite sure what was going on at that point. Then you wake up on Monday and read the papers, and you could see the story was building and building. We were on at seven o'clock and it was almost like this big build-up to the show. Hopefully people were wondering: 'What are Carragher and Neville going to say?' But the fact that the show was scheduled almost twenty-four hours after the announcement meant everyone was a lot more informed, the momentum had built, and that possibly helped us in that we knew we were speaking for the people.

On Monday morning, when I woke up and saw Joel Glazer's name and quotes on the press release, I thought: 'This is serious.' He wouldn't put his name to anything if he didn't think it was going to happen. He's not the type to put his head above the parapet unless it was certain. That's when I thought: 'This is happening, they're going for it.' Obviously I'd gone off on one on the *Super Sunday* and by Monday, Carra had gone, and, to be fair everyone had gone. The media had gone, the fans had gone.

Seeing that they had announced it overnight scared me, but it also told me how hopeless they were. This cabal of billionaire businessmen, who've had great entrepreneurial careers and have the best PR and communications machines around them – to have launched this in such a mangled way, with no one willing to talk in public to defend the idea, was inept. The only one who did speak publicly was Real Madrid president Florentino Pérez, who looked increasingly manic over the next couple of days. And with the best will in the world, if you're defending a controversial idea in the global court of public opinion, you need someone arguing your case in English on the BBC, Sky and in English-language newspapers. Did they really imagine they could hide behind press releases and scripted statements? How could they misread the room so badly that they thought they could just go and create a league that no one else could get in to apart from them and that they would deliver it at Sunday night at half past eleven?

It's even astonishing to me that they would allow this to come out ahead of a *Super Sunday* with *Monday Night Football* following the next day. If you have a radical and controversial idea, one that's potentially going to have a bit of a backlash, you're probably best not doing it any time around those shows. What did they think we were going to say? Just get in line, doff our caps? We don't care about who we upset in moments like this. That means that sometimes Sky may get a little bit annoyed with us and I'm sure the Premier League do too. We are willing to go against the grain. And this Super League proposal was toxic; it was pulling the pin out of the grenade and chucking it into the room.

I was most annoyed that my own club, Manchester United. The first club to go into the European Cup, born out of workers from Newton Heath around the Manchester and Salford area, the epitome of a working-class club. It has always had great working-class British managers like Sir Alex, Sir Matt Busby. The club of the Busby Babes and the Munich Air Disaster. All the things that this club has been through that helps to galvanise communities. And what had they become? They should be the protector and defender of English football. That's my view. I knew it wasn't true any more. But to me Manchester United and Liverpool football clubs, the most successful clubs, the biggest clubs, they are your leaders, your pioneers. They are the institutions everyone looks up to, the leaders in the game. If they behave properly, the rest will follow. But if they go sour, the rest of the game becomes rotten. And we have to grab it back.

There's no doubt clubs were suffering at the time, including Premier League clubs due to Covid and the corresponding lack of fans on matchdays. But then, apart from the whole human tragedy emerging around them, which was infinitely more important, in the football world, other clubs were suffering worse than them and haemorrhaging money. Every week I would be on Zoom calls with League Two clubs, with owners who weren't sure whether their club would come through this. We collectively voted to abandon the 2019-20 season. It was a truly desperate situation. Both leagues then struggled without crowds in 2020–21. The costs to put a game on are still significant when you've paid for staff and stewards to open up the stadium. And with next to no income coming back into the clubs, it meant a perilous situation for the majority of the 48 teams in these two leagues. When you think that the majority of money in the lower leagues comes from gate income, it's a very different model than the Premier League where the TV income is enormous.

You really do find out about people when there are points of stress, particularly economically, in football. You find out the real character and whether the game really does have the resilience and camaraderie. Rather than say: 'Right, this is a moment where we all stick together as one,' what they decided to do was basically go along and strip the game of money, pulling it all towards themselves. It would have been the end of English football, as we know it, which has always been meritocratic. Promotion and relegation are sacrosanct. If you win, all well and good. But no one gets a free pass. It's not the NFL.

David Jones, presenter Sky Sports *Super Sunday* and *Monday Night Football*

When Gary said his piece on *Super Sunday*, I had no idea what was coming, We had been drip-fed news through the day and then the Premier League made a statement condemning the plans, and I thought: 'Oh. This is serious. Because they never say anything about anything.'

We had abandoned our half-time analysis and just talked about this one issue, because everything else seemed irrelevant. After the game, I just wanted to see how far Gary would go. Obviously, it's my job to push him a bit, but he didn't need a lot of encouragement. It was dramatic stuff.

On the Sunday evening, we convened on the way back from the studios and we agreed we needed to get Gary on *Monday Night Football* as it was the only story in town and we needed to tackle it head on. He was initially reluctant, but the rest of us got to Sky quite early the next day (Monday), each a bit shell-shocked, and by then Gary was on the train down.

We realised this was an opportunity to have an impact and give it everything we could. The head of football and the deputy head of Sky Sports joined us in our meeting, which had never happened before, because we wanted them to explain what was at stake. That added to our desire to tackle it head on. We don't use autocue on *Monday Night Football* but I had scripted my opening lines. Statements kept coming in from the Prime Minister, from Prince William, head of FIFA. I just thought I would collate all of them into the opening. And my opening line was: 'This is a *Monday Night Football* like no other.'

Because we were late getting to the studios and there were no rehearsals, I did a practice run about ten minutes before going on air. And Gary turned to me and said: 'That's good that, Dave.' And he never ever compliments me.

I came down to studios in London on that Monday around two o'clock, later than I would normally get there, because my appearance wasn't planned. So I missed the initial meeting, but the Sky bosses had come into it and said: 'Look, this is dangerous. This is basically something that affects everybody within this company and football as a whole.' Sky were livid with it, but I'd already gone on one the day before so it's not like I had deliberately synchronised my views with Sky. But for Sky, the prospect of owning rights to a Premier League without the excitement of Champions League qualification was awful. It's just not the same product.

Although I had shuddered when I saw Joel Glazer's name on the launch document, going into the show I was 70/30 that they would bottle it. It was so unpopular! Crucially, they didn't seem to have squared off the UK government. They were going to court in Madrid, stopping UEFA from punishing them, citing Spanish and European law. That seemed odd in the era of Brexit. Six of the clubs were English and so not bound by European law. If the British government made it illegal or even came out against it, it would be very difficult to proceed. It was almost as if the prime movers hadn't really thought that through.

I just kept thinking about Jürgen Klopp. What's Klopp going to say? There is no more charismatic communicator in English football. He speaks, people listen. He has the credibility of having won the Champions League, the Premier League, and his heart always seems to be in the right place. When Liverpool fans protest against the owners, he always understands why and seems to act as a go-between. He's spoken about his own idea of socialism, of his appreciation of football as the people's game. In that sense, he's a direct successor to Bill Shankly.

Liverpool players had been for a short walk in Leeds that day and had been taken aback by the abuse they received from the public. Though there were no crowds, they could see fans gathered outside the ground protesting when they arrived, the banners denouncing their club. So what Klopp said was crucial.

Monday Night Football, Leeds v Liverpool, 19 April 2021, pre-match interview with Jürgen Klopp

Prior to the match, Liverpool fans group Spion Kop 1906 had informed the club that their display of banners on The Kop, which had been placed there to represent the fans during lockdown, were to be removed as a sign of protest. Leeds United had warmed up in T-shirts reading: 'Champions League – Earn it', directed at Liverpool, and had left some T-shirts in the Liverpool dressing room.

Sky reporter, **GREG WHELAN:** Jürgen, not too long ago you said you hoped there wouldn't be a Super League. What are your thoughts, your feelings today?

JÜRGEN KLOPP: Didn't change. My feelings, my opinion didn't change. I heard first time about it yesterday, when you're trying to prepare for a game, a very difficult game against Leeds United. So far we've got some information, not a lot, to be honest. Most of the things you more or less can read in newspapers. Yeah, it's a tough one. People are not happy with that. I can understand that. But I cannot say a lot more about it to be honest because we were not involved in any processes. Not the players, not me, we didn't know about it. That's the case. The facts are out there. Now we will have to wait [to see] how it develops.

WHELAN: Just as a football man, what are your own instincts?

KLOPP: I'm fifty-three years old and since I was a profes-sional player, the Champions League was there. I'm not sure, 1993, or something like that was the [start of the] Champions League. My aim was always – as a player it was not possible – but as a manager was always to coach a team there. So, I have obviously no issues with the Champions League. I like the competitive fact of football as well. I like the fact that West Ham might play Champions League next year, no problem. The most important part of football are supporters and the team. So, we have to make sure nothing gets in between that. The thing that people think is not right is the competitiveness. I get that. I don't like that we may not be in the Champions League, but if we earn it, we want to be there, like anyone else . . . I heard already there are warm-up shirts; we will not wear them; we will not wear them. If someone thinks they have to remind us that you have to earn [it] to go to the Champions League, that's a joke, a real joke. And it makes me angry. So if they put it in our dressing room, if it was a Leeds idea, thank you very much. No one has to remind us. Maybe they have to remind themselves.

JAMIE CARRAGHER

You're always a bit more embarrassed when your own club's involved. That was the biggest thing for me. I said that if Jürgen Klopp is against this and we lose him on the back of it, Liverpool supporters will rip that stadium down, because he's the best thing that's ever happened to the club for thirty years. Because of where the club has come from, the socialism in the city, Bill Shankly's own socialism, the importance of the success of Liverpool and Everton in the 1980s when the city was being so ravaged by Thatcherism, because of all of that, it was embarrassing for Liverpool.

In the main, I think the owners have been good for Liverpool. I must say that. But because of our history in the city, the news really hit home in Liverpool, maybe more than for the other five clubs. Thinking about the club and where it had come from, that these new guys in town think they can just change what's been there for over a hundred years? We ain't gonna let it happen. Imagine five English guys going to the baseball over there and doing that with the Yankees and the Red Sox and ripping apart something that's stood for a hundred years? Ripping apart a league. That would never be allowed in their country. Not a chance.

I couldn't believe how naïve the English clubs were. I never saw this as a European Super League. I saw this as a Premier League Super League, in that no other country has six teams in it. We didn't *need* to be in this. Basically, it all stemmed from the fact that European clubs cannot believe the revenues that the Premier League generates. That a team which finishes bottom can still get a hundred million and almost have as much money as a top European club such as Juventus. Spain and Italy had three clubs each. England had six. That just tells you everything you need to know. Basically, what they wanted, we've already got. We didn't *need* to join it.

Because of Covid, they were becoming desperate, since they were losing hundreds of millions of euros. Look at Barcelona. Look at the revenue that Juventus has lost. And when you start becoming desperate you do stupid things. That's not just football, that's life. I wouldn't say I would give these foreign clubs a free pass on that. What they did is obviously terrible. But they were desperate. Why were our clubs railroaded though? How could they get talked into it by Barcelona and Real Madrid? How could they not see: we don't *need* them. They need *us*! That's what it is.

We knew we had to go big and unleash. But we also had to be strategic and say things that would mean that fans would be boiling as well. You can't do these things on your own. I've had a couple of experiences in business where the people have been against me. We wanted to regenerate Turn Moss for Salford's training ground and the local community came out against me, wearing Gary Neville masks. We had to listen and back down. If you haven't got the community or the people with you, then you aren't getting any message across, as good as it may be.

DAVID JONES

The game was so irrelevant. We were hearing from the managers, but we only wanted to hear from them on one subject. That's the only thing we wanted to talk about. Klopp had a little pop at Gary during his interview. And that's the only time I felt we had to be a little bit careful, because we didn't want a situation where this got overtaken by Klopp v Neville. So I had to row us out of that water. I had written a checklist of all the key points I wanted us to cover and I still felt we had a couple to get through in the last half-hour; indeed, we picked up some more momentum in the last half-hour of the show. It was all unrehearsed so it did stand out as a broadcasting experience. It was totally unscripted and very much the case of feeling it as we went. It was fun, as we don't often get to do that on our show. There is a structure normally. This was unique, an entirely unprecedented show. It felt like the whole of football was completely united and it was a good feeling: as though you were all fighting for the same cause against something that was incredibly unjust.

We knew that on *Monday Night Football* we had to say things that would hit home and that tugged on the heartstrings of historic clubs. So we referenced Shankly, Sir Matt, Sir Alex, Klopp – people who always spoke or speak about wider society, who have had great social impact in football, to whom the idea of breaking away, of not looking after your own, is ludicrous. Basically, managers stepped into a socialist view of the world. We had to tap into that sense of history and responsibility. And we wanted to get to Manchester City fans, though they are relatively new to the elite. The work that their owners have done with Sheikh Mansour's money in east Manchester, regenerating that area, is incredible. Why does Sheikh Mansour need another £50 million or £100 million? They've created a community in east Manchester and built so much goodwill by putting wealth into our city. They've done all that amazing work at City with cheap tickets, affordable football, great leisurewear, great pre- and post-match experiences for fans. Everything they do is really good. Why would you ruin all that for £50 million pounds when buying City was a £2-billion-play for the state to gain acceptance in the Western world?

When the Super League proposal all started crumbling a day later, City began claiming that they were the last, as if this was some sort of acceptable defence of their position. The fact is, I think City panicked and got railroaded into a terrible decision which demonstrated a lack of self-confidence. They should have stood strong. Paris St Germain didn't go in. Bayern Munich didn't go in. Borussia Dortmund didn't go in. They were on the right side of history.

People might say it was a strategic political play by PSG, because they are owned by Qatar, which is invested in the 2022 World Cup and so couldn't afford to upset football's authorities. But ultimately they didn't baulk and they didn't go in. And the German teams didn't go in, so everything we think about Germany, with the fan model of ownership, the affordable tickets and travel prices, that model stood strong in a moment of stress. That tells you their core foundational beliefs are steadfast and worthwhile. Fundamentally, their ethos held together, their ethics held strong. Our ethics and foundational beliefs proved to be rotten. Our clubs were shown to have the moral compass of alley cats.

It was really important that the players spoke out and James Milner did a really good job that night. He was short and to the point. When he was asked what he thought about the Super League he said: 'My personal opinion is, I don't like it and I hope it doesn't happen.' That became a slogan for the Liverpool players who then Tweeted their opposition the following day.

DAVID JONES

We felt we could have an impact on the parties that were involved that night in the game, so primarily Liverpool. We could send a message: 'You can put a football match on, put your players up and managers up, but we're not actually interested in that because you're threatening the fabric of English football.' It was never going to be the type of night where we ended up talking about the race for the Champions League spots.

The fact that there were no fans there made our job a little bit easier, as there weren't the usual rhythms and noise. It was such a sanitised event, being played out while we drew breath ready to talk more. When we came off air there was a collective feeling that we couldn't have done any more and we also felt that the tide was turning that evening, because of the way Klopp and Milner has spoken. I think there was a gathering sense of early momentum; the sands were shifting. There was a sense of what the next twenty-four hours might bring: watch this space. There was clamour building and we had been at the heart of that on Monday night. So then we were all sitting back watching the dominoes fall.

The big moments after the game were when Patrick Bamford and James Milner came out and spoke against it. And Klopp clearly wasn't in favour. And that was it, they were dead. I knew some of these characters like Daniel Levy, Ed Woodward and John W. Henry would wilt. They couldn't handle this.

JAMIE CARRAGHER

We came off that show thinking or hoping we'd played a part. By the end of it, I was convinced it wouldn't go ahead. Maybe it was off social media, looking at my phone when the game was on. Obviously, we had done our first hour. We weren't 100 per cent sure how it would go and then you see the interviews with Milner and Bamford. Just at the end of the show, I said something like: 'This is gonna fall like a pack of cards. This is finished.' And it did. Actually, it was interesting watching it the next day, I'm not a very emotional person in terms of welling up, but there was a sense of emotion when I saw the crowds gathering outside Stamford Bridge the next night. Chelsea were playing Brighton and though fans still weren't allowed in the stadium, thousands had gathered to protest. When I saw sporting director Petr Čech coming outside to speak to the fans, I thought: 'This is *massive*.' It felt like a huge moment, like a big political moment. I always remember when David Cameron walked out on the back of Brexit, watching that moment. It felt like that. I didn't cry. But I was a bit like: 'Wow, this is powerful.' Chelsea put the statement out first, saying they were out, and then you knew the rest would crumble.

I was proud and a little bit emotional, because it felt like it was one of the first times that the power of the people had shown itself. The people had taken on the big dogs, if you like, these owners, these multi-billionaires who normally just throw their weight around and get what they want. And it was England, it was nowhere else; it was here, in our country: it was our supporters that stopped it. I think it's something that we should all be immensely proud of. I know speaking to people within the game that a lot of people around Europe were like: 'Wow, that's what English football did, what their supporters did up and down their country for our game!' It just shows the power of the supporters and I think that's something we'll always look back on and remember. It was great to be a part of it and be part of the fight that stopped this ludicrous idea going forwards. It was all about greed and I'm really proud that it was our country that stopped it and not Spain or Italy.

Me and Gary are pretty similar. I don't think we're too worried about what social media says. I don't think we're swayed too much or that we would allow it overly to affect us. Social media is a bit of a different world, a bit mad. But it was the one time I can ever remember when everybody came together. I don't think it'll happen again. It brought everyone together, just a couple of days after the announcement. I'm sure when the next game started it all went back to normal. Or the following weekend. But it was a really good feeling to get everybody together because it doesn't happen, ever, in football. You weren't just getting messages off people to do with your own club. It was from clubs up and down the country and messages from CEOs of different clubs, thanking us. Not thanking us, as such, but more for me and Gary being part of that show.

John W. Henry did a video after the Super League to apologise and I think it was the worst thing he ever did. That will haunt him one day when he shows his true colours. Liverpool fans at the moment are euphoric because of the Klopp era and what's happening at the club, but one day he'll regret that enormously because it demonstrates how disconnected he is from the people at Liverpool. Then there was Joel Glazer speaking to Manchester

United fans at a fans' forum and pretending that he cares about them. You know what you can do with northern people? You can smack them in the face with the truth. We might not like it, but we'll say: 'At least he's told us the truth.' They would be better off saying: 'This is how it is.' What you can't do is feather us and tickle us with what many thought were lies. And that's what it seemed these lot tried to do. I wish they'd had some bottle, had done a press conference, stood there together to talk about the Super League and how it was good for the game. Instead, they wilted like . . . I don't know . . . like a Solero in 90-degree heat. They melted inside twenty-four hours, which meant that they hadn't actually planned well, they weren't well organised, they didn't have good communication. Clearly they hadn't examined or thought through the ramifications outside of their own little bubble. All that told me is what they really are, which in my view is dangerous for football and people who don't see anybody else's perspective.

John W. Henry and Joel Glazer will make enormous money out of the sale of these clubs one day and that's capitalism. However, so long as they own those clubs they've got to respect the English pyramid. They've got to try and act in the best interests of football and stay true to Manchester United's and Liverpool's principles and values. They have to build a winning football team but at the same time be part of a league structure that looks after smaller teams. There are some things when you buy into a football club like Manchester United that maybe aren't specified in the terms and conditions in the small print, but they are still expected of you.

It was disgusting. They must have seen Bury go bust, Wigan and Bolton under stress, and their scheme would have pulled away more money from these clubs, rather than resetting the game and redistributing the wealth more widely through the pyramid. I get it. I'm all for a competitive market. For all the Red Nev stuff, I'm a capitalist. The free market is too embedded. I invest in businesses and I invest in football clubs. I'm not against owners gaining a return and we know the biggest are always most likely to succeed but it's important that you act with dignity and fairness.

Football has to come away from the idea that it's just a business like any other. It's not. Football clubs have to be treated differently. I don't think I'll ever make money out of Salford. I doubt I'll get my investment back. But it's not my goal to make money and if I do, it will be because we have done something unbelievably right. The best analogy I can give is that clubs should be like listed buildings. They should be protected assets and treated differently as such. You can't go to a town hall in London, Manchester or Leeds and just knock it down. It's a symbol of the city. Leeds United, Manchester United, Liverpool, Everton, Barrow, Bury, Wimbledon, Exeter – these clubs are so important to the fabric of those cities, towns and communities that they have to be protected, which means owners cannot just come in and do what they want with them.

We have to stop talking about football as a business unless we can talk about it in equal measure as a community asset. You go to Bury, talk about football in such places, and they all bleed football. They bleed Everton, they bleed Liverpool, they bleed Manchester City. It's a release in people's lives, a place to come together with friends. Football clubs should not be compared to Tesco. You can't just set up a competing club in Trafford to compete with Manchester United. Manchester United is like a religion. For many people in 2022, football clubs are more important to their town than the church. So, you cannot treat football clubs like Tesco. If Tesco goes out of business that would affect the employees, who would suffer. But there would be food on the shelves in other supermarkets. It wouldn't affect the whole city or the whole community. If Manchester United seek to change the fundamental principles of English football, it will harm millions for ever. That's why football clubs have to be treated differently and boundaries must be set.

But they haven't gone away, you know. Those same powers that were recording apologies and attending a fans' forum in a fit of manufactured contrition will still be plotting. We stopped them this time but they will come again, probably thinking their money gives them the right to tear up 150 years of our history. Real Madrid, Barcelona and Juventus are still fighting their corner, taking UEFA to court in a bid to get Europe at least to agree that the principle is legal. So all the energy and anger we managed to gather together previously needs to be retained and gathered up again. We need to shape the future of the game. With an independent regulator now promised by the government, we need to seize this opportunity. Our voices, the ones they labelled 'legacy fans' in their shiny PowerPoints, need to be heard. We need to make them understand why a club like Bury is important. Why owners need to be controlled. Ultimately, football is only what it is because billions of people around the world love it.

2

THE CONQUERING HEROES

'Hitherto Bury had apparently been holding themselves;
now they gave the crowd something of an idea of what
they were capable of. They appeared to have suddenly
realised that they were THERE TO WIN THE CUP. The
next fourteen minutes were an overwhelming display of
attacking football.'
**Bury 6 Derby County 0, FA Cup Final
match report, *Bury Times*, 1903**

My great-grandad, Tom Taylor, was born too late for Bury's first
FA Cup final and would have been just too young really to remember the clubs finest hour in 1903. Doubtless though, he would
have heard from his parents the stories about the fans and their
grand day out to London. Tom was born in 1900, the year of that
first Final against Southampton, and the town would have been
still fresh with those carnival memories as he grew up. It would
have been quite a day because by then the FA Cup was, despite
the first final only being played twenty-eight years before, a
massive part of the nation's popular culture. I like to think he
would have been proud that two of his great-grandsons would go
on to play in the Final.

If you read the contemporary reports you get a sense of how
big this was for Bury in 1900. 'No fewer than 1300 persons left

Bury on Friday and on Saturday morning for London on special trains organised by the Lancashire and Yorkshire Railway company,' the *Bury Times* had reported.* 'Groups of excursionists wore colour brimmed hats.' Flags proclaiming 'We Are The Shakers' – that being the club's nickname – adorned the carriages. London papers were commenting on the 'invasion of London by Lancastrians' and were especially taken by their 'thick blunt speech'. Indeed, thousands had descended on the capital, 'all busy seeing the sights: St Paul's Cathedral, Westminster Abbey, The Houses of Parliament . . .'

On the way down, the Bury fans would read the London-based *Daily Chronicle*, tipping Southampton for the Cup. Typical southern bias in the London-based media. 'Our faith was strengthened finding the football prophet of the *London Chronicle* again confidently expressing his belief that Southampton would win the Cup,' the *Bury Times* recalled. 'The Shakers have won so often when the Cockney oracle had been against them that we have always preferred him to favour the enemy.' I like that. It's almost like Sir Alex, in the sense he engendered that 'they're all against us'.

On the Saturday morning, open-top omnibuses hauled by horses along The Strand were seen with 'Play Up Bury' banners decked over the front, while from noon Victoria Station was 'besieged by people' all heading down to the Crystal Palace for the match. I'm sure the Londoners loved welcoming a huge group of northerners into their city for the day! The trains it seems were 'crowded to excess for several hours' as the network struggled to cope with numbers, even with the special trains laid on. On arrival, 'many took a short time looking through the Palace buildings and afterwards strolling through the grounds'. The Crystal Palace, built in 1850 for the Great Exhibition, was still an

---

* All quotations from the Bury Times unless otherwise stated.

architectural wonder with its glazed exterior, it being another thirty-six years before it was burnt to the ground.

As would become traditional, FA Cup Final day was blessed with warm weather, a heatwave in London leaving reporters worrying about the impact of weather on the match. As it was, 68,945 spectators had made it to the Palace. Not quite the record, set the year before, but still more than double what the Final had been attracting ten years earlier, confirming this relatively new event as one of the principal dates in the sporting calendar. The match itself was never a contest. Those travelling Bury fans would enjoy a magnificent day out. Jasper McLuckie scored from a corner after nine minutes with Willie Wood adding the second after sixteen minutes. When McLuckie scored his second and Bury's third after twenty-three minutes, the *Observer* would describe it as a 'brilliant piece of play'. Three-nil down at half time, Southampton improved somewhat in the second half but were still described as 'woefully weak' as 'Bury's forwards swooped down on Southampton's citadel like a flying column'. In the eightieth minute came the denouement, a corner 'beautifully placed' by Jack Pray, from which Jack Plant 'revolving at the far side sent in an express ground shot which beat Robinson [the Southampton goalkeeper] all the way and the fourth goal was registered'. Lord James, formerly Bury's MP and a Liberal politician who had served under Prime Minister William Gladstone, presented the trophy to Bury captain Pray, and made a speech, which was 'heard with difficulty owing to the enthusiasm of the crowd', after which Pray led the crowd in 'giving three hearty cheers for the losing team'. The players then retired to the Royal Crystal Palace Hotel where the victory was 'fittingly celebrated'.

Back in Bury, meanwhile, those who had not been able to travel were milling around Silver Street where local shops were putting up goal alerts received by telegraph from London. 'Each goal announced was received by cheers and when the third goal arrived the enthusiasm of those waiting was almost unbounded.' The final result, relayed at quarter past five, was 'greeted with loud and long-continued cheers. Long after the announcement, the streets were more than usually crowded and even when people had returned to the usual Saturday night avocations there was an air of enthusiasm and jollity about them, which showed that something quite out of the ordinary had occurred.' One man was heard to say: 'Southerners'll not need to ask where Bury is again, they'll know reet enough, aw reckon.' The team itself did not return to Bolton Street Station in Bury until seven thirty on Monday evening, when the streets were 'densely crowded' with special constables required to close off approach roads. The Mayor of Bury, James Byrom, regaled in his chains of office, was there to greet them. Captain Pray emerged carrying the Cup as the crowds on the platform shouted out 'Play up, Bury' and 'Good lads.' The mayor naturally offered a few words, according to the *Bury Times*. 'Bury was noted for many things . . . (A voice: "Black Puddings" and laughter),' he said amid some light-hearted heckling. 'It was noted for Bury blankets . . . for Bury simnels [cakes] . . . and they now had the champions of England at football and held the English Cup.' The Besses o' th' Barns band struck up 'See the Conquering Hero Comes', now better known as the tune to the hymn 'Thine Be the Glory'. Three horse-drawn carriages awaited, one for the band, the others for players and officials, and, with Pray holding the Cup aloft, they set off through the town. 'The scene outside the station was exceedingly animated' as the carriages proceeded up Silver Street and toured the town, finishing at the Queen's Hotel. 'The cheering was tremendous with Pray's frequent waving of the trophy above his head.'

Of course, success would bring jealousy from the less successful and smaller clubs. 'The mystery is,' reported the *Manchester Guardian*, 'that the doings of twenty-two good footballers, procured mostly from Scotland, to play for two limited liability companies at Bury and Southampton, should stir the public imagination as it does and be invested with so profound a territorial significance.' Too many foreigners, not enough home-grown talent, the commoditisation of the game: all were live issues for Victorian football. Mancunians were doubtless jealous that their less successful teams, Manchester United and Manchester City, were no match for the likes of Bury. 'The writer doesn't seem to know the facts,' wrote the *Bury Times* in what reads like a Victorian version of a Twitter spat, as the rival papers deployed alternative facts. 'The majority of players were English' and the local paper contested that Scottish-born George Ross was more or less a Bury lad, having lived in the town since the age of two. Still, the sheer scale of recruitment of more technical Scottish players was an undoubted factor in Bury's rise. Amid the success, however, there was an ominous and perhaps prescient note. The Cup Final receipts of £983, 16 shillings and 6 pence, combined with the semi-final receipts of £350, 1 shilling and 6 pence, helped to pay off the club's debts of £1,230. Seems like even in their glory days, Bury were overspending.

Not that the fans worried too much. This was Bury's era of domination. The year 1900 turned out to be merely the appetiser for an extraordinary record-breaking FA Cup Final three years later. Bury's feats in 1903 would not be matched by any club until Manchester City in 2019. 'SIX GOALS TO NOTHING' roared the *Bury Times*, on this occasion Derby County being the hapless victims of The Shakers' overwhelming force. 'Another record broken!' it added, for Bury hadn't even conceded a goal in the run-up to Cup Final, thereby equaling Preston's record of 1889. Not even Pep Guardiola's team managed that. And as the *Bury Times* pointed out, Preston's achievement from a different era was 'against much inferior opponents'. This time 'seven long trains' were commandeered to take the Bury fans down to London and 'nearly 2000 persons left Bury alone on Friday afternoon and night and Saturday morning en route to the Crystal Palace'.

Once again, 'King's weather conditions' of 'bright warm sun prevailed' on Final day. 'Nearly all the occupants [of the trains] wore the blue and white favours of Bury.' The Cup Final was becoming the sporting event of the year, with the *Bury Times* reporting that fans from all over the country, not just from Bury and Derby, would make their way to the capital. 'Between 30,000 and 40,000 excursionists invaded the world's greatest city', with trains coming in from Birmingham, Sheffield and from various locations in Lancashire as well as from Bury and Derby. 'The trippers brought with them a large stock of provisions', including '40 barrels of beer and 200 cases of bottled beer and mineral water and jars of whisky galore'. It added: 'Remarkable scenes were witnessed in the metropolis as crowds flowed into local restaurants and before many hours these were cleared out of all refreshments.' These reports sound so familiar that you can almost feel the excitement of the day. I can clearly remember my first trip to Wembley to watch an FA Cup final because it was one of the greatest finals of all time. Manchester City fans will be amused to find out that it was for the 1981 replay between Spurs and City, with that great goal from Ricky Villa. Walking down Wembley Way, the anticipation and excitement was enormous, even though I wasn't a fan of either club. For these people it was a day out and commute to Crystal Palace. But the rituals haven't changed much over generations.

In 1903 thousands spent the morning 'doing the sights of London' and 'whichever way one turned, one met Bury people. It was impossible to get away from residents of one's own town.' Special extra booking offices eased the rush at Victoria Station this time, as people crowded towards the Palace and the ground slowly filled up to 63,105 fans, 'the sight . . . a magnificent one'. Flags 'were ever conspicuous especially of the Bury colours'. And the roar that greeted that Derby team was 'easily outclassed when the Red Rose representatives were led on by Captain [George]

Ross'. The pitch was poor, making it hard for the players to control the ball, and though Bury were in the ascendant, they were only 1–0 up at half time. Willie Wood's cross on twenty minutes reached Ross, whose volley evaded Derby keeper Jack Fryer, who had declared himself fit despite an injury but who seemed impeded in goal.

The second half was altogether different. 'Hitherto Bury had apparently been holding themselves; now they gave the crowd something of an idea of what they were capable of. They appeared to have suddenly realised that they were THERE TO WIN THE CUP. The next fourteen minutes were an overwhelming display of attacking football.' The second goal came on forty-eight minutes, Derby keeper Fryer dashing from his goal to intercept a through ball to Charlie Sagar. The pair collided but Sagar got a toe to the ball, which 'slowly found its way into the net'. Both the centre forward and the keeper needed treatment after the collision, Fryer having seemingly aggravated his original injury, which may have had an impact on subsequent proceedings. With no subs allowed, Fryer was still off the pitch and full back Charlie Morris had taken over in goal when Joe Leeming scored the third on fifty-six minutes 'in the easiest fashion' when Morris dashed out of goal and Leeming simply 'tipped the ball over his head'. Fryer, having seemingly seen enough of the stand-in keeper, 'immediately returned' but 'another minute had barely passed when [Frank] Thorpe sent in an electrifying range finder and Fryer only just succeeded in reaching it . . . by flinging himself at full length. But his almost superhuman effort was of little avail . . . as [Willie] Wood, running in, had an open goal and before Fryer could rise the ball had been netted for a fourth time.'

'The blow was a severe one to Derby prestige and courage while it aroused additional interest among Bury's supporters and non-partisans', who now scented another record. Just two minutes would elapse from the restart before Sagar found Plant, who made it 5–0. This proved Fryer's swansong, and in his 'broken-down condition' he had to go off; Leeming would make it 6–0 on seventy-five minutes.

This was an FA Cup Final record, which stood until 18 May 2019, when Manchester City beat Watford 6–0 in the Final. Coincidentally, four days before Vincent Kompany lifted the Cup for City, Bury were in the High Court facing a winding-up petition and it turned out they would have played their last ever Football League match just two weeks previously.

Back in 1903, the media backlash against losers Derby was merciless, with the press unsparing in their criticism. 'Candidly the match was a fiasco,' wrote the *Daily Chronicle*. 'Nothing like it had ever been seen. Bury defeated Derby County by six goals to none and it might have been twenty. That it was not is testimony to the mercy exercised by the victors rather than the defence of the losers.' The *Bury Times* was equally unforgiving about Derby's efforts, labelling them

> unworthy of a great team. Not a single section of the team rose to the greatness of the occasion. Their efforts all through the game was spasmodic and weak; there was nothing to redeem their play from mediocrity and at times it even sank below that. The great reputation of Derby County was scattered to the winds and they were generally acknowledged to be the most-disappointing team in the country.

This I suppose is the equivalent of a Twitter pile-on combined with a *Sun* back page comparing your manager to a turnip.

Not that Bury much cared. Back in the town, crowds had gathered in Silver Street, as in 1900, to hear any news that could be relayed about the Final. In 1985, the year of Bury's centenary,

George Horridge, then club president, who would have been a contemporary of my great-grandad, wrote:

> I remember both the FA Cup Finals well. In 1900 when Bury beat Southampton four goals to nil I was sitting in the nursery awaiting the result, aged six. In 1903, I was in Silver Street, which was crowded with people waiting for notices to be put up in the shop window of the Duckworth and Collins shop as to how the game progressed. In the second half Bury scored five goals and on each occasion, as the notice was put up, a great shout went up from the crowd.

Once Lord Kinnaird, the president of the FA, had presented the Cup, the team retired to the White Swan, Norwood, and from there, making their way through a large crowd, they were driven up to The Trocadero near Leicester Square, in those days a glitzy restaurant rather than a nightclub. The West End, it seems, was already the destination venue for celebrating footballers. A group of Bury fans who had made their way up from Crystal Palace to the restaurant were invited to join the party, which was apparently so engrossing that a visit to the Palace Theatre was abandoned as the celebrations continued into the night. 'Needless to say the English Cup did not escape without its baptism of champagne.' The following day there was a boating expedition to Hampton Court and the Bury party by now 'included a number of ladies'. On Monday the team departed St Pancras for Birmingham as they had a league game at West Bromwich Albion, and at the London station they were sent off 'with ringing cheers by a large crowd which had thronged the platform'. The Cup, it was reported, was placed on a table in the saloon carriage so it could be visible for the spectators on the platforms.

On arrival at Birmingham, the team were driven to the match through the city and were greeted by cheering crowds. They proceeded to beat West Brom 3–1, despite their late nights and celebrations. The next day, as their returning train went through Derby, home of their vanquished opponents, 'the station was densely thronged with people who were unstinted in their congratulations and cheer and as the Bury players departed . . . they brought away the feeling that Derby folk are the best sportsmen they have yet had the good fortune to meet'. The same occurred in Manchester, where many Bury townsfolk had travelled, impatient to greet the team, but the grandest reception would be on their arrival in Bury. This time there was a degree more organisation, with only specially invited guests led by the new mayor, Councillor Duxbury, greeting them at the station before speeches and another parade of the Cup around the town.

My great-grandad would have heard all these stories growing up as he watched Bury take on the best teams in the country in the Football League's First Division. In time, he would open a butcher's shop on Bolton Road, marry Josephine, and in 1924 his daughter, Mary, was born. She would be known as Mollie and that was my nan. As Mollie grew up, Bury found themselves in the equivalent of the Championship, having been relegated in 1929, just three years after having achieved their highest-ever league position of fourth in the old First Division. Still, they were a decent side, going close to promotion on a number of occasions, agonisingly so in 1937, when they finished third, behind Leicester City and Blackpool. Only the top two were promoted. The Second World War then intervened.

In 1945, as the war drew to a close, Mollie would marry Bill Harper, my grandad. He had fought with the Royal Fusiliers, come back injured three times during the Second World War and three times returned to fight. On returning from the war, he took over a newsagent on Ainsworth Road. Their first child was a daughter, Wendy, and a few years later they would have another daughter, Jill - my mum. In time, she too would be taken to Gigg

Lane. 'I remember my dad taking me there from the age of five or six,' she said. 'My dad was a newsagent so he had a delivery van. We lived in town, so all his friends who were going to the game would jump in the back of the van and we would drive to Gigg Lane. I would be in the back with them. When we got there, my granddad [Tom Taylor] had a bit more money. He sat in the reserve chairs, in the middle stand, but we just used to sit on the wooden benches in the main stand. Back then, nobody went to away games because the first team played at home on the Saturday and, the Saturday after, the reserve team played at home. So, your season ticket got you into that too. That's how it was.' In the 1960s, my grandad and mum would watch players such as Alec Lindsay and Colin Bell play for the club. Lindsay would go on to win the league, FA Cup and UEFA Cup with Liverpool, while Bell, one of England's greatest midfielders, played in England's 1970 World Cup team and won the league, FA Cup and Cup-Winners' Cup at Manchester City. From 1969 to 1973, Grandad and Mum saw the first phase of Terry McDermott's career, the player going on to win five league titles and three European Cups at Liverpool.

My mum would grow up and marry a Bolton fan, Neville, my dad, whom she met at Bolton Casino. They would live in Bury, in a two-up, two-down terraced house on Ainsworth Road, near the newsagent, just around the corner from Lonsdale Street, where my nan and grandad lived. My brother, Phil, and I used to play out at the back at the garages with our neighbours, the Fords, until eight o'clock at night while Mum and Dad were in the house. I was outside in the streets and sometimes in the park, though not as much, because it was a bit rough over there. But in the back streets, we literally were out there all hours God made. We played football against the garage doors. When we were playing outside, my dad would come home sometimes in his lorry and he would beep his horn. He had CB radio and I used to get on his knee and play with the radio. I would travel with him to the big trips away sometimes and the CB radio would come on and he would let me speak in it. I always remember sometimes he'd be out there, he would park up outside the back and he'd be on his CB radio for, like, thirty minutes when he came home. Your dad coming home at the end of the day is a big moment when you're young.

My mum and dad were friendly with a couple called the Robinsons, Terry and Brenda. Terry, who had a business selling farm equipment, had become involved on the Bury board of directors and in 1979 had been asked to take over as chairman. By now, football had changed and Bury were in what was then the Fourth Division, or League Two, more a community club than an FA Cup contender. Still, a core of three thousand fans were invested in the team. 'Mrs Allen, who was the old chairman's wife, wanted the club to carry on in the way it had been run under her husband and after a little while she asked if I'd be interesting in taking the chair,' said Terry. 'I said I wasn't experienced enough. But, as it happened, the chairman decided he'd go on his holidays and that Monday we got a call off the bank manager. The club had reached the limit of its overdraft. Times back then were a little more trusting, and the overdraft was without guarantees. So I came out of the meeting with Mrs Allen and a guy called Ian Pickup, and we both had to give undertakings on our houses to get an overdraft facility to keep the club running. I said to Mrs Allen, "I think it would be better if I became chairman because I could lose my own money."'

My dad, as well as being a lorry driver, was a trained engineer, and had also become involved in arranging benefit events for local Lancashire League cricketers. That led to him being employed by nearby Burnley Football Club as a commercial manager. But pretty soon after, Terry persuaded him to work in the same role at Bury. My dad was now in the boardroom and my mum would do the catering on matchdays. That meant Saturdays were a work day, but with three young children to look after there was no option but to bring them along. So we would be dragged along in tow. We'd play football in the corridors as my mum made sandwiches and prepared the food, while my grandad, Bill, was a doorman on the car park. I'm beginning to understand why my life is so busy. It's just something I inherited growing up.

Bill was the nicest person I've ever met in my life. He worked until he was eighty-five, three weeks before he died of lung cancer. He had standards. He probably got up every single day and put his tie on. He lived in a private house on Lonsdale Street in Bury, again just opposite the park, two-up/two-down across the road from where I lived. He never ever once asked for support off the state, but wanted to be entrepreneurial and work. Basically, Labour's economic policy of the late 1970s destroyed his 'newsagent' livelihood. They taxed business, I think, at 40-odd per cent, and it killed him. He sold the shop, got a job and said that he would never, ever vote Labour again. He was a Labour voter and he became a Thatcher voter. So did my nan. And they were good people who were important, from my point of view. They gave me so much in terms of normality and standards. They looked after us when my mum and dad were playing netball or cricket. Nan and Bill, we used to call them, Nan and Grandad. They would be on the side-lines watching us play cricket, football.

Saturdays was Gigg Lane. Dad would be sorting out guests and sponsors, Mum would be doing the catering. Tracey would sometimes go to see a friend, but often she would be there. Phil and I would be in the walkways under the stands, eating sandwiches, playing football until the crowds came in. Then we would get to watch the match. We had a front-row perspective from childhood on what being a lower-league football club meant. Bury was a family club, same people working in it for twenty years. My mum would be doing the buffets in the sponsors' lounge and the boardroom. My mum's dad ran the car park. My mum's mum helped with the sandwiches. My mum's sister helped with the sandwiches. My dad was always down there watching out the front with the sponsors.

There was a pasty shop in Bolton called Ye Olde Pasty Shoppe, and my mum used to get the pasties from there; we always used to go in the back and get a pasty from my nan. That was the highlight of the day. We would play football in the morning and, if United were playing away, we'd go to watch Bury. It's a special club. We used to stand in the Manchester Road End on occasions, behind the goal, and experience it with the fans. I'd go to away games with my dad and the chairman in the car. If United were shifted to a Sunday match, you'd go and watch Bury on a Saturday. I went all over the country to away games watching Bury, to Cardiff, Grimsby, Tranmere, Bournemouth, Bristol, Swansea. Because we were obsessed with football and my dad was a big part of the club. It was a family club. It was a club that I would say was at the heart of the town.

But Bury was also a big stress in our lives. My mum and dad would bring it home with them. The club were always living hand to mouth. They were always trying to raise money, save money. They were always scraping around to cut costs. It was always a scrap. It was stable for a period, but then Hugh Eaves, who was the owner a long time ago, had financial troubles in his other businesses. This is when a lot of lower-league clubs get into trouble; namely, when financial stress occurs in the owner's other businesses and then it impacts upon the club.

I remember lots of arguments, lots of stress, fans getting to my dad, fans abusing my dad, abusing the chairman. There were invariably two or three thousand fans and they were a noisy bunch – passionate and loyal but a cantankerous bunch. From the age of five to eleven, it was United, and weekends were passionate, peaceful but enjoyable. But when my dad joined Bury it became the opposite because they had to win or get bigger crowds or secure a commercial deal or win an FA Cup match to get extra money. There was always a desperation around the club. I lived that with Philip and Tracey and my mum and dad, probably for most of our lives from the age of eleven onwards.

My dad and the chairman used to go into the social club after every single game. My dad had a heart attack at the age of forty-two and that is partly because of Bury Football Club. He was overweight and lived his life in what would be a northern man's way. He was a lorry driver, ate and drank. So I can't say Bury caused it. But when you put stress with that, it's devastating. And the stress of Bury was enormous. I remember that when my dad had that heart attack on the Monday, there had been an incident on the preceding Saturday with one of the players' fathers, who had tried to get into the sponsors' lounge. My dad had said: 'You can't come in.' There had been a massive row. It was always like that at Bury. That incident occupied his mind all Sunday, and on Monday he had the heart attack. I'd joined United by then, probably just got into the first team. And at that point I said: 'Dad, you're leaving. It's gonna kill you.' And my dad left the club to come and work for me, but he never really left because my mum was still there. And he was still chairman of Save Our Shakers, their foundation, which had to round up local businesses to save them in 2002 by putting in hundreds of thousands to buy the ground, then give it back to the club. Different boards came in. Different owners came in. They were never financially secure enough in their own lives to be able to give it a go and they were always struggling to keep hold of the ground. The principle for my dad was that we always have to keep hold of the land and the ground. 'Once we lose that, we're done,' he would say.

And just before he died, in 2015, he had to do the unthinkable, because there was nowhere else to go, no one who could take over at the club. Save Our Shakers had a golden share in the ground and he had to give it to Stewart Day, which released the ground and control of the club. Basically, that's when I first sensed they could end up in trouble. I said to my mum after his death, 'Get out,' because my instinct told me not to trust what was going on and I wanted to protect my mum as I knew the impact the club had had on my dad's health. My mum is independent, strong willed and could never leave because of my dad. My dad had always saved the club and had a stand named after him. There's all the memories she had there. I'd been asked to lend money to the club just before he died. I'd put money in before to Bury a couple of times as a loan during my United career to help out and get them through. I gave them this money knowing that I might not get it back, but, to be fair, I did. In reality though, this time I didn't trust the ownership and I felt the 100 grand requested was just going to go into a bigger hole and this was well before the crisis that finished them.

I get asked regularly why I didn't save Bury, why didn't I step in, it's your home town club, and so on. Bury was unsaveable. Even before the ridiculous ownership period of Steve Dale. The company was rancid, the accounts all over the place, money was disappearing left, right and centre, and in the end no new owner could take the chance not knowing what they were about to enter into. This should never have been allowed to happen. The football authorities have failed Bury, as they have many others, with the lack of financial monitoring and regulatory controls which protect these historic community assets.

So this is a story about Bury. But it could be about their opponents in 1903, Derby County, who would go on to win the FA Cup in 1946 and the league in 1972 and 1975, yet face points penalties in the 2021–22 season that saw them plummet down the leagues in financial chaos. It could be about Chester City or Macclesfield, who were also liquidated. They reformed as phoenix clubs and thrive now.

We could say something similar concerning Portsmouth, FA Cup winners in 2008 yet in administration facing a winding-up order in 2009. All of their stories will resonate with football fans. Most clubs have their own horror stories: Exeter City, Wimbledon, Wigan, QPR, Chelsea, Manchester City, Bolton, Aldershot, Coventry, Darlington, Plymouth, Crystal Palace, Middlesbrough, Brighton, Bournemouth, Southampton, Leicester City, Ipswich Town, Wrexham, Rotherham, Cambridge United, York City, Hull City, Millwall, Doncaster Rovers, Gillingham, Barnet, Tranmere Rovers, Newport County, Southend United. Bad owners and mad owners have taken them to the brink of extinction. They have all suffered catastrophic financial events that have threatened their existence. Most have been in administration. Port Vale and Palace have managed that twice since 1998. Today, it's Oldham going through the mill as they slip out of the league with an owner who seems to despise the fans. These are proud clubs, many have won major honours. Two of them were Super League plotters! A number are in the Premier League. All have stories like my great-grandad's. Families will have followed them through generations. They all play vital roles in their community. This nation would be a lesser place without them. And yet we allow them to be treated like playthings of chancers and dreamers. The sheer length of the list demands that there has to be change.

3

CASH MACHINE

'Roman Abramovich has parked his tanks on our lawn and is firing £50 notes at us.'
David Dein, former Arsenal vice chairmain

There's an old line from an advert I remember: '1966 was a great year for English football: Eric Cantona was born.' So, if we're marking significant dates in the development of our game, in understanding how we got here, let's talk about 2003. As far as English football is concerned, the twenty-first century started a few years late, in 2003. It's the year everything changed. It's the year the game we have today emerged.

That year, 2003, was also a period of change at Manchester United. David Beckham, who had been my best mate since we were teenagers, left that summer to join Real Madrid, and though it wasn't a shock, it was huge for me on a personal level. We had signed a skinny teenager to replace him. You worried a little as to how he would cope in the Premier League. His name was Cristiano Ronaldo.

Manchester United had won the Premier League in 2002-03 but my own form was patchy. Arsenal's Invincibles were coming the following season. I had led a strike of England players before a Euro qualifier in 2003 because of Rio Ferdinand's missed drugs test. But all these developments were superficial compared to the seismic changes that were happening elsewhere. Two takeovers were instigated that year, one in a flurry of publicity and lavish spending; the other, quietly, and opaquely, happening on the stock market.

In July 2003, a short press release from Chelsea announced that a previously unknown thirty-six-year-old Russian tycoon had bought the club for £140m. Back then, £140m bought you a Premier League club. Now it gets you Kylian Mbappé.

There was a storm coming in Roman Abramovich and his cash. Chelsea announced themselves that summer by spending an unprecedented £150m on Hernán Crespo, Damien Duff, Juan Sebastien Verón, Claude Makélélé, Adrian Mutu, Scott Parker, Geremie, Joe Cole, Glen Johnson and Alexei Smertin. We'd never seen anything like it, not even in the days of Jack Walker at Blackburn. The Arsenal vice chairman David Dein summed it up well when he said: 'Roman Abramovich has parked his tanks on our lawn and is firing £50 notes at us.'

Abramovich was the first foreign owner of a major Premier League club. Sam Hammam, from Lebanon, had owned Wimbledon through their rise up the divisions to the elite, and Egyptian Mohamed Al-Fayed bought Fulham for a quaint-sounding £30m in 1997. But Fulham were in the third tier, the equivalent of League One at the time.

In 2003, we thought the game was big but it was a parochial affair in terms of ownership. 'Big-money owners' meant someone like Walker at Blackburn, who was worth £600m. Former Manchester United owner Martin Edwards had inherited his wealth from his father, who ran a meat-processing and packaging business. Ken Bates, the former Chelsea owner, was a property tycoon. David Dein and Danny Fiszman, Arsenal's owners, were diamond dealers. All were multi-millionaires, but Walker had put their wealth into perspective and made them look relatively small time. Now, his own level of wealth looked paltry compared to that of Abramovich, who himself would later be put in the shade by Sheikh Mansour and Mohammed bin Salman.

Abramovich changed everything. Or rather, once José Mourinho was in place from 2004, everything changed. He was special. Immediately there was a steeliness to Chelsea, a clinical sense of getting the job done in how they recruited players; even in how they took Manchester United's chief executive Peter Kenyon off us. Everyone thought that you needed an Arsène Wenger or a Sir Alex Ferguson to be successful in England, managers who dominated the club and would be there for decades. Chelsea changed that. Thirteen different managers (or fifteen, as Guus Hiddink and Mourinho came back for second stints) won nineteen major trophies in nineteen years under Abramovich's ownership. Before he arrived, they had only won nine in their whole history. (We're really not counting the two Full Members' Cup wins in 1986 and 1990 as major trophies!)

The quality of football went up, too, which is a good example of how investment has improved the Premier League. José caught us by surprise in the 2004–05 season. Chelsea won the league with ninety-five points. We had a formula of how to win titles against great Arsenal teams. After Christmas was when we got ourselves together and went on long winning runs. Up to then it was just about staying in touch. We knew we could reel teams in. We always said people will drop points in the run-in. José changed that (and now Pep Guardiola and Jürgen Klopp have taken it to a different level). But José was the first to have that relentlessness. This was the only period when I wondered: 'Will we win a title here again?' We had had the Arsenal Invincibles in 2003–04 and then this Chelsea team, who could outspend us. We had to rise to the challenge. And we did. Sir Alex Ferguson rebuilt Manchester United on the back of that. Big choices were made. We changed tactically and went to a 4–3–3 formation. It was the first time we became a truly European club, despite the fact that we had won the Champions League in 1999. It was a British formula, then, playing 4-4-2. By 2008, when we won the Champions League again, United were a European team, with underlapping and over-lapping full backs, two passers in midfield and no recognised centre forward. Cristiano Ronaldo set the tone for the positional interchange of the front three. Football-wise, it was revolutionary. But something else was going on as well in the business world. A quieter, stealthier revolution, was being planned.

On 2 March 2003, Red Football paid £9m for a 2.9 per cent share of Manchester United. The Sunday Telegraph reported that the man behind the company was someone pretty much unknown in the UK at the time, Malcolm Glazer, owner of the Tampa Bay Buccaneers, the reigning Super Bowl Champions. By November 2003, Red Football had increased their stake to 15 per cent and were meeting United's new chief executive David Gill.

I don't think I even knew what that meant at the time. I would have followed the news about United. But it just would have been a corporate thing for the boardroom to worry about. The players dealt with Sir Alex and only concentrated with what happened on the pitch. I couldn't have dreamed how important this Glazer family would become to our lives at United. This is how naïve we were back then. We thought the Premier League was already important, but overseas broadcasting was around 14 per cent of what the domestic TV deal was worth. In 2003 Premier League clubs received under £3m a year from overseas TV deals. In 2021-22, United and Chelsea would earn around £90m and, for the first time, the value of the rights sold abroad would be worth slightly more than the UK rights. Smart people saw this coming. Most of us in the UK didn't. We already thought we were pretty big. How could it get any bigger? But Abramovich and Malcolm Glazer changed the cosiness of the domestic game. From opposite sides of the old Cold War, they had seen the value in our game even if they had very different motives for why they did.

The Premier League was founded in 1992, which itself was a land grab by the biggest clubs, annexing power from an inept Football Association. To understand the difference it made having entrepreneurs at the helm, rather than Football League officials, in 1988 ITV had paid £44m to secure a four-year deal to show live matches from Football League Division One, the old top flight. With the formation of the Premier League in 1992, BSkyB, the forerunner to Sky, driven by Rupert Murdoch, agreed a £304m deal for five years. As it turned out, because of complications over the overseas deal, they only paid £191m for the five years. But still, it was a huge increase, more than 300 per cent.

But the globalisation of the Premier League and the opening of the floodgates to overseas billionaires began in 2003. Unfathomable riches would pour into the game. There were people like Abramovich, who had cashed in on the old Soviet Empire. Others, like Thaksin Shinawatra, the former Prime Minister of Thailand and later found guilty of corruption, arising from what he claimed were politically motivated charges, had money to spend. American financiers, such as John W. Henry, who had done well out of the 1990s boom in derivatives money, would look to invest. And new financial instruments were developed in the North American banking world, allowing people to borrow much more money than previously and take more risks, which only encouraged the flow of cash. The world's wallet was opening up and the Premier League found itself a grateful recipient.

What brought these untold riches into our game? Now, it seems clear what brought Abramovich. He had a pressing need of a visible asset in western Europe. In February 2003, another Russian oligarch, Mikhail Khodorkovsky, an oil baron like Abramovich who had been enriched in the chaos of the Soviet Union's breakdown, complained about corruption in a public forum with President Vladmir Putin. Khodorkovsky, just like Abramovich, had made his money under a dubious auction overseen by the previous Russian President, Boris Yeltsin. Indeed, even Abramovich's own lawyers called the sale of previously nationalised industries 'rigged' during a High Court hearing in 2011. But the response to Khodorkovsky's call for a clean-up was swift and severe. Putin, whose staff had encouraged Khodorkovsky to raise the issue, turned on him and accused Khodorkovsky of corruption himself.

Within weeks Khodorkovsky's company was being investigated for fraud and his associates arrested. By October 2003, Khodorkovsky was himself arrested. He was convicted in 2005 and spent eight years in prison on what most people in the know thought were politically motivated charges. It was a powerful reminder of the power President Putin exercised over the oligarchs. If it had been the wild east under the previous president, Boris Yeltsin, Khodorkovsky's fate demonstrated there was a new sheriff in town.

How did Abramovich survive? The same tax breaks used by Khodorkovsky and that were being used to destroy him and his company seemed also to have been used by Abramovich and Sibneft. As Catherine Belton claims in *Putin's People*:

> The threat of the Russian authorities imposing enormous back tax charges seemed always to hang over his [Abramovich's] Sibneft. By 2004 the Yukos oil major acquired by Khodorkovsky was being dismantled and taken over by the state precisely over such back tax charges. Khodorkovsky had been arrested and jailed for fraud and tax evasion after falling out with Putin, though his business model was no different to Abramovich's. The risk Abramovich's Sibneft could face similar charges appeared acute.[*]

Abramovich's oil company Sibneft was also about to be taken over by the Russian state company, Gazprom. But while Yukos was seized forcibly as an asset and Khodorkovsky bankrupted and imprisoned, Putin authorised the Russian state to buy Sibneft

[*] Belton, C. (2020). Putin's people : how the KGB took back Russia and then took on the west. William Collins.

from Abramovich in a deal worth $13 billion. 'The deal was done in a multi-step process that began barely two weeks after a Moscow court finally pronounced the guilty verdict against Khodorkovsky in May 2005,' writes Belton.

> The Russian government announced that it was going to borrow $7 billion from international banks to raise its stake in Gazprom to a controlling 51 per cent. Gazprom, in turn, announced that it was going to use the cash it received from the government for its shares for an acquisition of its own: rather than bankrupting Abramovich's Sibneft and then seizing control, it was going to buy it. The deal seemed to underline how much Abramovich's fate differed from Khodorkovsky's.

All this has been known for years. Everyone at the Premier League knew it. Let's be honest, we were all too busy enjoying being awed at Chelsea's spending power and enjoying Mourinho's arrival in the Premier League to be too concerned. Though there were some in the media who did shine a small light on Putin's suspected links to Abramovich, that wasn't the main headline when he came in. 'Which players is he [Abramovich] going to buy?' was the question that preoccupied us. But 2003 was also the year that the Queen hosted President Putin at Buckingham Palace for a full state visit. It wasn't just football that looked away. The City of London was busy enriching itself, doing deals for oligarchs. The Conservative Party would later be collecting donations. The ruling Labour party were ingratiating themselves. Just one snap shot: in August 2008, Lord Mandelson, the architect of Tony Blair's New Labour and at the time EU trade commissioner, would meet with aluminium billionaire Oleg Derispaska on his luxury yacht just off Corfu. Aspiring Conservative politician, George Osborne, soon to be Chancellor of the Exchequer was also there, along with banker Nat Rothschild. Everyone seemed to be on board: the City of London, the ruling elites and the Russian oligarch, all rubbing shoulder to shoulder on a luxury yacht in the Med. It's a picture of Britain at this time. Osborne denied he ever sought donations and Mandleson said he always followed the UK's Ministerial Code and that politicians have numerous meetings with business people. But that all changed on March 10th 2022, when the UK Government announced that it had sanctioned Abramovich and Derispaska. On Abramovich, the Government said: 'He is one of the few oligarchs from the 1990s to maintain prominence under Putin.' The Premier League followed a few weeks later, disqualifying Abramovich as a fit and proper owner. The facts hadn't changed, just the politics.

I have no qualms at all about Abramovich being kicked out of this country and out of English football. The shame is that it took a war and the death of thousands of innocent people in Ukraine to expose nineteen years of Russian money-sloshing into the Premier League and also into the City of London, the UK legal profession and the Conservative Party. All those smug city bonuses, donations to the Conservative Party and centre forwards paid for by Russian oligarchs. No one cared at the time.

I wasn't calling for Abramovich to be ejected from the game a year ago. Though Chelsea became a pain in my playing days, disrupting Manchester United's dominance, as a pundit I enjoyed their rise and the journey under Abramovich. People still remind me about my slightly orgasmic commentary at the Nou Camp when Fernando Torres scored to put them through to the Champions League final in 2012. Almost all of us were guilty of turning a blind eye and not seeing the danger of what might come in nineteen years' time.

And here's the irony. I'd love to say that I wouldn't have wanted him at Manchester United. But if, in 2003, with the gift of foresight, you were offered the choice of Abramovich or the Glazers as owners, who would you take?

The Glazers' takeover at United was as different to Abramovich's at Chelsea as it was possible to be. They saw something no one else in US sports business could see in 2003, that their world of National Football League (NFL) and even National Basketball Association (NBA) franchises was limited to North America and that the world was much bigger than that. Football, as the world's most popular sport, and Manchester United, as arguably the biggest club, along with Real Madrid and Barcelona (clubs that weren't for sale), was the perfect gateway to the revenues this new era of globalisation would bring.

Jim O'Neill, who in 2003 was a partner at investment bank Goldman Sachs, is a lifelong United fan from south Manchester who tried to buy out the Glazers in 2010. He was also on the board of United in 2004–05, when the contentious takeover battle was raging, and he recalls that the initial reaction was bemusement and scepticism. 'They weren't billionaires, that's for sure,' said O'Neill. 'They had nothing like the wealth of Abramovich. In terms of money, they were more like Jack Walker's level. And up until the last months of the takeover, the general view of the board was: "Who on earth are these guys?" They were misread, frankly.' At the time, a much more high-profile group was snapping up United shares. J.P. McManus and John Magnier, Irish racehorse owners and initially friends with Sir Alex Ferguson – though they would have a bitter fall-out – had built up a 29 per cent stake. Everyone was expecting them to take their shares over 30 per cent, which would have triggered a full takeover. 'The view was that McManus and Magnier had the controlling position and at board meetings no one really talked about the Glazers,' said O'Neill. 'I remember some conversation where it was wrongly assumed that the Glazers had been dragged into owning a significant number of shares without out really wanting to, so they were completely misread. Some people thought McManus and Magnier might dump their shares and some in the board thought that the only reason why the Glazers started buying more was [to keep the price up] because if they didn't they'd be sitting on a very large loss. But the Glazers were very savvy. I would say that not grudgingly. They rather cleverly realised that United's content brand was just spectacularly bigger than the board had understood. United had no debt at the time. I remember speaking to J.P. McManus and asking him: "How come you're so keen to buy Man United?" And he said: "The thing is they're just so cash rich. And they had no debt. It's unbelievable."'

American investment banks, prior to the financial crash of 2008, were enjoying the benefits of a lightly regulated market that made it easy to borrow money. Leveraged buyouts were all the rage. Essentially, you used the value of a company to borrow money to buy the very same company you were borrowing against. It meant you could buy a huge company that you could never normally afford with your own assets alone. In theory, it wasn't dissimilar to having a mortgage on a house, except, of course, the sums, and therefore the risk, were much greater. And the special kind of new financial instrument the Glazers used meant you could put off the interest payments and just add them to the debt. These were Payment in Kind (PIK) notes. The interest rates were eye-watering. United were paying 14.25 per cent on their PIK notes when the Glazers took over the club in 2005. You could roll over the interest payments year on year, so the debt was increasing massively. Essentially, the Glazers were betting the future of the company on the fact that it would be worth so much more in ten years' time, at which point paying off or paying down the huge debt wouldn't be an issue. The Glazers bet big on United, in my view potentially jeopardising the club, but they won.

'The PIK notes became a way of borrowing a lot of money from a bank, paying a very high rate of marginal return,' explains O'Neill. 'It was very attractive to highly acquisitive individuals who didn't have much cash. But it only worked if you could own a cash-generating asset and pay off a lot of the debt you borrowed quickly and refinance the terms. They became very popular in the early noughties and Glazer jumped on the back of that.' The man who worked on the details of the deal at J.P.Morgan, the investment bank putting up the money, was a junior banker called Ed Woodward. 'He organised the PIK financing,' said O'Neill. 'Post 2008, when the markets tightened up, they couldn't have done it as they did. But at the time, it was smart. It lives on in the Chelsea deal. The American owners seemed to understand the media rights and the appetite for it better than anyone else. They were aware of that [imminent burgeoning of international TV rights], though nothing like the scale that it became. The last board meeting at United, when we were trying to fend off the offers from the Glazers, I told the board we could gather together a group of investors and borrow £250m ourselves. We would easily have been able to have done it but because of the pressure of time the board thought I was being stupid.'

In May 2005, the Glazers announced they had reached an agreement with McManus and Magnier to buy their 28.7 per cent stake in the club and also the shares of mining entrepreneur Harry Dobson, taking their share total to 62 per cent. By the end of that month, they had more than 75 per cent of the club which meant they could take it off the stock market and take it private.

As someone who is a capitalist and now a businessman, who lives in that world and who has debt in certain areas of his life, and mortgages, I don't think I can look at the Glazers and say they've done anything wrong in buying Manchester United. I wish they weren't the owners. I wish United had better owners who were putting every penny back into the club and not taking dividends out or leveraging the club with debt. But they've not done anything that's outside of the rules. In the last few years I've now eventually become convinced they're not fit to own the club.

As players at the time, we were aware of the McManus–Magnier and Glazer camps building up their stakes who both had around

29 per cent. But these were different times. We were aware in a passive way. It was very clear to us that we didn't get involved in the business side of the club, and what happens in the boardroom. That was a line you didn't cross in Sir Alex Ferguson's club. In the year after the Glazers took full control, we signed Patrice Evra, Park Ji-sung, Nemanja Vidić and Edwin van der Sar. Not expensive signings but smart ones. The following summer we signed Michael Carrick. We were on a roll regarding top signings! We would win three successive Premier League titles from 2007 to 2009 and the Champions League in 2008 with the great Tevez, Ronaldo, Rooney team. We were back in charge of English football and everything seemed fine.

But there were warning signs that this might not be good. David Gill, the chief executive, had initially come out against the Glazers, saying we shouldn't be putting all that debt on the club. Some fans were outraged and protested vehemently against the family and their model. Looking back, they were right. We'd met the challenge of Chelsea head on, had seen off Arsenal, who were in decline, and were back in charge. How bad could the owners really be?

I can sit here now and wish I had lived in different world, where social media had existed and players spoke up more; that I had paid more attention and not just dismissed it. After all, I had been a United fan since childhood and owners had always been unpopular with the fans, even when we were winning, whether it was Martin Edwards or later the plc board. It didn't seem new to me or particularly worrisome that the fans didn't like the owners. I just thought that was football.

And the truth is I didn't have it in me to speak out. Footballers now have much more character and presence about them. We harp back to characters of old. But there's more to character than playing on with a bloodied bandage around your head. I maintain that players today are stronger willed and have more personality than players of twenty-five years ago. They consistently stand up for issues beyond football, as we've seen with Marcus Rashford on child poverty, Raheem Sterling and Tyrone Mings on racism.

I was a strong-willed footballer, sometimes referred to as Red Nev. I was the union rep and had some basic business understanding at that young age. I was willing to take on the FA and threaten a strike. But, at United, you didn't cross the boundary into off-the-field issues. None of the strong personalities questioned it. Even the most out-spoken footballers around wouldn't get involved in club ownership issues. Whether that be at United or any other football club for tht mater.

I don't think I can regret that now because football was in different times than it is today. You did what you were told. You were told to be here, do that, focus on football. There was no social media. You were very much a footballer one hundred per cent of the time. It wasn't a thought that crossed my mind. Not one player in twenty-six years at United broke rank on issues relating to the board. This isn't an excuse, but just like with other societal and political issues, we kept quiet. It's not something I'm proud of looking back.

And I could justify the Glazers' game plan in my head. I believe in a free society, in capitalism, that you can buy something, that we have listed companies that can be bought and sold. I believe in debt, borrowing to grow. I have debts, mortgages and loans. Loans aren't necessarily bad. My biggest problem is lack of attention to the club and United's decline under the Glazers' ownership.

I always knew that Sir Alex was a phenomenon, a genius. What I didn't properly appreciate was that his presence covered up for the ineptitude of the Glazers. When Sir Alex left in 2013, David Gill, the chief executive, left at the same time and Ed Woodward became executive vice chairman with David Moyes as manager. My first serious doubts about the character of the owners was really in 2014, when they sacked Moyes after ten months. I felt that wasn't the club I had known. Yes, he had a bad run of form and the football was poor, especially compared to what we were used to. But I think if David Gill had still been in charge he would have been given longer. I was prepared, though, to set aside Moyes' sacking, as there were was always going to be turbulence in the post Sir Alex Ferguson era.

But some personal encounters at that time, I thought, showed the Glazers to be petty and small-minded. I had retired in 2011 and had immediately begun developing some business plans. I was working to open our hotel, Hotel Football, which is opposite Old Trafford and was a project backed by myself, Phil, Paul Scholes, Ryan Giggs and Nicky Butt. Initially, we were working with a fan's group to build a supporters' club with offices on top. The fan couldn't go ahead with their share of the investment so I took the plans to United, while David Gill was still chief executive, and offered them a 50 per cent share. Word came back that they weren't interested so I found another partner in Peter Lim.

We had planning permission to build offices, but it didn't really make sense as people wanted office space in central Manchester, while Old Trafford is a few miles from the centre. So we decided to make it a hospitality venue, namely a hotel, and applied to have the planning permission changed. I always attend planning meetings to present my case and when I turned up on this day in 2012, Manchester United were at the meeting. Not just an official, but Michael Bolingbroke, the Chief Operating Officer, the second most important executive, who had been sent along to object. At the time Ryan and Paul were still playing for the club and Nicky was on the coaching staff. I thought that was incredible. To be fair, if Joel Glazer had turned up and told me he had a problem, I could have talked it through. But to send one of their executives to argue the case rather than turn up themselves smacked of throwing one of the team under the bus. Asking someone of Michael's status to attend a planning meeting where they were always going to fail with their objection was cowardly and unimpressive. The decision to object must have been sanctioned from the top and, at United, that is Joel Glazer. Their argument was that our hotel didn't fit their vison for the area. Which, judging by what they have achieved in the ten years since, seems to have been to maintain the environment as an industrial wasteland.

Trafford Council approved our plans unanimously. I held my tongue about it and didn't speak out. But it got worse. Once we had built the hotel, United realised what a mistake they had made. They were horrified. And people at the club told us that they had been banned from visiting the hotel for lunch or coffee. We weren't allowed to book Manchester United tours direct from the hotel. The club wouldn't take our bookings. It was unbelievably petty. Again, I believed it was an order from the top.

I realised for sure then that these aren't the people who should be owning Manchester United. Not because my life was being made inconvenient. That was unimportant. It was the narrowness of the vision, what I thought was the spite directed at people they knew loved the club. And that after we had been open with them and offered them partnership. That demonstrated to me how small-minded they were and how they lacked any creative plan for anything. They didn't seem to understand anything about Manchester, the wider community and the area. I have to say that over the last couple of years, with Richard Arnold coming to more prominence at the club, the relationship has changed.

Despite the fans having been against the Glazers for ten years previously, it only really sank in around 2014 just how bad the situation was. Even so, I never called for their heads. I would criticise their football decision making. But I kept my personal issues with them quiet. The final straw was when they seemed willing to destroy English football with the Super League. That's when I knew I couldn't hold back any longer. Their greed and poverty of vision was just scandalous to me. The idea that you could just cut off the rest of English football and create something that, while it may suit America, is an act of cultural vandalism appeared an extraordinary testament to how little they have learned about England in the nineteen years they have been invested in the club.

There are many things I don't especially criticise them for. I understand business far better now than I did then. And there has been investment in the team. They have trebled the income since they took over. According to Kieran Maguire, who lectures in football finance at Liverpool University, they have spent £830m paying interest loans. And yet, since 2016, the club have paid annual dividends to shareholders, worth £154m. Another £11m was paid out in dividends in June 2022, most of which goes to the Glazer family, and that's after the club lost £23m in 2020 and £92m in 2021 and won no trophies.

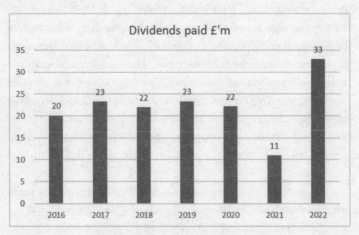

Graphic courtesy of Keiran Maguire

This might well be allowable under company law but as Jim O'Neill says, it seems that, basically, Manchester United has been reduced to being a cash machine for the Glazer family. There are directors on the board, such as Edward Glazer, Darcie Glazer Kassewitz and Kevin Glazer, who appear to have zero interest in the club but sit there anyway and are paid for the trouble. Avram, and especially Joel, might be more involved as Co-Chairmen, but essentially it's seemingly all about taking money out. No other major European club is run this way; not Barcelona, Real Madrid, Bayern Munich. Not even Liverpool, who have American owners. And we're told Todd Boehly at Chelsea won't run things this way.

I have no problem with dividends being paid out by clubs that are successful, in great shape, with a plan and a stadium in fantastic condition, and a training ground as good as it can be, with the team going well and investment set aside for the future. If all that is in place and there is spare cash, then there is no problem with owners, who put the money in and took the risk, benefiting. Clubs like Burnley did that for years under their previous owners and no one batted an eyelid because they were well run. But United aren't in my view.

What should never happen is that the owner is creaming off money, even if it's allowed under the rules, while staff are struggling and the club needs investment. You can't take millions a year out when the ground is rusting, the training ground needs refurbishing and the team is in disarray. My problem with dividends is when the stands aren't painted, the facilities are below par, the hospitality is second rate. Equally, not all debt is bad but imagine if that £830m in interest payments could have been spent on building a stadium like Tottenham's? Not only would the club be in a much better state, but it would be worth more money. So the Glazers would get their money eventually. It could be a win-win for everyone. Instead, the only people winning are the Glazers. The team certainly aren't.

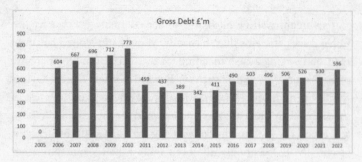

Graphic courtesy of Kieran Maguire

It's clear to me they should sell the club. They need to hand it over to new owners and to do so responsibly, making sure the club passes into good hands, debt-free.

But if they're going to keep the club, I would say the following are essential:

1. They stop taking dividends out for an initial period and they rebuild or refurbish Old Trafford to become the best stadium in the world.
2. They pay off the debt by selling shares in the club to fans and make the club debt free.
3. They rebuild the stadium.
4. They redevelop the training ground into a world class facility.
5. They present a new sporting plan for the next five years and allow it to be scrutinised.

I may be completely wide of the mark, as this is just a gut feeling. However, I do feel that the Glazers are either going to have to sell for a huge profit or dilute by a significant percentage by bringing investment in, in the next year or two. The cost of the five points above that I've listed are, if done properly, substantial. There is no way I can see them raising further debt at the level required.

They've committed to a new plan and stadium redevelopment. The timing, I feel, is right with the significant spend needed, revenues dipping, lending becoming increasingly more difficult with the economy, and Chelsea having set a precedent for a bumper price. I personally feel the window is quite narrow for the Glazer family to sell. Fingers crossed that we are seeing the end of the Glazer reign at Manchester United. The only question then is, where is the suitable successor with the money, vision and sporting principles that United require?

4

THE FAIRER SEX?

'Complaints having been made as to football being played by women, the FA Council feel impelled to express their strong opinion that the game of football is quite unsuitable for females and ought not to be encouraged . . . the council request clubs belonging to the Football Association to refuse the use of their grounds for such matches.'

FA Council, 5 December 1921

Alice Kell was of one of English football's first superstars. Long before Sir Tom Finney, she was the darling of Deepdale, Preston. Prior to Dixie Dean, she shone at Goodison Park.

Prior to England winning Euro 2022, the two most significant dates in the history of women's football in England are Boxing Day 1920, and the FA Council meeting on 5 December 1921. The former date showed clearly, more than a hundred years ago, the potential and star power that women's football had; the latter showed how patriarchies abuse power when they feel under threat from the rise of women.

Goodison Park, Boxing Day, 1920, is an indication of what might have been in the past century if the men who then ran the game had had vision. On that day, Kell led her team, Dick, Kerr Ladies, out at Everton's ground to play St Helen's Ladies in front of 53,000 fans. But such was the excitement surrounding these women's teams, an additional 10–14,000 fans were outside, locked out. Liverpool's men's team played at home later in the day with Dick, Kerr Ladies guests at the match. It attracted 50,000; Everton had played Arsenal the day before and got 35,000.

Goodison wasn't an aberration. There was an equal mania for the women's game as there was for the men's. The women's team of the Dick, Kerr & Co. manufacturing plant in Preston had drawn 25,000 to Deepdale for an international match against a French representative team the same year. They played in front of 22,000 in Paris in a return fixture. Dick, Kerr Ladies games at Accrington, Blackpool and Blackburn typically attracted 15,000. The game at Goodison was the second-highest attendance recorded for any football match in England, male or female, outside of FA Cup finals. The Football League's record attendance at the time was for the Manchester derby between City and United in November 1920, with 63,000, though, of course, had they had a bigger ground, Dick, Kerr Ladies might have beaten that. The average attendance for men's professional teams in Division Two, the equivalent of the Championship, was 16,380 in 1920–21.

Kell was typical of the women drawing crowds to the game. Born in Preston in 1898 into a working-class family, she lived with her parents, Joe and Clara, four brothers Tom, Alf, Sid and Reg and two sisters, Ethel and May, but grew up playing football with her brothers. Tom, her elder brother, enlisted in the Loyal North Lancashire Regiment when the First World War broke out, though according to family members he only did so after being called a coward and presented with a white feather, having not signed up in the first wave of enlistment. He was killed on 15 June 1915 after a bayonet charge and his name is listed on Le Touret Memorial in Pas-de-Calais.

Kell was working at the time at the Dick, Kerr factory

manufacturing shells, destined to bombard German lines on the western front. The company had been formed in 1898 by William Bruce Dick and his nephew John Kerr as an offshoot of the Britannia Engineering Works, based in their native Kilmarnock, and was to provide parts for the electrification of tramways and railways. With the outbreak of war in 1914, the Admiralty approached the factory owners to switch to the production of ammunition.

Kell was part of an early wave of what might now be described as feminist empowerment, one of the so-called Munitionettes, women drafted in to do the heavy lifting of manufacturing work, providing munitions while men were away at the front. And it was literally heavy lifting at times, lugging 50kg coal sacks around at the factory to keep the fires burning. They worked amid toxic chemicals – the women working with TNT often suffered from jaundice, and were known as canaries, due to their skin turning yellow. Some would die of jaundice while others lost their lives or eyes or fingers due to accidental explosions.

As a footballer, Kell was widely deemed to be exceptional. 'She worked with a skill that no professional player could have excelled,' reported the *Lancashire Evening Post*. Grace Sibbert is the young woman to whom Kell and the Dick, Kerr Ladies team owed their opportunity to play. Sibbert and other young women would join with the lads playing football in the tea breaks at the factory. In October 1917, with the men's works' team suffering a run of defeats, Sibbert is said to have goaded the lads in the works canteen. 'Call yourself a football team?' she teased the men. 'We could do better than you lot.' Piqued, the men's team challenged them to a game. Sibbert, twenty-six, was the driving force in organising the women. It might have been a diversion from weightier matters. Sibbert's husband, Jimmy, was a prisoner of war at the time. There is no record of the result, though there is a historic photo of the women's team and it must have gone well, for they had no intention of stopping.

A suggestion was made that a charity match of the Dick, Kerr women's team against the neighbouring Arundel Coulthard Foundry take place on Christmas Day 1917 at Deepdale, Preston North End's ground, in aid of convalescing soldiers. It is striking that in these early days there was no chauvinistic opposition recorded. Preston waived the £5 cost for hiring the ground and advertised the game at the stadium. Kell, who along with her childhood friend, Florrie Redford, was widely recognised as the best player, was captain of the team. It's difficult to imagine what they might have expected, but you suspect had they attracted a few hundred spectators, it would have been deemed a success. Yet 10,000 fans turned up. According to Gail Newsham, in her book *In a League of Their Own!*, Kell had to calm down some of her teammates, who were overwhelmed by the size of the crowd, with a steadying team talk. The *Lancashire Daily Post* sent a reporter along, and though there were elements of men patronising women, it wasn't the predominating sentiment. 'At first the spectators were inclined to treat the game with a little too much levity and found amusement in almost everything from the pace [of the game] . . . to the "how dare you" expression of a player when she was pushed by an opponent,' wrote the *Post*. 'But when they saw the ladies meant business and were "playing the game" they readily took up the correct attitude and impartially cheered and encouraged both teams.' Dick, Kerr Ladies won the match 4–0 and £600 was raised, around £50,000 in today's money. A 1917 scrapbook* report recorded the fact that it was the biggest crowd at Deepdale that year and commented that although the majority of the 10,000 crowd:

---

* A scrapbook was collated by the team's manager, Alfred Frankland, and was passed on to Gail Newsham by Kath Latham who had taken on the running of the club in 1957.

no doubt went with the object of being amused . . . all agreed at the end that the quality of the football shown was much better than expected. One or two individual performances indeed were surprisingly good, particularly in regard to 'ball control' . . . These outstanding players showed that they had made consider-able progress in the dribbling art and that they could put a good deal of power in their kicks.

More fixtures were hastily arranged in 1918, against Barrow and the Lancaster Ladies, which attracted 5,000 spectators.

All of these details have been collated by Newsham in her book, a meticulously-researched history of this story, which is still not as widely known as I feel it should be. This chapter could only be written because of her work. When we surveyed football fans, 65 per cent said they knew nothing about these events at all. Only 20 per cent knew a fair amount or a great deal. This scandal is still a relatively unknown story in English football and yet its context is vital when we discuss the women's game in this country. 'I have often said we need to inform people more on the history of women's football,' said Newsham. 'Generations of people have been brought up to believe that football isn't a game for females, but I firmly believe this is a throwback to the FA ban in 1921 and everything they subsequently said and did to prevent women from playing. Only by telling the true and rich history of the women's game, and highlighting the injustice, can we hope to change long held attitudes that have been born out of a lack of knowledge of the historical facts. No other country in the world has this kind of history and it should celebrated more widely. What the Dick, Kerr Ladies achieved is no less important than that of the current play-ers today.

And while one player, Molly Walker, was reportedly shunned by her boyfriend's family for showing her legs in public, generally there seemed to be widespread enthusiasm for the women's game.

Preston North End, for a 20 per cent cut of the gate, were happy for Dick, Kerr Ladies to use Deepdale, and further fixtures against Lancaster and Bolton at the ground attracted 5,000 and 6,000 spectators, proving that the game had support beyond the novelty of the initial fixture. It is interesting to note that the *Lancashire Daily Post* felt the need to publish an article entitled 'Ladies Football Justified', yet its tone indicates the groundswell of support and civic pride in the rise of the Dick, Kerr Ladies. 'When the munition girls began to invade the football field, some of the old shell hacks scoffed at their usefulness both in the playing sense and as an attraction,' the article read. 'In Preston the movement had been fostered instead of derided and in the Dick, Kerr's eleven we have had perhaps the best ladies team in the country.' Likewise, the company itself was fully supportive of the women's team.

When the war ceased, there was no question of games ceasing, and the firm made a ground available for the women to play and train at, Ashton Park, according to the company's 1919 Annual General Meeting minutes. This also records that the factory general manager, Mr J. Conner, invited the team to a social evening where each player was presented with an engraved gold bracelet. According to Newsham's book, Kell was interviewed in a newspaper around this time for an article entitled: 'Should Girls Play Football?'

'I can best answer this question by asking, "Why should they not?" We love a game of football better than any other sport in the whole world. I know that the girls who play football are the best and most willing workers at Dick, Kerr's. I have repeated assertions of this from the foreman at our works and if fresh air and healthy recreation have a beneficial effect on men, surely it confers the similar benefits on girls? Several leading gentlemen of Preston who were rather opposed to the idea of ladies playing football at the outset are now distinctly with us. Were [sic] as they criticised at first, they now have nothing but praise for us. Several of them were astounded at the quality of football shown in our matches. We are true sportswomen. We do not retaliate. If we get bowled over, we treat it as a joke. If girls play football in the right spirit it is bound to be good for them and ought to make them more equipped for the battle of life.'

'I believe that the Goodison match at the end of 1920 would have sent shock waves throughout the football establishment,' said Newsham. 'There you had the two Merseyside clubs with home fixtures over the festive period, yet 53,000 still turned out to watch a women's football match when both local teams had home fixtures against top opposition. Throughout 1921 the FA made it increasingly more difficult for clubs to let their grounds for women's matches but the Dick, Kerr Ladies played sixty seven games of football that year and almost 900,000 people came to watch them. But by the end of 1921, women's football would be seen in a very different light.' These young women were creating history at every turn. In April 1920, after an approach from the Fédération des Sociétés Féminines Sportives de France, a select team of French women travelled to Preston to play what appears to be the first ever women's international football match. Twenty-five thousand came to Deepdale to watch Dick, Kerr Ladies win 2–0. By contrast, the England men's team that year attracted 35,000 for their game against Scotland at Hillsborough. Fifteen thousand then turned up at Edgeley Park, Stockport, for the second match of the tour, a 5–2 win for Dick, Kerr Ladies. The two teams drew their next match in front of 12,000 supporters at Manchester City's Hyde Road ground before the French finally won the last game of the tour 2–1, in London at Stamford Bridge, in front of 10,000. There was an appetite for the women's game all over the country. The first foreign transfer also came out of the tour, France goalkeeper

Louise Ourry staying on in Preston to continue playing for Dick, Kerr Ladies. She would only return to Paris when a return trip was made later in the year, a crowd of 22,000 turning up to see the teams play out a 1–1 draw in Paris.

All this was achieved with the support of Football League clubs – who were happy to allow women's teams to use their grounds, even if they took a cut of the gate receipts – and with the encouragement of male owners of the factories and male supporters. Indeed, one local newspaper writer, not identified specifically but, given the cultural backdrop, likely to be male, revelled in the success of the team, just as he would in that of Preston North End, who won the league and cup double in the first season of the Football League in 1888–89, going unbeaten all season. 'It's coincidental to think that in leading the way among the ladies teams of the land, Dick, Kerr's are but emulating what "Proud Preston" did in men's football way back in the 1880s,' he wrote. 'Preston North End were then known as "The Invincibles": Dick, Kerr Ladies are the Invincibles of today.' The writer adds, noting the crowds they attracted, that 'something will have to be done . . . to increase public accommodation'.

In short, it appears that there was no groundswell of opposition to women's football from most men. By contrast, it seems as though they enthusiastically embraced the development. Not all men, however. There was a select group that was very much opposed. By 1921, there were grumblings at the FA who were worried about where the huge gate receipts were ending up. These games were styled as charity matches and the FA seemed prepared to permit that, but not something that might evolve into professional competition to the men's game. They couched this is concern that some female players might be being paid. That, in itself, is bizarre. Though the amateur/professional divide was still hugely significant in British sporting culture at the time, football had been one of the first sports to accept professionalism, such was its popularity and the amount of money being generated. However, that only apparently worked for men.

Newsham says there is evidence that some money was going to either managers or players. She interviewed Lydia Ackers, a St Helens player in 1920, who said that West Cheshire's team manager came in before the game to ask them how much they were being paid, to which Ackers and her teammate replied ten shillings, the amount to cover expenses and time off work. 'But he was asking for much more [money than that],' Ackers recalled. Clearly, there were people sensing there was money to be made from these charity games, but it almost certainly wouldn't have been the women themselves who principally benefited. Alice Kell was adamant they only received expenses and pay for time missed at work: 'We play for the love of the game . . . It is almost impossible for working girls to afford to leave work to play matches in Scotland, Ireland and up and down the country and be the losers. I cannot see the slightest reason why they shouldn't be compensated for their loss of time.'

Yet the FA, headed by Lord Arthur Kinnaird – the same man who presented the FA Cup to Bury in 1903 – were working up a head of steam over the matter. They only agreed permission for a game between Dick, Kerr Ladies and the South of England, to be played at Bristol City in September 1921, on condition that the club was responsible for receipts and payments. And they reprimanded Winchester FC in November 1921 for hosting a match between Plymouth and Seaton Ladies without their permission. Doctors were enlisted in the FA cause, which increasingly came across as not just patriarchal but also paternalistic. To twist the knife, they were female doctors. Dr Mary Scharlieb, a Harley Street physician – some way removed in social class from the factory girls of Dick, Kerr – wrote: 'I consider it a most unsuitable game, too much for a woman's frame.' Dr Elizabeth Sloan Chesser wasn't in favour of a ban, but wrote: 'There are physical reasons why the game is harmful to women. It is a rough game at any time but more harmful to women than to men. They may never recover from the injuries they receive.'

With their paternal sense of duty bolstered by medical opinion, and reinforced also by their inflexible belief that they were the protectors of amateurism – a curious position for a sport already professional – the sixty men of the Football Association met on that fateful day of 5 December 1921. 'Complaints having been made as to football being played by women, the Council feel impelled to express their strong opinion that the game of football is quite unsuitable for females and ought not to be encouraged,' read the minutes of the meeting. 'The Council are further of the opinion that an excessive proportion of the receipts are absorbed in expenses and an inadequate percentage devoted to charitable objects. For these reasons the council request clubs belonging to the Football Association to refuse the use of their grounds for such matches.'

There was outrage. Alice Woods, from St Helens, who was the first woman to win an Amateur Athletics Association competitive race, an eighty-yard sprint in 1918, and who was playing for Dick, Kerr Ladies at the time of the ruling, said: 'We were all disgusted with the FA after we had played all those games for charity. They said it wasn't a game for ladies. But we all thought it was because we were getting the spectators that the men didn't get, especially in the outlying districts in small rounds. We always had terrific crowds.' Kell wrote:

Girls have a right to play football if they desire. We play for the love of the game and are determined to go on.

They did fight back. A Ladies Football Association was founded. Women could still play games at smaller, non-FA grounds, though typically they could now only attract around three thousand fans. Dick, Kerr Ladies went on playing at their Ashton Park ground. An English Ladies FA Cup was set up in 1922, but Dick, Kerr Ladies were not entered. It is unclear why. Perhaps they already had their sights on bigger horizons; a tour to the USA and Canada was being organised. In 1922 they travelled to North America and played games in New Jersey, Rhode Island and New York in front of crowds between five thousand and nine thousand. They were due also to play in Canada, but the FA there refused them permission. Meanwhile, Stoke Ladies would win the inaugural ELFA Cup, but without the support of the men's game and the impetus that playing in front of large crowds gave the women, the ELFA fizzled out. Talk of a league faded. Dick, Kerr Ladies would go on playing and touring and in the early 1960s no less than Sir Matt Busby watched them play in Blackpool, commenting that Val Walsh was of the best players he had ever seen. The team eventually disbanded in 1965, ironically just six years before the FA would rescind their ban on women using their facilities in 1971. The history is important and Newsham's book is a vital document of what happened because once you know this story, it changes how many people feel about women's football. Broadly, fans are supportive of the men's game supporting the women's game. Our survey found that 61 per cent supported that proposition, 21 per cent of people being strongly supportive. But once you relay just a few of the facts about Dick, Kerr Ladies, the number of people who strongly agree that men's football has an obligation to support the women's game rises to 34 per cent. The overall figure of people who agree or strongly agree rises to 71 per cent. Once you know the context, there is an overwhelming majority of people who understand that football has a historical debt to pay to the women's game. Yet the possibility of a thriving, professional women's game had been strangled at birth by the game's very guardians.

Girls who wanted to play football were actively discouraged. I know because my mum was one of them. In fact, she became a bit of a story. 'I was about nine years old and I started playing football for St Stephen's, which was my junior school, and I played right wing,' she explains. 'I was quite good, good enough to be in the school team. I don't think the other teams realised I was a girl, or it didn't bother them. And the boys on my team were fine. They were not bothered because I was quite a fast runner. I was quite nippy and had a good cross on me.

'Then one school came to play us, saw me and said that they wouldn't play or rather that they wouldn't let me play. They said because we're playing against a girl, we can't kick and we can't tackle and we can't do this, that and the other. It was a home game, I remember, because I had to change in, like, a little office, I didn't change with the boys. And when I had got changed they said: "No, she can't play." They just said: "Oh, there's a girl there. We're not playing." That's how it all came about.

'I just thought: "We're all the same really. What difference does it actually make?" You're a nine-year-old and I'd played with the boys and trained with them at school and that. I didn't play for any other team, it was just the school then. I just felt let down because we all played outside together in the streets at that time.'

It became a bit of a local issue, according to Mum. First, the *Bury Times* came calling and eventually the story became so big she ended up in London on the BBC *Tonight* programme with Cliff Michelmore, the 1960s equivalent of *The One Show*. 'That was quite a big deal because we flew down – in 1960 – and I remember it was like going on a crop-spreader,' she recalled. 'I can remember it being very bumpy coming back and feeling sick. Before that trip, I'd only been to Fleetwood for my holidays.

'I didn't really want to go. I don't like the limelight, but my mum said I had to! So, my mum came and I think my nan came with me as well. And we just went down for the day. I remember the bit we did on TV. At that time I didn't feel an injustice that I couldn't play football. I was just annoyed. I wouldn't have gone parading out and making a big issue of it. I think I kept playing for the football team after all that but then the year after I didn't because netball was my the thing. The football dwindled out. Maybe it seemed best that I didn't play. There wasn't any women's football and I think that's probably why they stopped a girl playing.'

My mum typically has tried to play her own experience down. When she told me this story as a teenager, I didn't really think anything of it. This was a period where sexism, misogyny, racism and other major societal issues were just glossed over and swept under the carpet. Looking back, this unacceptably was the norm. However, in 2022 as I speak to my mum and listen to her recount her story, it's a horrible read. When I think of my sister's emergence in sport, my brother's journey with the England women's team and both my daughters excitement they freely enjoy playing various sports, including football, it's depressing that my mum was discouraged and prevented from exploring her own passion for the sport.

Sylvia Gore, who died in 2016, played for Manchester Corinthians in the 1960s and the effects of the ban were clear. 'We played on park pitches in Frog Lane and had nothing,' she told *FourFourTwo* magazine. 'We just had an old hut and we used to get washed in buckets of water that the manager brought across. We had no heating, nothing.'

It wasn't until 1969 that a new women's FA was formed on the back of resurgent interest in football following England's 1966 World Cup win. The inaugural winners of the women's FA Cup in 1971 were Southampton Women's FC, whose only connection with the men's club was that its founders were supporters. In an echo of the men's finals 77 years before, the final took place at Crystal Palace athletics stadium, built on the original football stadium and, as in the original men's FA Cup, a Scottish side reached the final, Stewarton Thistle. The first ever official England national team's international took place against Scotland in Greenock, 1972, exactly one hundred years after England had played Scotland in the first men's international. Gore scored the first ever international goal for England in a 3–2 win.

There were many heroines in those years. Sue Lopez was a founding member of the successful Southampton Women's team; she also played in Italy, where she at least got paid expenses. Setting up Southampton was hard. 'We used to play at Southampton Common and it had a pub called The Cowherds,' she told *FourFourTwo*. 'That tells you what it was like back in Victorian times: people's cattle probably did feed on this bit of ground. The football pitches were really rough, with no nets, and we used to play at places like that most of the time.'

In 1993, the FA finally took on the responsibility of running the women's game, and in 1994 the Women's National League became the Women's Premier League, the forerunner of the Women's Super League today.

About that time Faye White was discovering her first ever women's team, Horsham Ladies, as a fourteen-year-old girl. White would go on to become one of the icons of the English game, captain of the national team, winning ninety caps, leading them to the Euro 2009 final, as well as at Euro 2005 in England and at World Cups in 2007 and 2011. At Arsenal, she won the Champions League, ten FA Women's Premier League titles as well as the inaugural Women's Super League in 2011 and nine FA Cups.

Initially, she trained with her older brother's team because there was nowhere else to play. She only sought out Horsham Ladies because, at fourteen, she was still playing (and holding her own) with and against sixteen-year-old boys.

'My parents were happy and didn't have a problem with their little daughter playing football,' said White. 'But it was just wider society. It was like: "You shouldn't play because you're a girl." The messages were: "You can't play, it's a boys' league." ' Undeterred, with the help of PE teachers, Faye set up a girls' team at her secondary school. 'My PE teachers tried to adapt but the curriculum didn't allow it and they were trying to find ways to let us play.' By the time she left, however, a girls' league had been established for local schools.

'It's just what is seen and learned,' says White. 'There was no set-up for girls and I did feel quite alienated. I was referred to as a tomboy. I would think: "Why am I a tomboy just because I love sport?" Every moment I had, I wasn't playing with a doll, I was out in the garden playing football or rounders. I still did things that girls did, but because I was sporty, active and competitive, I was a tomboy.' Faye was widely accepted among the boys she played with, even if her brother got a bit miffed when she turned up at the family day at his Scout camp and won the sports' competition. 'I tried Brownies and Girl Guides and it just didn't fit with me because we had to learn how to clean up, wash toilets and sew. I was like: "I don't want to do that! I just want to play!" '

When White joined Arsenal in 1996, the same year that Arsène Wenger took over the men's team, she paid subs to play and train under manager Vic Akers, who as well as being kit man for the men's team, coached the women. 'We found Vic's notebooks a few years ago where he would write down the team and who had paid their subs!' says White. Bear in mind, though, that Arsenal were innovators compared to most clubs. 'We started to be paid a match rate and Arsenal were so forward thinking, they created jobs for the women in the set-up, allowing us not to have full-time jobs. I was a fitness instructor at the time and I had to take unpaid leave to play for my country.'

In 2009, the FA introduced central contracts for international players, worth £16,000 a year. 'I was working for Arsenal and earned a salary doing a nine-to-five job. I would then train in the evenings. I had a playing contract with Arsenal, which was a daily rate; then central contracts were subsidised and that allowed some of the girls to go part time,' said White. 'Around the 2011 World Cup, I got quite a lot of sponsors coming in, together with some significant sums of money – as much as £10,000 in some instances. But not like what the girls are earning now! During my career, though, as an England captain, I had quite a good living.'

These days the top women, such as Sam Kerr in the WSL, would be on around £350,000 a year at Chelsea, similar to a mid-level Championship player. Reviewing the progress that has been made, White says: 'I suppose I am satisfied but that's because I grew up knowing what limitations I had and I know it is so much better now. Young girls will be able to play in their own environments. I have met a lot of women who have said they never played because they had to play with the boys. Or that they would have loved to play more, but there just weren't any teams for them to join. Think of the number of women who have missed out.

'There was still a lack of opportunity in the 1990s. Nowadays, five-year-old girls are getting coaching, but I had absolutely no coaching until I joined that first women's team at fourteen and then Arsenal in 1996. I catch myself sometimes. I have to change what I'm saying. I'm speaking, like, it's when I grew up and girls haven't got the chance. That's gone now. But I do still think there's so much more? that can be done. I went back to Horsham recently and met someone at Horsham Sparrows, and their attitude was: "We are just a football club. Not a girls or boys club. We're 50/50 in our membership and we try to put the message out there that we're a football club and we don't differentiate." That's how it should be everywhere. My nine-year-old son has grown up knowing that Mummy played football, but I remember him coming home one day and saying: "But Mummy, boys are better at football than girls!" And I thought: "Where's he got that from?! He hasn't grown up in a home where that's the accepted wisdom." So you pick it up in the playground somewhere. Let's try to get across the message that it's just football we're watching on TV today; not women's football or men's football.

'I always had this feeling, especially when I was England captain, of having to promote the women's game. When I joined the England team, the stereotype was that it was butch and that players would have short hair and like baggy clothes. My thought was: "I still have long hair!" The US team were in the ponytail era. The assumption was always that you would want to mimic males, and I thought: "That's not how I feel! I just want to play football and feel feminine. I'm still a girl." I saw the change to fitted kits to show that we are feminine. I've done many interviews where it was: "How would you compare to the men. How would you compare to Thierry Henry? What would the score be if you played them?" I would think; "Why are you saying that? We wouldn't say something along those lines to Steffi Graf. Do we do so with tennis or athletics?" We don't want to play against the men, we know they're faster and more physical. I feel it was like that throughout my whole time, though you would get less of those kind of questions it towards the end.'

My brother Phil was England Women's team manager from 2018 to 2021, taking them to the World Cup semi-final in 2019, and he has strong views on the history of the women's game. 'It's actually quite disgusting the way that women footballers were treated in this country,' he says. 'The FA banned them for fifty years. Fifty years! And people don't know that or don't realise the extent to which female footballers have been suppressed. That's fifty years of development, fifty years of visibility, fifty years of learning, and it's no wonder now that the women's game is playing massive catch-up. That's generations of footballers that were missed.

'When we had just come back from reaching the World Cup

semi-final in 2019 there was massive investment and interest in the women's game. That was when I started to learn about Dick, Kerr Ladies. Like most people, what struck me was that they were getting 50,000 watching them play so many years ago. I'm thinking: "I wonder if that had continued whether the women's game would've been equal to the men's game now?" It was shut down because of sexism. It was shut down because of everything that we're now fighting against. It wasn't shut down because of financial reasons, like they said; it was not that women were being paid. It was shut down because the leaders back then wanted to suppress women. They felt they were getting too powerful, too popular, and they didn't like it.

'Had the women's game been supported I think you would have had the leagues growing side by side simultaneously. You would have had a Premier League. You would have had Champions Leagues. Everything. It would have grown at the same speed. All the things that the women's game is now catching up on – visibility, finance, greater technical and tactical depth – would be there. Everything would have been growing at the same speed.'

It's hard not to wonder what might have been had the FA just got behind women's football in 1921, even cynically, as a cash-generating exercise. 'What did the ban do? We'll never know', says White, ' I have always wondered whether my path and that of future players would have been very different had women's football been allowed to evolve like the men's game.'

The FA now is obviously a very different organisation. 'Throughout my career the FA have been integral in driving the women's game to get coverage,' said White. 'I see the people who work for the FA now, and they have a huge passion to drive it forward, so we can't keep hitting the FA over the head for what people did years ago. That decision did affect us, but they're not the people who are running it now.'

The potential of women's football is evident. A big

breakthrough was the 1999 Women's World Cup final when 90,185 watched the USA beat China at the Rose Bowl, Pasadena. For White, her big moment of realising what might happen came just as she retired, a crowd of 70,584 turning up to watch the Team GB women's team play Brazil at Wembley for the 2012 Olympics and then 80,203 watched the final there between USA and Japan. Since then we've had 77,768 for England v Germany at Wembley in 2019, and in March 2022, Barcelona v Real Madrid at the Nou Camp broke the world record with an extraordinary 91,553 and then broke it again the following month with 91,648 in the semi-final against Wolfsburg. We had sell out crowds for England at Euro 2022. This year's FA Cup Final attracted 49,094 and Tottenham v Arsenal in 2019 drew a crowd of 38,262. Still, though, the record for a club game in England is held by Dick, Kerr Ladies. Kelly Simmons, FA Director of the Women's Professional Game, spoke on Alex Scott's BBC documentary about the need to build on this momentum. 'Now that we're coming back from Covid, we have to get the attendances growing again,' she said. 'Before Covid we were at Tottenham v Arsenal, 38,000 in that fantastic stadium. It was one of those special moments and that's what big games in this country will look like long term. That's where we want to get to.'

My brother, Phil, is characteristically unequivocal on the issue. 'Football should be able to see the potential, going right back to Dick, Kerr Ladies,' he says. 'If you can get 70,000 people into Wembley for a women's game, they're going to make money. Barcelona got 91,553 for their Champions League quarter-final against Real Madrid and sold out the semi against Wolfsburg.' But it's about making these women visible so that they can then start making money, become heroes, become legends. We're still light years behind. We've still so much to do.

'The pandemic set women's football back a little bit in terms of visibility. Everything went into the men's game when we had the pandemic. It came right from the top with UEFA, whose approach was: "Let's just focus on the Euros for the men." So, the women's Euros, scheduled for 2021, just got bumped on a year. And the women had to take a backseat. The Premier League opened up for the men in the middle of the pandemic, but not the Women's Super League. The testing facilities for the women were different from those for the men. I felt that the women's game had lost momentum.

'You still encounter blatant sexism. One story that got attention when I was England manager was my insistence that we fly business class. We flew to most games in Europe on EasyJet and I was like: "This is just not right. It's not right." And I'm not a snob. I flew backwards and forwards from Spain on EasyJet all the time. But this is the England Women's National Team and we're flying on EasyJet. We came back from Russia through Austria. It wasn't even a direct flight. And I'm not just comparing us to the men's team, who of course fly by private jet. The England men's under-21 team flew private charter. What message does that send to girls? That an eighteen-year-old is more deserving than Lucy Bronze, voted best player in the world in 2020. I'm not being awkward, I'm not being one of those activists. I'm just saying it's fundamentally not right. I was really calm about it all the time, but I just made the point. And nobody could argue with it. Nobody could tell me that it was right. I would never fight for something that we didn't deserve.'

It was only in February 2022 that the US women's team secured equal pay with the men's national team after a six-year legal fight. The US women's team has won four World Cups and four Olympic Games. The US men's team came third at the inaugural World Cup in 1930 and since then has made just one quarter-final. The England women's team has had equal pay since January 2020.

The issue gets more complex in club football, as White points out. 'With national teams, I think it is different and has to be equal,' she said. 'For England, whether you're a man or a woman, you're playing for your country and it has to be equal. But at club level, we can't get equal pay if we're not getting the same number of people watching. I know some people disagree with that, but I think it's about growing the crowd base and growing the game itself at the right pace rather than always comparing ourselves to men.

'It's trying to get balance. There was a time when, in the WSL, people were talking about imposing a wage cap as the right way to make things more even, so that other teams could get into the league.' Steve Parish, the Crystal Palace owner, made this point to me when we spoke for this book. Palace's women's team is in the Championship, but it will be hard for them to compete should they make it to the Premier League, because of the salaries Manchester City and Chelsea pay, essentially running their teams as a loss leader. It is hard to justify investment.

'I have heard one of the clubs saying we won't invest unless we can control what we pay players,' said White. No one wants to regress the growth of women's wages, but equally, just as in men's football, a league where Chelsea and Manchester City share the trophies every year won't build a lucrative TV deal. The £24m deal between Sky and the FA to screen the WSL is, of course, a fraction of the men's deal. But it does show the game can stand on its own merits. Emma Hayes, the hugely-successful Chelsea manager and respected TV pundit, believes that even though White's Arsenal team are still the only English winners of the Champions League, back in 2007, that the WSL is world leading. 'The combination of the FA expertise plus men's football clubs being involved has propelled our game beyond other countries,' she told Scott on the BBC documentary.

Yet there are some tough questions to ask about the future. At present, huge attendances are often driven by free or cheap tickets. 'We always sell our sport so cheaply to get numbers in but I think we have to reconsider that model,' said Hayes.

White wants the game to grow organically, rather than fall into the trap some franchises have done in the USA. In 2009, LA Sol paid Marta, then the world's best woman player, a ground-breaking $400,000 a year. The club then folded in 2010. 'You don't want that to happen here,' said White. With clubs such as City, Chelsea and now Manchester United, there is more security. But there have been examples of clubs ditching their women's team when they lost interest in them or when the men's team fell on hard times, as with Fulham in 2006 and Notts County in 2017. Both clubs now have reintegrated women's teams into the club.

The fan-led review by Tracey Crouch recognised the salary issue, reporting that:

> Concern was also raised that a damaging wage race was developing in the women's game. This in turn resulted in a concern that if the women's game became uncompetitive, with success concentrated in a few wealthy clubs linked to men's teams, this could hurt the commercial development of women's football . . . there was a related concern that, as spending increased on wages, opportunities for home-grown talent were being restricted by the influx of foreign stars.

It also cited the case of prize money in the FA Cup. In 2021, Clapton CFC, from the seventh tier, did brilliantly to get through to the FA Cup third round to play Plymouth. They needed to win to pick up the £1,250 prize money – they lost 5–0 – but even that wouldn't have covered their travel and accommodation. As a result, the Vitality Women's FA Cup prize fund will increase to £3m per year from 2022–23. Before, it was £309,000.

Tracey Crouch's review made it clear that the women's game

needs its own independent review to set the path for the next twenty-five years. That can't come soon enough. For English football to be strong, the whole of football needs to be strong. If it's the people's game, it needs to represent all of the people, not 50 per cent of them.

For White, the future is positive, especially after the amazing Euro 2022 win. It is the girls in the playground she wants to help, and Baroness Sue Campbell, the FA's Director of Women's Football, has set a strategic objective that by 2024 every girl should have equal access to participate, compete and excel in football. The FA Girls' Football School Partnerships will help to achieve that. 'That's the one thing that would drive participation and playing numbers, and mean that it becomes the norm for kids growing up, which will help to effect that cultural change,' said White. 'We can have just as many girls playing in primary schools as boys, and they can experience football, not just netball and hockey. Obviously, we could do with more sponsorships and the glamour side of all this. But once these girls come through, it will make a massive difference.'

We've come a long way, but not far enough. We need to ensure the next steps of the journey don't take another century to come to fruition. At least the Faye Whites of today won't be alone in the playground when they want to play football. From Alice Kell to Sue Lopez, Faye White and Lucy Bronze, amid the many other trailblazers, we need to acknowledge that the fight has been long and hard up to this point. And to ensure that the men's game is battling shoulder to shoulder in the future, bearing its weight of responsibility.

5

THE BIGGER PICTURE

'Your next Class of 92 TV programme should be about making Salford sustainable.'
Andy Holt, Owner of Accrington Stanley FC

Before the Super League proposal, we had already had one brief convulsion in the game. On Sunday lunchtime, 11 October 2020, a story was dropped on the *Telegraph* website by Sam Wallace. It was a revolutionary plan called 'Project Big Picture'. The Premier League were willing to advance £250m to the Football League, the EFL, to get them through Covid. They would give £100m to the FA to kick-start a grassroots revolution and investment in the women's game. And the future share of combined TV revenue of the Premier League and the EFL would be split, 75 per cent to the Premier League and 25 per cent to the EFL.

As ever, communication is everything in the eye of a crisis. The proposals leaked and one person put his head above the parapet to defend it: Rick Parry, chairman of the EFL. Parry has had a circuitous route to become chairman of the EFL. He was the chief executive of Liverpool and was the first chief executive of the Premier League back in 1992, when it was originally formed. Perhaps people regarded him with suspicion because of that. By Wednesday, only three days after its announcement, the idea was dead, killed by the Premier League.

Let's be clear. It wasn't perfect. The scheme had arisen out of talks between the FA, the EFL and Manchester United and Liverpool, though it seemed Spurs, Arsenal, Manchester City and Chelsea had early warning. The problem was it presented, what looked like, a power grab by the Big Six. The League Cup would probably have been discontinued, or carried on without the biggest clubs. They were going to change the voting structure of the Premier League so that the nine longest-serving clubs would have the power. As 'long-term stakeholders', if six of them agreed on reform, it would become policy. The Premier League would have been reduced to eighteen clubs, so half would really be bit-part members just making up the numbers. But more money for a new independent women's league, fan charters, Financial Fair Play regulation, more clarity about ownership rules and spending were all included in the plan. As the document said: 'A reset of the economics and governance of the English football pyramid is long overdue.' Who could argue with that?

I remember when Parry presented the proposals to the EFL clubs on Zoom. As an owner I was there and some people outside the meeting thought it might be Parry's suicide note. He had been involved in talks and there were those who felt it was selling out the pyramid. But it was never like that. He had kept us up to date on progress but he was working on something behind the scenes to correct the financial disparity. And, with the proviso that some changes needed to be made, we were in the main behind the proposal.

What killed it was the idea of reducing the Premier League to eighteen clubs and a change in voting rules which would have favoured the big six. The fourteen were never going to go for this dramatic change in the voting constitution and the potential for 2 of them to be kicked out of the league with less opportunity to return. This was like asking turkeys to vote for Christmas. I think another issue, and this happens a lot with failed proposals, is that not all clubs were brought along for the journey. The fourteen clubs of the Premier League outside the Big Six, were not included in discussions as I suspect the 'Project Big Picture' instigators felt it would be an immediate roadblock. But there would be losers in all this and something had to be done to address their concerns. My view is that Big Picture had some merits and it could have been a proposal to negotiate from, rather than being seen and presented as a conclusion of how the game could be reshaped. It landed horribly. The government, seeing the reaction of the majority of the Premier League clubs, condemned the 'back-room deals'. And the FA joined them in disowning the plan. The then chairman, Greg Clarke, wrote to the FA Council, to express his opposition.

> With the knowledge of senior Board members and our CEO, I participated in the early stages of discussions. However when the principal aim of these discussions became the concentration of power and wealth in the hands of a few clubs with a breakaway league mooted as a threat, I, of course, discontinued my involvement and counselled a more consensus-based approach involving all Premier League clubs and its Chair and CEO.

Clarke is no longer at the organisation, after his disastrous House of Commons Committee appearance in which he referred to 'coloured players', repeated stereotypes about young female players and described coming out as an LGBT player as a 'life choice'. However, his opposition here was a curious stance because he may have been the visionary who saved the game had he played it differently.

'The initiative was started by Greg Clarke, Chairman of the FA,' said Parry when we met on Zoom to talk over the issues of this book. 'Listen, I give him great credit for identifying there was a problem. He recognised that there were tensions within the Premier League that the bigger clubs were unhappy about.

Everybody knows that the Premier League can't seem to vote on anything easily. There is a massive tension and, ironically, Greg was concerned that if we don't do something to address the challenges maybe they'll go off and form a Super League. So he was actually quite prophetic in that.

'He invited me to a meeting, so this wasn't smoke-filled rooms. This wasn't something underhand. If you're invited by the Chairman of the FA you think: 'Okay, this is good. This is entirely legitimate.' And Big Picture for us, and for the FA, frankly, was fantastic because it had the redistribution that we wanted. It had 75 per cent to the Premier League and 25 per cent to the EFL. It had better financial controls. It had the abolition of parachute payments [the extra TV money relegated clubs get from the Premier League]. All the things that I've talked about were in it. For all the cries of anguish over the voting structure, the fundamental problem was reduction to eighteen clubs in the Premier League. I think that was the bigger source of concern because that's something the clubs will never vote for 'cause two of them are going to drop out.'

There you have it from the horses mouth and something that doesn't surprise me. It's how I've always viewed the FA. An organisation that lacks backbone when the going gets tough and runs for the hills. Why didn't Clarke just come clean and tell us what we all know, that the game needs restructuring and that he was leading on this from the front?

There's so much distrust and suspicion in football, which meant we chucked out the baby with the bathwater. Remember this was mid-pandemic, we were all still in a state of worry and confusion, and fans weren't in stadia. We had no clear idea when they would be back. It's perhaps not surprising there was a lack of rational discussion.

The reaction to it was more evidence that football can't govern itself. Every time it brings a proposal forward, whether it be FIFA, whether it be Big Picture, whether it's Super League, the game just doesn't trust whoever is bringing up the suggestion. And the fans trust the authorities even less because they have been so screwed over. That for me is the biggest and the largest piece of evidence that football can't really reset, can't restructure.

And there were some key sneaky details in there. Going forward, each Premier League club could sell eight games a season alone, outside of the current overseas TV deal. If you strip the best games out of that deal, it wouldn't be worth a lot. So it definitely needed some negotiation. But the split of TV money was good. The idea was to bundle up the EFL and Premier League rights; 25 per cent would go to the EFL and 75 per cent to the Premier League. That would allow proper redistribution of money through the EFL, and to abolish parachute payments.

'There was an awful lot of emotion around the proposals for the voting structure,' said Parry. 'The way they had framed the governance was that half of those clubs would have votes on a restricted number of the bigger issues, so it would be the nine clubs who'd been in it the longest at any point in time. The concern was, if you're voting on the next TV deal, is it fair that clubs who've been in it for thirty years have the same number of votes as a club who's just going to be in it one year and then drop out? Are they going to take a longer-term view? My view was: "Well, that's democracy." One club, one vote was for me a fundamental principle. But I could get where they were coming from. All of that was negotiable, though. I think the six would have backed off if there'd been major pressure. The disappointing thing is that people ran for the hills and didn't support the project. It was worthy of a proper debate. It shouldn't have been killed off before we'd even brought the ideas out into the open.

'Interestingly, a lot of the Championship clubs, who might have been concerned about going up into a Premier League that's only got eighteen clubs, which meant they might miss a promotion opportunity, because it would have been two teams guaranteed going up plus a play-off against the sixteenth club in the Premier League, weren't,' said Parry. 'The Championship clubs were thinking: "No, we're alright." And on the governance, why shouldn't the long-term clubs have a greater say? We're comfortable with that. We're not going to be competing with them logically. The fairer system, the redistribution within the Championship, outweighs those concerns.'

Even though the majority of EFL clubs supported it, among the big players no one stood up to argue the case. John W. Henry, one of its principal architects, said nothing. And then Liverpool backed down, as did Manchester United and Joel Glazer. It's inexplicable and baffling to me how the owners of these two giant football clubs can be quite happy to do deals with parties behind the backs of the game, but we are never publicly able to hold them to account or even hear their visions for English football. They obviously have a burning desire for change, yet don't feel it's the right thing to publicise, explain, consult with fans or the wider game their thoughts. This isn't leadership. They wonder why the proposals fall over with fans distrusting them even more.

'The EFL was essentially left to support it, promote it, which I was more than happy to do, and most of our clubs were more than happy to do the same, because of the attractions,' said Parry. 'So we might have had a situation where we had six of the biggest and seventy-two of our other clubs saying much the same thing and fourteen clubs who, for the time being, were the biggest objectors. I think the six should've been prepared to come out and support [it] and stand their ground. I've made the point repeatedly. Listening to John Henry and Joel Glazer talk passionately about the importance of the pyramid and how crucial it was to maintain League One and League Two – bearing in mind we were looking at the challenge of Covid, during which people were talking about mothballing the two leagues for a season – was actually really positive. And for me really revealing. But it's no use me telling the world what they think. They've got to tell the world themselves for it to be convincing. They've got to put themselves in the court of public opinion if they're to be persuasive.'

I trust Parry and he wouldn't say that without good reason. It is intriguing to think that John W. Henry and Joel Glazer could see a bigger picture. Shame though that they then blew any credibility they may have had with Big Picture by backing a Super League, which would have destroyed the pyramid. 'Oh, listen, Super League was a bad idea,' said Parry. 'There's no two ways about that, because it cuts across everything we believe in in terms of fair competition and merit; by definition, to have a winner you've also got to have a loser. You cannot have a sporting contest where everybody is guaranteed security and success. It doesn't work.'

The pyramid is so integral to our game, not just because it builds community and strengthens our society but also because, on the basic entertainment value of the content, it adds jeopardy. I believe European football has thrived more than NFL or basketball precisely because of this jeopardy, the fact you can go down or lose or drop out. Clearly, the idea of jeopardy is extremely relative: the last ten Champions League finals have been won by five clubs, Real Madrid, Barcelona, Liverpool, Bayern Munich and Chelsea. But the pyramids that support the elite are part of the success of our game.

That said, there may well be an issue nagging away at some readers, which they might view as the elephant in the room: my own club, Salford City, which I part-own with Peter Lim. Peter, our Singaporean partner, owns half of the club and Nicky Butt, my brother Phil, Ryan Giggs, David Beckham, Paul Scholes and I share the other 50 per cent. We run at a loss. The club has been backed by owner injections from Peter and the CO92. Our goal has always been to get to the top of English football. We went through non-league quickly, securing four promotions in five seasons. Fair to say, League Two has been harder. We have one of the biggest budgets in the division but have yet to make the play-offs in what has proved to be a very difficult league for us. And since we took over in 2014, we've made five managerial changes. The first two managers lasted five and a half years, but since then we've sacked three in two seasons, something I would never have imagined, especially since criticising the likes of Roman Abramovich for doing precisely that. Still, it gives Jamie Carragher something to tweet about.

As such, I felt it only fair to give a platform to one of our arch-critics, Andy Holt, owner of Accrington Stanley. The original Accrington were one of the founder twelve members of the Football League in 1888, such was the strength of football in the north-west. So it's a town with football history. Accrington Stanley, a separate club to Accrington, were formed in 1891 and played in the Football League from 1921 to 1962, when they resigned mid-season because of financial issues. The current club is a phoenix club, founded in 1968, to revive the club that went bust in 1962. Holt took over in 2015, when the club was on the verge of folding again. They were in League Two at the time and now, with a very different philosophy to mine, he has guided them to being a stable League One side, twelfth in 2021–22. So he's done what I want to do, but crucially he's done it on a budget. Accrington spend what they earn and he's sees what we do at Salford as distorting the competition.

'What you don't get, Gary, is that when you stop spending on Salford, they'll be jacked up to such a position it will be unsustainable,' he said. 'Somebody's got to come in and want to lose ninety-one grand a week. So all these owners, like you, Gary, and even the new Burnley owners, their dreams are to make it a worldwide brand competing with the likes of

Liverpool and Man United. They have all these airy-fairy dreams that forget the real purpose of football in the first place, to me. It's a social sport. It brings fitness and health, physical and mental wellbeing. It's a community and it creates bonds between people from different clubs up and down the country. It plays a massive part in every supporter's life and every community. So, if Accrington lost Accrington Stanley, it's devastating for the town. It is a necessity, then, that I don't play with that and I don't take that lightly. I believe that by gambling, you're taking that responsibility lightly. You concentrate on sporting success because you've come from Man United and a background where they just buy what they want and do what they want. If you lose, you can go and buy some more, and that's your background – not your early life, but your training at Manchester United. It's a merry-go-round. They know when it finishes you can end up like Bolton, you could end up like Wigan, you can end up like Derby.'

I take the point but at Salford we only ever give two-year contracts. If we give a three-year contract it's very rare. We know it'll cost us probably around £4–5m to transition the club back to what would probably be a million-pound-a-year budget rather than a £3m-a-year budget. We would also have to cut back our football staff costs and non-football costs in that transition period to pull it back to a sustainable level. With that transition pot of money in reserve, the club would still operate but just more within its means and without large owner injections. It's that transition fund really that owners need to put in place if they're going to have a go.

This isn't enough to satisfy Holt, however. 'If you're doing this then you should have bought a club that has a chance of matching your ambitions,' he said. 'You're building the club beyond its reasonable sustainable limit. And you raise the bar for other owners, who have to sit by being pushed down the league by other owners being irrational. Other owners are unlikely to honour a pledge like this and their largesse punishes other clubs trying to do the right thing.

'Your next *Class of 92* TV programme should be about making Salford sustainable. The journey from a £3m budget to a £1m budget will kill morale and guarantee relegation for the club and their next owner. It's set up to fail. The club that you've built has to be able to sustain going up leagues and going down and have the ability to cope with stresses that come later on down the line. If you build it up too big, the crash is too hard. Look what happened at Bury, it's what happened at Bolton and it's what happened at Wigan.

'Clubs should be able to spend money they generate; they should be able to invest money to generate money in outside-club activities. The pinnacle for Accrington Stanley, in my opinion, is bottom of the Championship; that's what Accrington could achieve in our wildest dreams. The lowest we should accept is top of the National League, top half of the National League. I think we can sustain the club there now that we have the facilities. So we've got to set all our costs and business model around somewhere in the middle of that to be able to come up with variance either side, and that's not what you're doing. You're setting the budget for the top end and losing a fortune.'

Here's the irony of all this though. Andy wants an independent regulator. So do I. He wants sustainability in football. So do I. He wants better governance in football. So do I. In broad principles, we agree with each other. Where we disagree, however, is that he says clubs should only spend the money they generate. That is a form of sustainability, I can't deny that, but I find it constrictive as it removes the ability of Blackburn to win the league under someone like Jack Walker or of Leicester to thrive under Vichai Srivaddhanaprabha. Jack Walker wanted to win the league and invest back into the town where he grew up, which is just down the road from Accrington. Is that wrong? I don't think regulation should stop anyone from doing that. Is it wrong that Vichai Srivaddhanaprabha wanted to fund Leicester, get them into the top-flight, and win the Premier League and the FA Cup?

We talk a lot about Chelsea and Roman Abramovich, Manchester City and Sheikh Mansour and Newcastle and Mohammed bin Salman when we discuss owner-funded clubs. But some of the greatest stories in English football history have come from owners funding their own clubs. It's part of what has made our system great. In trying to hold Sheikh Mansour to account, I don't want to ban Jack Walker.

The issue for me is how do you control owner funding so that it's sustainable? Personally, I don't think that means you ban it altogether and it seems Andy could agree to some owner funding. 'You could have a cap,' he said. 'If Manchester United's budget is £500m and they are the top budget, that's the cap for everybody. It doesn't necessarily have to be the highest budget. It could be set at £400m. But there has to be a cap.' If what Andy is saying is that we should place limits on owner funding to ensure it is sustainable, although that was not my position before I started this book I could, and maybe would, accept it for the good of the game. The suggestion is that if an owner funds a team, it shouldn't be allowed to go above the turnover of the biggest organic club in its division. In League Two in 2021-22 that would have been Bristol Rovers and when the accounts come out, people will see that's roughly where the funding of Salford is at. I think we were second to Bristol Rovers in spending. So, I could live with that.

I know Andy's other issue is that one day something could go wrong, the funds run out and Salford crash through the league or do a Bury. It's true that if you borrow too much against a club and run out of cash, you can destroy a community asset. But we haven't borrowed too much and anything we have put in is personally secured across seven owners. A regulator can ensure that an owner doesn't borrow against the club's assets. Again, I could live with that. It's a good rule. Put money in, but make sure it's your own or put a guarantee in place.

Andy is right to worry that an owner could lose interest and walk away. But a strong regulator, with real-time financial monitoring, can guard against that. Anyone funding a club needs to put up the money guaranteed at the start of the season. But they also need to set aside plans to transition the club over the length of its playing contracts, which would usually be two to three years in League One and Two. Then, if they walk away, the club can adjust over three years.

People do downsize and transition in life to a smaller model. That can be a manageable path. It's just that, without regulation, football invariably manages it badly and a team crashes through the league with the threat of administration and liquidation. But, again, with a strong regulator that needn't be the case. No team should start a season without funds in place. No owner-funded model should be allowed without that transition plan. I would fully support that.

And even if Salford did go back through the leagues or we had to go back to a budget of around £800,000, which is similar to Barrow and Morcambe, my passion wouldn't change. I would see that as being a different chapter in our history. We came from the Northern Premier League Division One North and in some ways, I enjoyed the purity of that level more. We had an £80,000 a year playing budget when we first bought the club! We can do that again. As long as Salford survives within the community, that's fine. They would have the stadium as a legacy. But for that to happen, all seven owners would have to lose interest.

Or, alternatively, maybe one day we sat down and decided to

run an Under 23 team in the style of Athletic Bilbao, in that we only recruit from Salford, Manchester and the North West. Maybe we would end up in the National League North. I would still be passionate about it. Some of my favourite moments with Salford were visiting Brighouse Town or Ossett Town.

We have roots in our club. Paul Scholes was born in Salford; Ryan Giggs lived there for 45 years of his life; me, my brother and Nicky Butt grew up at the Cliff Training Ground with Manchester United, which is in Salford; David Beckham lived in Salford for eight years. We found a business partner in Peter Lim, who wants to invest in our local club. I think a blend of local passion, entrepreneurism and wealth is a good model.

I know Andy is 100 per cent committed to his community, but I would also say we've built up a football club with an academy, we've founded a university in Trafford and we have a foundation delivering community projects all over Greater Manchester. We've put our money into Manchester, Trafford and Salford and I also see myself as a custodian, just like Andy. I just do it differently. I've put significant money into Salford. I value where I came from and the roots I have. My mum and dad invested their time and love into Bury and I want to do the same for Salford. Believe me, I don't go to Oldham away to look good! It's because I want to! You'll find me sat with Sky commentator Martin Tyler on the gantry before a Premier League game watching the Salford feed. It's not a rich man's passing hobby. It's a huge part of my life. I don't believe my principles are that different to Andy's though. We just differ on how sustainability is achieved. But even then, if Andy wants limits, I can buy into that if it helps the greater good of the game.

Ultimately, I believe Andy and I have a lot in common and agree on the core issues. That's why it's been useful writing his book. With a limit of 280 characters on Twitter, it's hard to debate and you can end up simply restating your own positions. With time and space to explore the issues more deeply, nuance emerges. Hopefully, in time, we can build a better game. We both want that. And I'll look forward to enjoying a drink with him at Accrington Stanley next time we play. Of course, that's assuming we get out of League Two!

6

BURIED

'Having fully considered all available options, including a
number of late expressions of interest provided to the
EFL, the EFL Board has unanimously determined with
enormous regret that Bury's membership of the league
be withdrawn.'
English Football League statement, 27 August 2019

The night they killed Bury it was the Carabao Cup second round.
The call came from the EFL's head of legal Nick Craig at 11.07pm
and my mum took it. 'Jill, I'm just telling you that you're out the
league,' he said. 'I've tried the chairman. I can't get hold of him so
I'm ringing you.' My mum, who had worked for the club since
1986 and who eventually became club secretary, tried to dissuade
him and tell him that there was an alternative bid waiting to buy
the club. He said it was too little, too late. She remembers: 'He
said he'd been busy all night because the Grimsby game has been
called off with a flooded pitch. I told him again: "We've got a bid
in!" But he said, no, it was too late. And then we got an email the
morning after to say that all our players' contracts were cancelled
and that was it.' Bury FC, founded in 1885, breathed its last in
2019 at the venerable old age of 134.

For months, the key officials at the club had been asking the
Football League to remove Steve Dale, the man who had taken
over the club in December 2018, nine months previously. He had

stepped in to buy Bury for £1 when Stewart Day found himself in financial difficulties. 'We pleaded with the EFL all summer long to remove him,' said my mum. 'They had files on him. We said, "Will you remove him?" That's what they're there for. They kept saying: "We're there to help you."' The reality is that the EFL didn't have the power to do that. Dale had no previous experience in football, but that wasn't a disqualifying factor under the EFL's owners' and directors' test. Nor was the fact that more than 20 companies of which he had been a director had been dissolved, in liquidation or agreed a Company Voluntary Arrangement. 'I'll save the old girl,' Dale promised everyone after he had acquired the club from Day. But in an interview with BBC Five Live, shortly before the club breathed its last, Dale outlined his true feelings. 'I never went to Bury. It's not a place I frequented. So for me to walk away from Bury and never go back is a very easy thing to do. I don't do anything up there. I didn't even know there was a football team called Bury to be honest with you. I'm not a football fan.' None of that disqualified him from being the club's owner. Since then the rules have been amended. But for Bury, it was a case of the horse having bolted long before that stable door was shut.

Throughout Dale's ownership, Bury's financial viability grew ever more fragile. He was an enigma, barely showing his face at the club and rarely communicating.

The irony was that Bury completed one of their best seasons in recent history. Under Ryan Lowe's management, they had finished second in League Two and had reached the semi-final of the EFL Trophy. The Professional Footballers' Association, the players' union, had partly covered wages in March, but in April and May, promotion was secured with unpaid players knowing they could risk an injury that would jeopardise any future career prospects. By June 2019 a winding-up petition had been issued from the tax authorities, HMRC, and almost everyone at the club was urging Dale to sell to some of the interested parties. Club captain Nicky

Adams described on Twitter how the players had gone 'from elation to complete and utter dismay' at the end of the season. Instead of planning for a League One campaign, which for some would have been the pinnacle of their career, they were desperately seeking new clubs. Lowe pleaded with Dale: 'Mr Chairman, we know you have no regard or consideration for us as players, our families or our futures, but please just accept the offer and walk away from our club before you bring it to its knees.'

The twist was that it was perhaps their very success that killed them, as the independent review into Bury's collapse by Jonathan Taylor QC makes clear. 'Despite the players still not being paid their March and April wages [the PFA loaned them half of the outstanding amounts], Bury FC ended the season on 30 April 2019 by winning automatic promotion to League One,' Taylor writes.

> Other clubs expressed significant frustration that Bury FC had achieved this success while failing to meet its financial obligations, but the EFL did not have power to deduct points or block promotion itself, and there was no precedent for asking a Disciplinary Commission to impose a points deduction based on the club's various breaches of the Regulations.

During Day's ownership of the club from 2013 to 2018, the amount spent on players' wages had soared from £1.9 million when he took over to £4.5 million when he sold it for £1. Turnover had also increased, but not by the same margin, from £2.1m to £3.2m. So, by the time Day sold the club, for every £1 that Bury earned, the club had committed to paying the players £1.24. The shortfall was made up by a £2.38m investment – effectively a loan – from Day's businesses, principally student property lets. When the property business began to fail, Bury was simply the last financial car crash at the end of a long line of businesses. Bury had literally been writing cheques they couldn't cash. In addition, from the moment Day had taken over in 2013, Bury had been consistently late paying fellow clubs, had deferred wages on several occasions and had to borrow to survive. Taylor's inquiry provides a long list of EFL interventions. One detailed table spread over a number of pages is entitled: 'EFL interventions in response to Bury FC defaults in payment of football creditors Basic Award deductions and Regulation fines – 2013–2018'. Football creditors in this context means other football clubs. Success was built on an overdose of wishful thinking at best, a fantasy at worst. The ultimate decision in 2019 on whether they should be given more time or be expelled from the League was taken by the EFL Board. Yet in late September 2019, the EFL clubs were then asked to vote whether Bury should be readmitted into League Two the following season. They voted against. Understandably, by that stage, goodwill among the latter, many of whom had put up with Bury's defaults for years, was in short supply.

Day was a property developer and, off the back of success in property, he wanted to take Bury up the leagues. I had met him in 2013 and he was full of optimism and ambition. But I walked away from the meeting worried, even back then. Bury could never have grown to be a club that could compete in the Premier League. It's not got the bandwidth. It's not got the size. Since the end of the Second World War it had always been a League One (third-tier) club at best. And if it wasn't a League One club, it was going to lose a lot of money so whoever owned it would need to have big pockets. When Day was in financial trouble, Dale came in, supposedly to save the day. The heart of the structural failure of football here lay in allowing Bury to overspend, allowing them to take loans they couldn't afford to pay back and allowing a new owner to come in who wasn't fit for football. My mum tells the story of the ownership change between Day and Dale happening in an afternoon. She was one of the people who had to sign the release form, and Steve Dale came in and promised to save the club. He was never saving the club.

Bury fans were understandably angry. A lot of them were angry with me. I'd spoken out on social media when the Super League idea was mooted, and frequently campaigned for an independent regulator of the game. 'But where were you when Bury went down?' they asked. Well, I watched it at close hand actually. I knew three or four years before it was going to go down. I knew one day that the mismanagement of Bury was going to cause a problem. What I did expect was that football would save it. I expected that the Premier League might help. I expected football to come together to put an arm around Bury, at the very least allowing it to continue to save itself. But it didn't. The structural failings of the governance of football centre around the lack of power to intervene by the EFL, which in essence is made up of the clubs itself.

After Bury went bust, the League One and League Two owners came together and said: 'We've got to put regulations in place to not let this happen again. Save ourselves from ourselves.' Football club owners, including myself, we know we make emotional deci-sions. We try to push the boundaries and we do indeed need saving from ourselves. And we need saving from ourselves because foot-ball clubs are more important than just a business. The reason I've become involved in pushing for football governance reform is because of my unease around what happened at Bury and because of the disconnect between the Premier League and grassroots. What happened at Bury can never be allowed to happen again. No owner should be able to take hold of a football club, borrow against it, overspend beyond the means of the club, without having some form of financial or cash or bank guarantee in place to be able to fulfil their obligations. It's really simple. If you go and borrow against your house, and what you owe goes over 70 or 75 per cent of the property's value, the bank will stop you and say: 'No, you have to find the cash because actually the security against the asset isn't enough.' It should be the same in football. Real simple. This is your revenue last year. This is what you've got to spend next year. Eighty per cent of it, 90 per cent of it, whatever it might be. Once you go above that, you've got to put cash in up front.

Football clubs were an easy target for the financially slick. There is some debate in Bury as to who was to blame for the demise. Was it Stewart Day, who overspent and overcommitted? Or was it Steve Dale, for being so obstructive and not seemingly ever having any interest in the club? My mum felt Day was foolish rather than anything. 'I always got on very well with Stewart Day,' she said. 'It was more naivety and getting sucked in rather than him being bad. That's what I thought. Other people said he'd misled us, but I think he was just drawn into making Bury a successful club. He went to every game. Him and Glenn Thomas, his business partner, moved their office into Bury so he could be there doing both, though they later decided that didn't work. But he was mainly at Gigg Lane all the time or at Carrington, Manchester City's old training ground, which we leased off City in 2015. That was the best thing that had ever happened really. The facilities were fabulous. We had five or six pitches. We used to run our Centre of Excellence from there, the first team trained there, they had all the meals made, the breakfasts made, the lunches made. He wanted that. He wanted players to join Bury because of the facilities and set-up. Before that, they were training at Gigg Lane, the stadium, and Lower Gigg, the old training ground, with just one pitch, where they would have to carry the goalposts on their shoulders, then go to the local shop afterwards and get a butty. Here they had proper meals. He wanted to make it into a really good professional club that people would be eager to come to and win games with. I think he wanted to make Bury a successful club. He just wanted to do his best and hoped that we would get further and make more money.'

Steve Dale was different though. Though I was always worried about Day, I had a terrible feeling about Dale from the start. 'Your first words,' my mum recalled, 'were: "Don't believe him." And I said: "But Gary, he's putting this money in, he's signed an agreement."' I was adamant with my mum. I looked at his record and could only see a bad trajectory. But in person, these types can be very convincing. 'We all had interviews with him,' said my mum. 'He introduced himself. He owned that many companies. He had 278 cars. He owned all this property in Manchester. He would turn up in a Rolls-Royce. And of course you sit there and believe it.

'Maybe I'm naïve really. But his spiel was so good. Yet whenever we needed money he was always ill. He was in hospital or he was ill or something like that. Luckily, from December to February, we lasted with the money we had, our EFL distribution money, our Premier League solidarity money and we'd won some competitions, so we were okay. Everybody was paid in February 2019 and then from March onwards, the money was running out and people were only being paid part of their salaries. The players didn't want to play because they weren't getting full pay. All the staff weren't paid full salary. But the manager at the time, Ryan Lowe, just said: "Come on, let's go and do it." And they ended up getting promoted. Steve Dale was saying: "I'll save the old girl." He used to call the club "the old girl". I used to ring him up constantly and say: "What about this? What about that?" "Don't worry, I'll save the old girl." And all summer long we were in conversation with the EFL putting all our salary costs and management together, with plans going forward. And all they wanted was proof of his money. Ultimately, he didn't have any.'

It was at times like this that we really missed my dad. He had seen off so many chancers at Bury, his insight would have been invaluable. 'If Neville had been alive, he probably wouldn't have taken over,' said my mum. 'It wouldn't have got to that stage. Neville would have done something. But we didn't know what could be done. The EFL were controlled by the chairmen and owners of the other clubs. To the very end, until we got kicked out at the end of August, we'd pleaded with them to help us get rid of him, so that we could then get people in. We had buyers. People who wanted to buy the club. And even after we got kicked out, we all still went in every day, trying to work out what we could do, whether we could appeal against it. I had a long conversation with Dale in September, but he told the EFL not to speak to me. He told the FA not to speak to me. So I thought, well, what's the point? If the owner said to the EFL, "Don't speak to Jill Neville," they wouldn't speak to me. By the end, everyone just ran out of patience with him, to be honest; he had come up with that much rubbish.'

Others, like Jon Walsh, former Bury season-ticket holder and fan of forty-five years, is more of the opinion that Day needs to be held responsible. 'I am more angry at Stewart Day than Steve Dale. The majority of the businesses Dale's bought, he's liquidated. He's an asset stripper. That's what he does. We got into a situation where we couldn't sell the club a week before we were due to be expelled. We had a number of companies that came in to buy Bury at that point. But when they looked at the financial complexities of it – long-term loans sold on a twenty-five-year 100 per cent return on a car park space outside a football ground in a northern mill town! – they couldn't proceed. There will be Malaysian investors in twenty-three years' time saying: "Where's my money?!" The financing was a fantasyland. You might think Stewart Day was a slightly over-ambitious owner; he was really, though, only hoping for the best and he just got caught up by what he did. But it continued even when there were warning signs. I was never a fan of the man because he had this inflated impression of himself that he was a Bury fan. He would stand on the touchline near the manager's dugout waving his Bury training jacket, shouting at the linesman. Some people loved that, but, to me, you're the owner of the club, mate. We don't need that. He wasn't a Bury fan and that's fair enough. There's more non-Bury fans in the world than there are Bury fans and I'm not going to hold that against him, but don't pretend to be something that you're not. The focus, though, is all on Dale. Dale's a terrible person because of what he does? But Dale's done what he does for a long period of time.'

It's also true that the EFL faced an invidious choice. There wasn't the infrastructure to keep Bury playing until something, such as a fans' takeover, could be organised. 'We didn't help ourselves,' said Walsh. 'People have this rose-tinted view of Bury that we got into trouble in the last two years. Bury had been in trouble since the late 90s. It was always: "Bury's going to fold; we're going to have to merge with Oldham; we're going to have to merge with Rochdale and become Manchester North End." Now when people look back they say everything was wonderful until Dale and Day took over. We had *huge* problems way back then. The problem is we had a very big ground that was too big for the league that we were in and we had too many debts that we couldn't afford to pay off and not big enough crowds. So I have a level of sympathy for the EFL when it got to a point where they said: "This can't carry on." Because if we had gone on for another year, unless another sugar daddy came in, we'd have just been a year down the line and then folding and not being able to pay people. The EFL were partly to blame in that they didn't do a proper test of the new owner and that's what I would focus on. Buying clubs for a pound should raise every red flag there is.'

Those rules have been changed since. Too late for Bury, however. What Bury needed was a structure that protected a community asset from the dreams of an individual. 'Every football fan will say: "You know what? With the wind blowing in the right direction and everything going right, we could get a run to the Premier League," ' said Walsh. 'That's why clubs over-extend themselves and that's why owners and people do these sorts of things. It's a real concern. The Super League and Bury are fantastic examples of how clubs always act in their self-interest. When Bury were expelled from the league, every club in the world was [supposedly] supporting Bury. "It's an absolute travesty what's happened to you." But fifty-odd clubs voted not to readmit us into the league. Now part of that is that Bury over-spent and there was a discontent from people who thought that we'd spent more than we had, which we had done, and therefore it was an unfair advantage. But it is also in clubs' interests to look after themselves so, with the greatest will in the world, not every one of the ninety-one clubs that sent us support on social media were going to allow us back in. It was never going to happen because it was in the financial interests of other people for the club not to survive.'

Jonathan Taylor's report is well worth reading. It explains why the EFL had run out of patience with Bury.

The EFL Board . . . met . . . on the evening of 27 August 2019. It noted Mr Dale's claim that there were other expressions of interest in purchasing the club, but also noted that these would require more delay, with no certainty of success, and that it was not possible to postpone any more fixtures, because it would not be possible to re-schedule them all. The EFL Board concluded that Bury FC's continued membership was no longer in the interests of the EFL and its member clubs as a whole. It therefore decided not to suspend the Notice of Withdrawal any further, but instead to effect the transfer of the club's share in the EFL, and thereby withdraw the club's membership of the EFL. On 26 September 2019, following a meeting of all clubs, the EFL Board confirmed that Bury FC would not be re-admitted to League Two for the 2020/21 season.[*]

Taylor also drew some conclusions about why Bury had ended up in such a parlous state; essentially, the financial controls imposed by the EFL at the time, known as the Salary Cost Management Protocol, weren't robust enough.

Some argue that Bury FC's fate demonstrates the tension between two competing visions of a football club: (i) as a business that seeks to generate a return for its owner's investment; and (ii) as a community asset of which the owner is just a custodian. However, I think that misses the real point. There are certainly grounds to criticise the owners who presided over Bury FC's financial ruin. With the benefit of hindsight, it can also be argued that the EFL could and should have intervened sooner and more forcefully. However, I do not see anything that the EFL could have done that would have made any difference, because the real cause of Bury FC's collapse is the fact that clubs are able to fund player wages not just from normal operating income but by means of cash injections from their owners. This can make clubs completely reliant on owner funding to remain competitive on the pitch. If such an owner becomes no longer ready, willing and/or able (for whatever reason) to provide such funding, the club is inevitably plunged into deep financial crisis. In such cases, unless a new owner comes along with sufficient funding to meet the club's commitments, there is nothing that the EFL can do to save the club. The real question the Bury FC case raises, therefore, is whether the Salary Cost Management Protocol rules need to be revised to remove, or at

* THE BURY FC REVIEW. (n.d.). Available at: https://www.efl.com/siteassets/image/201920/governance-reviews/bury-review..pdf---adobe-acrobat-pro.pdf.

least limit, the risks attendant on reliance on owner funding to underwrite player expenditure.

Tracey Crouch's *Fan-Led Review of Football Governance 24 November 2021* also dealt with the issue.

> One of the most difficult issues to deal with is the question of owner subsidies. There are examples within the English game where wealthy owners have transformed clubs into champions (Manchester City and Chelsea) or even allowed a smaller club to operate above its natural means to the benefit of its city and supporters (Brighton & Hove Albion). The openness to invest-ment and opportunity for development of clubs is generally perceived to make English football attractive for investment. On the other hand, the many clubs where owners have ceased to be willing or able to continue to fund losses have encountered deep difficulties.
>
> Further, even where an owner is able to continue to fund an individual club, the activities of that club may cause disruption at other clubs as they overspend in order to compete. This will ultimately inject wage inflation, destabilise football and it is questionable whether or not a credible regulator could allow this.

She suggested imposing stricter limits related to the size of the club, known as capital and liquidity requirements. And, if you do want to subsidise a club, as I have done at Salford, the money will need to be paid up front. 'This will reduce the risk involved in reli-ance on owner funding,' she wrote in the review. 'A club will be able to invest in order to seek to improve its competitive position but this will no longer be gambling with a club's future. For a club to do this, money will need to be in the club upfront and committed.'

The review, which argues for a regulator in English football, then discussed whether there should be a limit to owner injections. It concluded:

> On balance, due to the fragile state of club finances, the review considers that IREF [The Independent Regulator for English Football] should have a proportionality mechanism when assessing owner injections. In outline, this would involve a limit being set on the level of owner subsidy based on the size of a club's existing finances (which would grow over time if the investment was successful and the club grew). In addition, if the activity of one or a few profligate clubs is objectively assessed as being destabilising to the long-term sustainability of the wider league, IREF would be permitted to block further owner injections on financial stability and proportionality grounds.

I agree with Jonathan Taylor and Tracey Crouch's analysis. I wouldn't end owners funding wages. I think that if an owner wants to inject money into a club that's fine. Obviously I've done that myself at Salford City. It's just that there should be much tougher controls around it. Overspending by owners should require safety. The EFL would have to sign off on any expenditure, which they do now, but as we've seen, they didn't then have strong enough powers to intervene. So Stewart Day could just borrow the extra money off alternative lenders at huge interest rates and as long as he could show that he was good for any extra money he wanted to inject into the club, it wasn't in the EFL's remit to establish how sensible those loans were.

If I do a property development and I have a loan from the bank, I have a monitoring surveyor, who every month will come and look at what I've spent, look at the work that's been done on site and then release the next part of the development fund to make sure I've not overspent. This is so simple and normal in every other walk of life. It's like a quantity surveyor in construction or a bank monitoring surveyor in development. These roles exist in every other walk of life. In our restaurants, we always want to hit around 30 per cent of food costs. Our financial director in the hospitality business understands what 30 per cent of the food cost is and monitors it to ensure we don't spend too much on food. How can it be that difficult for a football club? There should be independent monitoring surveyors, accountants and financial directors in a position to put controls in place.

It's not the lack of ability or the lack of resources to be able to actually implement it. It's the lack of willingness to want to do it. And I appreciate that the EFL is basically the clubs. The clubs have to vote it through. Which is, of course, why we need a regulator, as there are too many competing interests for there ever to be a majority to vote for it. Someone has to come in and knock the heads together. It's the same in the Premier League. You can see them squabbling over issues. Should there be relegation during the pandemic? Should we be allowed to cancel games because of injuries during a Covid surge? Should we allow Saudi Arabia to fund Newcastle? Left to the clubs and a disempowered executive leadership, it becomes a cat fight, everyone scrabbling to look after their own narrow, short-term interests. Jon Walsh nailed it when discussing Bury's demise. However much clubs might feel they look at the wider interest of football, ultimately they look after themselves.

There are exceptions. When we met at the start of Covid as League Two clubs, Port Vale had a great chance of going up. But it was clear that we couldn't finish the season, as the costs of putting in games without fans was just too high. So she [Port Vale Chair Carol Shanahan] voted to end the season and work out the promotion places on points per game, which meant Vale missed out. I was delighted, therefore, that they went up in 2021–22. 'I was new in the industry and it never crossed my mind not to do the right thing,' Shanahan tweeted. '[I] was shocked at the reaction it created and how unheard of it was. Still ploughing our own farrow and confusing the crap out of people.'

But most clubs will adopt the position that suits them at the time. I can't even blame them for that. For most executives it is literally their job. But it means football can't reform itself because no one will ever agree on something in the greater interest. Take Leeds chief executive Angus Kinnear. He likened the idea of a regulator in football to Maoism. Aside from the offensiveness of this – Chairman Mao's policies in China led directly to 45 million deaths – it's also stupid. I wonder how Kinnear felt on the last day of the season when Leeds were in danger of relegation? Might his position change on the distribution of TV money through the pyramid if Leeds were relegated and couldn't get up inside three years, when their parachute payments would run out? My guess is that it would.

Aston Villa chief executive Christian Purslow said that he didn't see why they should bail out failing EFL clubs. Yet back in 2020, during the season that was almost curtailed because of the first wave of Covid, there were Premier League clubs arguing they should play out the season with no relegation as, with no fans and unsure circumstances, the financial consequences were just too great. Might Aston Villa have been one of those clubs? They were certainly in a relegation dogfight that season, having only just been promoted the previous year. And had goal-line technology worked properly in their game against Sheffield United and registered a goal – for the first time in nine thousand games it failed – they might have lost that game and ultimately gone down, with Bournemouth staying up. I wonder where Aston Villa would be now but for that stroke of luck, and what Purslow's view might be in a parallel universe in which they had been relegated?

Go back a bit further in Villa's history, before Purslow's arrival, and the jeopardy of football becomes even more apparent. In the summer of 2018, after losing to Fulham in the Championship play-off final, Villa did not pay a tax bill on time and were threatened with a winding-up petition. They were lucky. New investors came in. But without the £57 million sale of Villa Park to NSWE Stadium Ltd, a company controlled by the club's owners, in 2019 they would have certainly breached the EFL's Profit and Sustainability rules, which would have likely meant a financial penalty. Essentially, that's the same trick Derby pulled – selling the stadium to yourself and leasing it back to get around the cost controls – which the EFL has now outlawed. Villa then beat Derby in the 2019 play-off final. Even given the enormity of that game, I doubt many fans knew exactly what was at stake. This was the game that broke Derby. Promotion would have saved them financially and all their gambles would have paid off. Not getting promoted led directly to the situation they're in now. So when Purslow says we don't need reform or that the Premier League can sort it out themselves, you can see why I'm sceptical.

The season Villa stayed up in the Premier League, 2019–20, they earned £112.6m. And they spent £108.8m on wages; 97p of every £1 they earned went to players, They lost £99m in their first season in the Premier League, a figure that was exacerbated by Covid. In the ten years running up to that season, the club lost £455m in total.* Nowadays, Aston Villa don't think they should bail out EFL clubs? If they had gone down in 2020, they would have been coping with a £108m wage bill with a massive drop in revenue and navigating a season behind closed doors. Yet this is the club telling us that prudently run Premier League clubs shouldn't subsidise EFL clubs that take unnecessary risks? Aston Villa could easily have been one of the EFL clubs arguing for a bail-out if it had not been for a dodgy goal-line decision. I wonder if Christian Purslow would have been banging on the door of the

* Swiss Ramble https://twitter.com/swissramble/status/1502177763146407937. [online]

Premier League demanding more money and telling us why they deserved it? They spun the wheel and it came up red. Well done them. But it could just have easily come up black.

When Purslow was busy telling everyone the Premier League didn't need an independent regulator, one of his key lines was that Tracey Crouch was conflating the issues around the European Super League breakaway – something he was vehemently against, because it would have damaged his club – with the demise of Bury, and that the two issues were completely different. Now, Purslow used to be chief executive of Liverpool. Had he been so at the time of the Super League, he would have been asked to argue that the breakaway was for the good of the game. Because he happened to be at Villa at the time, he was instead vehemently against the Super League. And he doesn't see the connection between Bury and the Super League?

To make it simple for Purslow, the link between the Super League and Bury is self-interest, the fact that no one in football can ever take a communal view. Bury were allowed to get into the mess they were in because EFL clubs had repeatedly rejected proposals for stronger regulation that would have prevented them from running up ridiculous costs. And they have rejected opportunities to strengthen the owners' and directors' test, which was so weak it allowed an asset stripper to take over a football club before the EFL could check the relevant finances. The Premier League clubs reject any kind of regulation because, at that particular moment, they're all right and doing well. But the vast majority of the Premier League clubs will need the support network of the EFL at some point. They don't think they will now. They all assume everything will be fine. But many Premier League clubs are one relegation away from a potentially catastrophic financial event. In the last twenty years, all but six of the Premier League clubs have been in the EFL, including Manchester City, who have dropped to League One in recent history.

Southampton and Leeds have been in League One and gone into administration. Crystal Palace have been in administration twice since 1999! Brentford needed fans to raise money and an emergency loan to stave off administration in 2005. Wolves plunged from the top flight to the bottom tier in four seasons in the 1980s and went into receivership. They had fallen from the Premier League to League One in two seasons before current owners Fosun rescued them in 2016. Brighton lost their ground to a property developer, had to play in Gillingham and were a game away from dropping into non-league football in 1997. Burnley were the same in 1987, escaping the drop into non-league football on the last day of the season. The Premier League clubs of today were the financial basket cases of yesterday. They just about survived, but how does this sort of chaos, with clubs teetering on the brink of extinction, forever relying on a knight in shining armour coming charging over the horizon to save them, help football? How is that a sustainable sensible business?

Jonathan Taylor's inquiry into Bury summed the point up well about the problem with EFL rules. At the time Steve Dale took over Bury, the EFL rules stated:

> Where there is a proposed change in control [of ownership], the club must submit 'up to date Future Financial Information' (meaning projected profit and loss accounts, cash flow data, balance sheets, and relevant explanatory notes), for the period covering the current season (or what remains of it) and all of the following season, that 'take[s] into account the consequences of the change of Control on the Club's future financial position'.

Crucially, however, Taylor pointed out that the rules said that the Future Financial Information must only be provided 'as far in advance of the change of Control as reasonably possible or, if such submission is not reasonably practicable prior to the change of Control, no later than 10 Normal Working Days thereafter'. Taylor's verdict on this was bemusement. 'In other words, the EFL Regulations do not prevent a person acquiring control of a Club before he or she has provided the Future Financial Information or proof of access to sufficient cash to finance the Club's operations,' he wrote. 'What is clear . . . is that it would be much easier to impose and enforce effective conditions if they are pre-conditions to approval of the change of control.' You could take over a 134-year-old club and have ten days before anyone asks you whether you actually have any financial means to sustain it. The clubs hadn't adopted better rules because it wasn't in the self-interest of the particular owners of clubs, even though it probably would be in the wider interests of the clubs as a whole. It took this debacle for the rules to change. Thank goodness. But not so good for Bury.

Football isn't like other businesses. It's communal. It relies on competition. In most businesses, if you eliminate your competitor because you perform better than them, that's just capitalism. Obviously, it's bad for the consumer, so that's why even pure capitalism needs regulation. But ultimately, your business has succeeded, another has failed and that's good for you: more market share, more profits, survival of the fittest. So, Apple iPhones outcompete BlackBerry and the winner takes all.

But football doesn't work like that. If Aston Villa theoretically outcompete every team in the country, so that they drive them all out of business, it's not so good for Villa. Because now they have no one to play and as such they themselves now have no business. Football really does depend on all its constituent members to exist. It's collegiate in the way normal business aren't. No club is an island, independent of the rest. And yet they behave as if they are.

The Premier League might well be the most successful league in the world but only because of its deep roots and history. The Big

Six weren't dropped fully formed into a franchise operation. They evolved out of an ecosystem that supported them. Pull up the drawbridge in 1903 and Bury would be in the Super League and Manchester City and Manchester United would be left outside it. Make the cut in 1996 and Newcastle and Villa would be in but Chelsea would be out. Do it in 2008 and City, Newcastle and Leeds would have been cut off for ever. Everyone relies on the ecosystem to survive and, sometimes, thrive. But only Liverpool, Manchester United and Arsenal have been at the top consistently over the last forty years and even Liverpool were at a point where falling into administration was a possibility in 2009. Purslow will know the details as he was brought in as Liverpool chief executive to sort out the £350m loan the previous owners were in danger of defaulting on.

I've sat in on League Two meetings and during the pandemic, back in 2020, when no one could see a clear financial future, we did vote for salary caps: a limit of £2.5 million in League One and £1.5 million in League Two. But the Professional Footballers' Association challenged that, went to legal arbitration and had it overturned. And it was a sledgehammer to crack a nut. Because £2.5m was the cap for League One but Sunderland, who were until very recently a League One club, regularly get crowds of 30,000. They could, probably, comfortably afford £6-7m a year in League One and still not be under any pressure. So that was a crude way of controlling costs. However, the current rules, the Salary Costs Management Protocol, could be strengthened and withstand a legal challenge.

The reason that independence is required in relation to Bury is that when someone like Stewart Day comes in, he needs to put a plan forward. When he puts a plan forward, that has to be costed. The EFL have a record of Bury's historical revenues, because you obviously have to submit them every year for the Salary Cost Management Protocol (SCMP) rules. It's really simple.

'If you want to pay five grand a week for a striker, that's great, Stewart, but we need to know where the money's coming from?'

'Well, I'm borrowing against the ground.'

'I'm sorry, you can't do that. Regulation 4.2 prevents borrowing against the ground for salary or transfers unless you put the money up.'

'Oh, well, I've found this alternative loan company that's happy to lend the money to me at 24 per cent interest a year.'

'No, sorry, regulation 3.5 prevents outside loans for salary or transfers unless they're guaranteed by a cash bond by the owner.'

I'm not against borrowing. Sometimes you have to. Tottenham have an £823 million loan secured against the ground. That's an eye-watering amount of money borrowed, but if it is structured sensibly and the new stadium raises their income by 50 per cent a year, it can be funded quite simply by the revenues that Tottenham generate. So borrow against the ground, yes, but for infrastructure projects only. And pay five grand a week for your striker in League Two if you want. But you have to have the money up front at the start of the season to cover excess costs over and above your projected income, which would ensure that you can finish the season.

In football currently there's no independence to create sensible regulation, there's very little transparency and there are ways in which you can get round the rules if you really want to. And Bury is a horror story of being able to manipulate the existing rules, which has led to a community being damaged almost irreparably. Let's hope it's not irreparable, but it's been damaged to a point whereby the historic football club in our community, in our country, is lost. And when I think of the stories and the people, it is mind blowing. Behind Bury Football Club are human beings, there are fans, there are people who work there, there are people who have lost their lives there, families who have watched it for a hundred years. There are players who have given their all for it and managers and coaches. All the people who have contributed to Bury Football Club over a hundred-odd years and it's *gone*. *Gone!* It went within four years of my dad dying. I knew that when my dad died it left Bury Football Club without its guardian and that this could spell the end of them. My dad had seen off previous escapes from what looked like dead-end situations. This time no one could save them.

7

POWER TO THE PEOPLE

'Without fans who pay at the turnstile, football is nothing'
Jock Stein

My first memory of going to the football is being aged four or five driving over Barton Bridge to Old Trafford and shivering with excitement – I even have goose bumps now thinking about it – and saying: 'Dad, are we nearly there?' Those words that every child says when you don't know where you're going. You know you're going to the ground, but you don't quite know *where* you are. 'Dad, are we nearly there?' Holding my dad's hand in case I get lost, standing outside K Stand entrance, getting in and up to the concourse, walking up the steps to reveal this magnificent stadium, looking out at this massive green pitch. Those red shirts would emerge from the tunnel for the warm up and my dreams would begin. The one word that I always use to describe travelling to a game as a kid: magic. It was in these moments that made me fall in love with Manchester United.

One day, when my mum had fallen out with my dad, she said: 'You're not going to the game today.' I was devastated, but my dad snuck me out into the garages at the back, got me in the car and we just went to the game. There were no mobile phones in those days, so she had no idea where we'd gone. Well, she probably knew. 'We're going to the game!' It was like going on holiday. Once over Barton Bridge, you knew you were nearly there at the ground. We would always go to Marina's Grill, at the top of Sir Matt Busby Way, and I would have steak pudding, chips, peas and gravy every Saturday lunchtime. It was the most special time in my life, that.

My dad knew a guy who had moved away to Tenerife who had two season tickets for a few years and we just kept them. I used to get in the ground a couple of hours before kick-off. My dad would be down with a few of the lads having a beer in the concourse at the refreshment stand and I would literally be sat in my seat with a programme. I would be sat there on my own, no bother from anyone, and I would wait to watch the players warm up. This would have been the 1979–80 season. I always remember when Arnold Mühren came in 1982; he would be warming up and could swerve the ball like nothing I'd ever seen, it was mesmerising. United always warmed up at the opposite end in front of the Stretford End. I remember playing against Aston Villa. I was so young I only remember weird things like Nigel Spink, the goalkeeper, had a massive kick and it was just scary to me that he kicked the ball so far, or Joe Jordan going up for a header in the left channel and flicking it on. But I just adored United, adored going to the game. It was everything.

Before I was a player, pundit, coach and club co-owner, I was a fan. And during all those jobs, I've always remained a fan. It's where it all starts for most of us in football, whether we're players, commentators, journalists, managers. Even some owners. We've all been fans, we've all felt that excitement and joy – and pain and disappointment – of following our team.

I remember going to away games as I grew older, such as the 1983 and 1985 FA Cup semi-finals at Villa Park. But back in the 1980s, being a fan was different. It was exciting, edgy and appealed to you as a teenager; standing on the terraces, being part of big crowds, big surges and chanting. But there was also the hooliganism, which was always around. You were often treated like scum by police, as well as by the very people you were paying to watch the game: the clubs. Fences penned you in, you were shepherded from one place to another. The idea that you might be paying for this experience seemed to be anathema. You were just one of the herd that collectively provided the money to run the club. And they knew we would turn up week in, week out, no matter how we were treated.

You can romanticise the 1980s, but to do so you would have to ignore the racism and violence and forget that terraces weren't safe places for women and families. Stadia were crumbling, facilities were awful, toilets were grim – women were lucky if there was a functioning Ladies. It wasn't a leisure experience. But football was heading for a massive wake-up call. Neglect of a stadium caused the Bradford City fire of 1985, killing fifty-six people. Two weeks later, hooliganism, combined with UEFA putting on a game in a decrepit stadium, caused the Heysel Disaster at the European Cup final between Liverpool and Juventus, where thirty-nine people died, mainly Juventus fans. And then came Hillsborough in 1989, ninety-seven Liverpool fans, due to the ineptitude of the FA, the police and the authorities, being crushed to death against the fences that penned them in.

That was the first massive governmental intervention into football. The fences came down, stadia became all-seater. Lord Justice Taylor wrote a report into Hillsborough, which exonerated fans, who had initially been blamed, and which lambasted the FA and police, making reference to the appalling attitude of the authorities towards fans. Though many of Taylor's recommendations were ignored, football was made to grow up and treat fans differently. It was a catalyst for the formation of the Premier League in 1992. The fact that terraces were going, which meant at most grounds attendances were reduced, meant that clubs had to look for other revenue streams. People like David Dein at Arsenal and Irving Scholar at Tottenham quickly realised television could be an even more lucrative source of income than gate receipts. That's why, for all our problems, we should never forget what the Premier League has brought. It took football out of the gutter.

Also in the 1980s, a quiet revolution was beginning. Fanzines started to appear, being sold around the grounds. The most famous, *When Saturday Comes*, was a national football magazine that campaigned for fans' rights and railed against terrible owners. Fans suddenly had a platform and a voice. When the Conservative government tried to introduce ID cards to control hooliganism, it was fans who argued against it and, with the help of *The Taylor Report*, saw them scrapped. A new organisation, the Football Supporters' Association, brought together fans and led these battles. It was more questioning and radical than the National Federation of Football Supporters' Clubs, which had grown out of club-sanctioned official supporters' clubs.

Fans began to ask questions and demand answers, rather than just continue as a servant class that did what it was told. Fan activism became a feature of the game, though it was limited because, unlike in Germany or Spain, few fans had any economic stake in their club at this stage. Perhaps the most significant example is the way Liverpool fans kept campaigning for a new independent inquiry into the Hillsborough tragedy which was published in 2012. Another example is that some fans could buy shares when their clubs – such as Manchester United, Arsenal and Tottenham – had traded on the stock market. But they were often regarded as a nuisance when they asked pertinent questions at annual meetings. All through the 1990s and 2000s, fans were organising. When Rupert Murdoch tried to buy Manchester United, Shareholders United Against Murdoch led the opposition and eventually evolved into Shareholders United and then the Manchester United Supporters Trust, which, along with the

Independent Manchester United Supporters Association, has led the opposition to the Glazer family's ownership of Manchester United.

On taking over, the Glazers took the company down the private-equity route, forcing fans to sell their shares, and thus did away with the troublesome Annual General Meetings. Stan Kroenke did the same at Arsenal once he had enough shares to do so. It's obviously, even to this day, too much hassle to engage with people who are paying to come through the turnstiles.

Supporters Direct was set up under the Labour government in 2000 to encourage supporter ownership. In the cases of Exeter City, AFC Wimbledon and Wrexham they helped fans save their clubs and remerge as fan-owned community assets. They helped FC United of Manchester set up as an opposition to the Glazer-owned Manchester United. Whenever there was a financial calamity or bad ownership model, at the likes of Portsmouth, Blackpool, Bolton Wanderers, Macclesfield Town, Oldham Athletic, Wigan Athletic and many others, supporters' trusts were in the vanguard helping to save clubs from extinction.

In 2002, the differences between the FSA and National Federation of Football Supporters' Clubs were put aside to create the Football Supporters' Federation. In 2018, Supporters' Direct came into the fold to create a united body, the Football Supporters' Association. And if ever a uniting of forces came at an apposite time, this was it. After thirty years of campaigning and knocking on the door, the moment for fans was about to come.

Tuesday 20 April 2021 was a big day for football fans. In 10 Downing Street, Boris Johnson sat in on a Microsoft Teams call with a group of fans from supporters' trusts and the FSA listening to their concerns about the proposed European Super League. Remember, in the mêlée of those few days, the clubs couldn't get a meeting with the Prime Minister. But the fans could and had a seat at the front table. How had that happened? How had they gone from terrace fodder to directing and influencing government policy?

For years fans have campaigned and told the authorities what was wrong with the game. They were broadly patronised. But many of those teenage fans from the 1980s had grown up into well-connected professionals and were experts in their own field. One was Tim Payton at Arsenal. Another was Kevin Miles, chief executive at the FSA. Miles was already extremely close to Tracey Crouch, as she and the Conservative Party had drawn on the FSA research to react to the crisis at Bury and create the Conservative Party manifesto commitment to a fan-led review in 2019. Payton's day job was as a sports politics lobbyist, working with the Department of Digital, Culture, Media and Sport (DCMS). Among other projects, he advised the department on Project Restart after Covid. He's also an Arsenal Supporters' Trust board member.

'Once news broke about the Super League, the major supporters' trusts, which pretty much overlapped as the Big Six clubs, were in contact,' said Payton. 'We had already had a dry run working together to fight Project Big Picture. We also had a victory when the Premier League tried to charge £14.95 for PPV TV games during Covid. So the infrastructure was there to coordinate.'

While I was sounding off on Sky Sports, making my opposition clear at the Manchester United game against Burnley, Payton and his colleagues went into action. 'You went in really hard, really early and I do think you gave the snowball a big shove down the mountain,' said Payton. 'It did make a difference. I think your position is where everyone would have been, but it put fire in a lot of bellies.

'We knew we had to get to the Prime Minister. On the Monday afternoon, Oliver Dowden [the DCMS Minister] did a statement in parliament that was very strong against the Super League, and that announced they would be launching the fan-led review headed by Tracey Crouch. I was chatting to the DCMS, as was Kevin at the FSA, because we know them. We were getting good support and access. Then, in the middle of all this, I had a request from Keir Starmer, the Labour Party leader, who was going to chair a meeting on Tuesday lunchtime and wanted us there. I thought: "Great." I went to the DCMS and said: "We have to meet with the PM! The leader of the opposition is meeting with us. When are you meeting with us?" And it was in the diary the next morning.'

Kat Law, who is a co-chair of the Tottenham Hotspurs Supporters' Trust, would also be invited, along with Kevin Miles and Duncan Drasdo of the Manchester United Supporters' Trust, as well as Richard Masters, chief executive from the Premier League and Mark Bullingham, FA chief executive, though the last two were pretty much second billing. It was the fans' voices that counted.

Law, a marketing executive, said: 'Tim had tipped us off on the Sunday lunchtime that the Super League was happening and we had been anticipating it anyway.' Because of fan pressure that had needed to be brought to bear on UEFA over the locations of the 2019 Champions League and Europa League finals, the supporters' trusts at Arsenal, Chelsea, Tottenham, and Spirit of Shankly at Liverpool, already had a WhatsApp group to coordinate things. 'We already knew each other anyway,' said Law. 'It was in lockdown, so I was having a walk. I was admin to the group so spent most of Sunday with Tim saying: "Add this person in, add that person in." We added in Manchester City and United. We already knew our position, but we had to make sure we were communicating with each other.

'Spurs didn't have a game so we couldn't do anything demonstrative like the Leeds or Chelsea fans could. We had to work on socials and on digital. We did a lot of podcasts, put out joint statements together and did loads of media. We put out an aligned message with Football Supporters Europe and the FSA, and I had to take an emergency half-day off work, because I couldn't cope with the volume coming through. Then I got a phone call from Kev Miles on Monday night saying: "Are you free tomorrow at eleven?" And I was like: "Why? I'm meant to be in work!" He said: "I want you on a call with Boris Johnson." So I was like [sighs]: "I suppose I'll have to make this call with Boris Johnson." Which was the most nuts call ever.'

Payton was asked to go first on the Teams call with the Prime Minister. 'I knew we needed something legal to stop them. The twelve clubs were saying: "We'll win this in court; you can't stop us." I specifically asked him [Johnson] if he would act to protect the FA if it expelled the Big Six clubs or took action against them. That's when the Prime Minister came back and gave the answer: "Yes, I think we must take action." And he used the phrase: "I'll drop a legislative bomb on it." I knew at that moment it was dead. I wanted to tweet it there and then, but I knew I had to observe protocol and wait for No. 10 to do it.

'I don't believe the Prime Minister would have got there without us. It wasn't just down to the six of us getting that meeting though; it was the noise across the media and everywhere. And we were all on the same side, with Richard [from the Premier League] and Mark [from the FA] coming in behind. We were all saying the same thing. But if I were to pick out the quote and moment that nailed it, it was the legislative bomb.'

When reports of that meeting filtered out that afternoon, there was consternation among the Big Six clubs. 'Arsenal phoned me up in a blind panic to ask what he meant,' said Payton. 'And, knowing my job, they even asked: "Can he do that? He can't do that, can he?" And I told them: "He certainly can. He passed Covid legislation in twenty-four hours . . ."' I don't know if they genuinely hadn't realised he could do it, I think it's more that they believed government would never do so. They must have known they'd get a big push-back, but presumably they'd factored into the equation a conviction that they would ride it out. They misread public opinion completely, misread parliament, misread the PM; failed to foresee his commitment to stopping it.

To Arsenal's credit, they did at least engage with fans in that period, with CEO Vinai Venkatesham speaking to Payton, though answers were not forthcoming. Arsenal were battling for a European place, playing Everton that week, both teams vying to make the Europa League. 'I asked Vinai: "What's the point of the game against Everton if qualification for Europe is already determined?" And he didn't have an answer.' For all the billions they had been promised from the Super League, the Premier League TV deal would have been ruined by their intervention.

By Tuesday night the wobbles had turned into a collapse of dominoes, with first Chelsea, then Manchester City, leading the retreat. Manchester United, Arsenal and Liverpool subsequently all capitulated together, leaving Tottenham with the ignominy of being the last club to bow to the inevitable.

'It was fascinating to watch,' said Law. 'But the effects have lasted a lot longer than that seventy-two hours. At Tottenham, it utterly decimated the relationship between the Trust and the board. We had been having conversations with the club about a breakaway for almost a year, mentioning it in meetings with them. And every time they said they don't comment on speculation, but that nothing was happening. We made it extremely clear what the fans' view was on the Super League idea in terms of meritocracy and sporting integrity. To find out that they were part of it was really distasteful. We had no choice at that point. We couldn't just say: "Oh it's fine, nothing's broken." There has always been a power imbalance – they still hold all the power – but the whole foundation on which our relationship operated was broken. We called for them all to resign and they hated us for that; the damage has never been patched over.'

It was during that Teams meeting that Miles could press the Prime Minister on the promised fan-led review. Payton also made a plea to the Prime Minister: 'I said that once we've stopped this, we have to address what is wrong. Can you make your review bigger? The manifesto commitment was to look at financial irregularity, but we have to look at everything.'

By Thursday 22 April the terms of the review had been established with the broadest scope, meaning it would look at owners' and directors' tests, assess the need for a regulator, look at fan ownership models, governance, fan experience, club finances and financial distribution through the pyramid. By 21 May the panel itself was confirmed. It would include Miles, Roy Hodgson (former England manager), Denise Barrett-Baxendale (Everton chief executive), Clarke Carlisle (former Professional Footballers' Association Chair), Dan Jones (former head of Sport Business at Deloitte), Dawn Airey (Chair, FA Women's Super League), David Mahoney (Chief Operating Officer, England and Wales Cricket Board), James Tedford (former Secretary, Southport FC) Godric Smith (Director, Cambridge United), and Danny Finkelstein, an independent member who has since been made a non-executive director under the new ownership at Chelsea.

For supporters, the main feature of the review's recommendations was that fans should have what is known as a golden share. That is, a community benefit society representing fans would hold a stake in the club and have the power of veto over the sale of the club stadium, relocation outside of the local area, joining a new competition that is not approved by FIFA, UEFA and the FA and/or leaving a competition in which it currently plays, and any changes to the club badge, first-team home colours and the club name. It also recommended each club should have a fan advisory board of five to twelve members, elected on a rotational basis, with which the club has to consult quarterly, with the chief executive meeting at least twice a year.

We will have to see what ends up in the final proposals as, while the government agreed with this part of the report in principle, its response points out that a golden share may be cumbersome for some smaller clubs and inappropriate. Likewise, while it supports the principle of a shadow board, the review says that the mechanism of fan engagement may need to be more flexible for smaller clubs. That said, the government has promised that when its White Paper – the draft form of their proposed legislation – is published, it will include a mechanism for fans to be able to veto those key decisions on the club's heritage.

'We've needed a new model of fan engagement,' said Law. 'We were working on the basis of grace and favour, which was basically: "If you like what we're doing and say nice things about us, come in, we'll meet you all the time, we'll put the kettle on and you can have a biscuit. If you want to oppose publicly, we'll throw you out and shut the door in your face." The important part [of the new government legislation] is that structure has some power and can't easily be ignored. Our acid test is: "Could any new structure stop the Super League from happening?" If it couldn't, it doesn't go far enough.'

This remains a defining moment for fans, one that needs to be seized. We don't have fan-owned clubs such as Barcelona and Bayern. Fans have always been outsiders, almost begging to be let into decision making. There have been successes in the past, notably at Exeter, AFC Wimbledon, Chester, Macclesfield, and York where clubs were saved by fans. But the fight against the Super League showed activist fans at their very best. The supporter-owned clubs in Spain didn't raise a finger to fight the Super League. Everyone around the world knows that it was English fans that killed the idea.

'The timing was right and everyone was shocked at the power of fans working together,' said Law. 'For too long authorities had relied on tribal divisions, so Arsenal and Spurs won't work together because they hate each other. On something like the Super League, all that was forgotten, and when fans move as one with a strong collective voice, there isn't anything they can't achieve. People within our fan base will do the same job as advisors to the club. We have PR professionals and crisis management executives. Unfortunately, the days of working in your local shop and having a season ticket at Spurs are well gone with the prices they're charging. So most of the fan base are fairly affluent and professional. We're constantly underestimated as fans. It happens all the time. You go into your meeting with the Premier League or the FA as fan reps and they'll be totally staggered that you might know what you're talking about.'

For too long, clubs have treated fans with contempt when actually they're the most engaged customer base you could wish for. There are people like Andy Mitten, who started up his fanzine, *United We Stand*, in 1989, the year of Hillsborough, as a fifteen-year-old and is still publishing thirty-three years on, making *UWS* one of the longest-running fanzines. I've known Andy since my early twenties, when he became familiar to United players on pre-season tours and from the interviews we would give to him, knowing we wouldn't be misquoted. We spoke on Zoom over the state of the game from a fans' perspective.

'I don't think I've ever been completely happy, because there are always issues and I come at those issues from a fans' perspective,' said Mitten. 'That's what's driven me since I've been very young. I can remember being a teenager at meetings because Manchester United were hiking their ticket prices up by 30 per cent. Those issues have always been important to me: ticket allocations, prices, football fans being messed about. It's why I started *United We Stand*. I thought fans were getting a raw deal. I thought that the government felt that we were all hooligans and I thought, I'm not a hooligan. It's pretty much not left me for thirty-three years. I've always fought the corner of fans, more recently on ticket prices for Champions League away games, especially in Spain. They completely take the piss. I just feel fans are looked down upon. Privately, I hear people at clubs talking about fans in a pretty disdainful way, and not just in England. Sometimes, with reason, sometimes the emotion of fans gets the better of them.

'I can point to areas where there's been a significant improvement: Manchester United's communication with the fans is far better than it's ever been. But football fans are always fighting against that prejudice, that discrimination, and I feel that I can articulate the voices which I hear by going to matches, by standing outside the ground, by speaking to real people – not online – in the real world. And people come up to me, they've got their issues, and if I feel they're genuine issues I'll try and fight their corner.'

We talked about some of the issues we have covered in the fans survey. Unsurprisingly, the issue of the Glazers and leveraged buyouts came up. 'I'm very uncomfortable with highly leveraged buyouts and not just with Manchester United,' said Mitten. 'I'm not a financial expert, but when I saw Burnley's buyout very recently, there's just red flags going there. I see the ownership model in other countries because I travel around. I see what it's like in Spain. I used to think that Barcelona was the perfect model [because the club is fan owned]. I've changed my opinion. The problem is you have human beings with egos. Presidents get elected on promises they cannot keep. This idea of *socios* [the members] all owning the club: yes, it does have some safeguarding advantages and there are some good parts of it, but because the presidents are being voted in every four years, major projects, such as ground redevelopments, get pushed back and back and back.

'I don't want to see what happened at Macclesfield or at Bury happen again. I love the meritocracy of football, that small-town dreams can become big and that clubs can rise. I'm worried that when the money comes down, it just floods straight through to player's wages, so I think there need to be checks there. Stadia have improved. Ticket prices have become less of an issue at the top level, yet if you go to an away game in the Conference you can be paying £19! You're paying more to travel away from home in the Championship – where you're still getting £37 tickets – than in the Premier League, where's there now a £30 limit. So there's all these knots that need to be ironed out. And in my own experience, as a Manchester United fan, we've seen a takeover that I don't think should ever have been allowed to happen and the divisions it caused within the fan base still run to this day.'

More recently, all these groups have played a full part with Football Supporters Europe in campaigning against the new Champions League rules, which would have still seen some clubs qualify on the basis of their European history. Their advocacy got that chucked out and the games reduced from ten group games to eight. Payton, like most, sees the campaign against the Super League as the start of something rather than a job completed; the next big struggle will be to address the distortion that UEFA money creates in domestic leagues.

'When we talk about money in the Premier League, I think too much of the debate is focused on the difference between twentieth in the Premier League and first in the Championship. I think we're going to have to think about what we do to smooth the gap between sixth and seventh, particularly with new European competitions. And because Liverpool have been so amazingly good and outperformed the metrics, I think it's been hidden that we're getting very close to the same problem with Manchester City as Germany have with Bayern Munich. You can see they add Erling Haaland in, Liverpool drop to Chelsea's level, and you have City winning by twenty points until Newcastle catch up with them.'

Fans, too, have issues to address. There is behaviour that will make female or LGBT fans feel uncomfortable and threatened. Speak to female fans, and a game can still feel like running a gauntlet for some. 'Most of the harassment and abuse I receive is online, trolling,' says Law. 'Being a woman who sticks her head above the parapet in football is still difficult. Martin Cloake, my co-chair, gets a lot less stick and we say the same things. Its abuse that is weight- and looks-based, very sexist and judgemental. Some guys just don't want to be represented by a "bird", as they would call me.'

The most intense and often aggressive area in any stadium is the segregation line between home and away fans. Some people, some women, would relish sitting there, as Law points out. But for some women, who can be randomly allocated a seat a few metres away from home fans in the away section, it can make for an awful experience. 'I've had female friends who have had money thrown at them while fans asked how much they were charging for a blow-job. All kinds of stuff like that. Most season-ticket-holding women don't want to be difficult and they don't want special rules put in place for them. They would just like people not to be arseholes. And it can't be up to the women to ask not to be put there; clubs need to sort out fan behaviour and pull people out.'

Spirit of Shankly, which was at the heart of the Super League protests, was, like so many fans' groups, born out of adversity when Liverpool almost fell into administration during the owner-ship of Tom Hicks and George Gillett. 'We didn't want the same issues that Manchester United had with the Glazers, burrowing money out of the club,' said Joe Blott, the current SOS Chair. Paul Rice, who chaired the Broadgreen Labour Party and was Chief Executive of Liverpool Commercial District Partnership, led the first meeting of 350 angry fans at the Sandon pub next to Anfield in 2008, the same pub where the club had been originally founded. From that grew a protest movement that saw Hicks and Gillett run out of town.

Liverpool's current owners, John W. Henry, Tom Werner and

Mike Gordon, know they owe much to the group, as their protests helped rescue the club and made its sale more pressing. 'L4 [Anfield] is one of the most deprived areas of the country, if not Europe,' says Blott. 'To lose Liverpool Football Club from that area would have been crippling for everyone. Just like it is for Bury, Macclesfield, Chester. The biggest victory was that we showed fans could and should have a voice and could make a difference.'

Under Henry, Werner and Gordon, SOS have forced the owners into U-turns on issues such as ticket prices, furloughing of staff, attempting to trademark the city's name and, of course, the Super League. And the boycott of an away game at Hull in 2015, because of the £55 price, led to the Premier League introducing its £30 cap on away tickets.

In 2016, SOS showed their power by managing to execute that most difficult, but definitely most effective, form of fan protest: a walk-out. Liverpool wanted to increase ticket prices from £59 to £77, so fans walked out in the seventy-seventh minute. At the time, Liverpool were winning 2–0 against Sunderland. They ended up drawing 2–2, with Jürgen Klopp citing the walk-out as having a major effect on the team and urging the owners to sort out the issue.

Blott points out that the idea came from Spion Kop 1906, who organise the flags at Liverpool, one of many Liverpool groups with whom SOS works. And they had no idea how it would go. 'It was nerve-wracking,' said Blott. 'I stood up on sixty-two minutes because I was so anxious I had got the time wrong! My seat is in the main stand, the one you progress to with rugs and blankets, so when I stood up, I thought I would be the only one. My mate stood up and all of a sudden there were loads behind us. I couldn't get out! I was looking round thinking: "This is bigger than I thought!" In our heart of hearts we were maybe looking at one to five thousand, which wouldn't have looked much. But there were twelve to fifteen thousand across the stadium, which meant huge swathes of empty seats. We never expected that. Because of unionisation, because of the way this city has operated over a number of years and a number of disputes, it's about organisation. I don't think they understood the power of what we have as a fan base.'

The upshot of the Super League proposal is that the owners take fans more seriously now than ever. SOS has worked with fellow Liverpool fan groups effectively to create a golden share even before it is imposed by a regulator. The owners are changing the company articles of Liverpool FC so that any owner now or in the future will need fan consent to move the ground, ground share or break away to a new league outside of FIFA, UEFA and the Premier League. They have to formally engage with fans over any change to the badge or kit, and the club's accounts have to be discussed with fans. 'There is a legacy now here for future generations, my children and grandchildren,' said Blott. 'It is a touchstone people can go back to and say: "No, it's written in the articles of association that you have to do this." And lower down the leagues, I think they have an opportunity to transfer our model. If you can do it with Liverpool, you can do it anywhere. We've gone beyond what people would have believed, we've changed the way the club thinks. They want the fan perspective when they make decisions. We've taken that shift towards fans to be part of the solution and not part of the problem.'

Payton at Arsenal still wants more. He once owned shares in the club, but the Kroenke family were able to force him to sell them when they took over the club fully. 'We still think the review missed the most important thing, which is structure not relationships,' said Payton. 'You can be let into a room twice a year, but if it's basically for talks in which they parry everything and don't do anything, what have you achieved? I wanted fans to have a right to own a certain amount of equity in their club. We know we won't get 50 per cent, because that's nationalisation. But I think there should be a right for fans to get up to 25 per cent of the club.'

When I spoke to Blott, fresh in the mind was the inept organisation of the Champions League final that saw Liverpool fans tear-gassed, locked out, dangerously crushed and attacked. Clearly, there is plenty more to be done. 'I'm excited, because, from a Liverpool fan's point of view, the deal we have is groundbreaking. That said, we've just been to a Champions League final in Paris and been mistreated by UEFA. So is it a golden age? No. There's so much that still needs to change. We know how fans are treated by other clubs. Their owners aren't for sitting around the table. We have nation states taking over some clubs and their means to an end is very different. What we saw from UEFA all the way leading up to the final in Paris shows that nothing has changed.' Bear in mind, these are the same fans who UEFA president Aleksander Čeferin was praising when they brought down the Super League, saving his competition, promising he would engage with them in the future.

'We've come a long way in the thirteen years of SOS, but there's still much to do. Let's use this as a platform to progress even further and seize the moment. If we can get the fan-led review through, if we can secure an independent regulator to hold football to account, that will be good. But, as fans, we have to be alive to the challenge of less honest and less scrupulous owners. It's important fans have a voice in every football club.

'We're approaching half time, 2–0 up, and the government have kind of said we can live with this. The big issue is the Premier League. They will be the opposition that comes out after the half-time bollocking and want to have a go at diluting any reforms or regulation. But fundamentally they can't regulate themselves.'

I agree. Fans have made great strides in recent years. And some clubs get it. They are beginning to listen. English fans have shown they can drive change here and in Europe. Fans have never been better organised and never had more leverage. Clubs should stop fighting them and start listening. So should the police forces and authorities organising games. There is much that could be achieved if club owners and the authorities reined in their egos and listened to those who are its lifeblood. Right now, there is a power imbalance. The fan led review calls for a greater presence and influence on the game from fans. The whole point of the review was for it to be fan led. It's now critical that these recommendations are seen through and implemented.

8

THIS IS HOW IT FEELS TO BE CITY

'We can do what we want.'
Simon Pearce, Manchester City director

In the summer of 2008 pretty much our only concern at Manchester United was whether we would sign Dimitar Berbatov from Spurs, a saga that had gone on for months and was now coming down to the last day of the transfer window. If you had told me that the power balance between the football clubs in Manchester was about to shift I would have laughed you out of Deansgate. The idea that Manchester City would ever be a threat to us was a joke.

Manchester City had the opposite of the Midas Touch. They had become a club excellent at grabbing defeat from victory. In 2008, we had just won the Champions League with arguably Sir Alex Ferguson's greatest ever team – I was sat in the stands! – which had Carlos Tevez, Wayne Rooney and Cristiano Ronaldo up front, Paul Scholes and Michael Carrick in midfield, and Nemanja Vidić and Rio Ferdinand at the back. We had just won a second successive Premier League title and would go on to make it three in a row in 2009, which would be Sir Alex's Ferguson's eleventh. He would add two more before he retired. City had finished ninth in 2008, behind Portsmouth and Blackburn.

United would get the Berbatov deal done on deadline day, 1 September. This was about the time that transfer deadline day became a major part of the sports media landscape, with reporters outside grounds, fans gathering to welcome new signings or to protest about the fact there were no new ones. In the middle of all this, Manchester City issued a press release: 'Manchester City can confirm that a Memorandum of Understanding has been signed between the Abu Dhabi United Group and Manchester City Football Club Limited. A period of due diligence for all parties, including the FA Premier League, has now been entered.'

City had a Middle Eastern sheikh as their new owner. To be honest, we just took it in our stride as their fans celebrated. We all knew how this would turn out. City were a joke. They had already had one sugar daddy come in, Thaksin Shinawatra, the former Prime Minister of Thailand, who had been overthrown in a military coup in 2006. He took over in 2007. They were going to be bigger than Real Madrid. Admittedly, they did beat us in the derby that year. But Shinawatra's assets were frozen, he was accused of corruption which he claimed was politically motivated, and the former owner had to step in to pay the players' wages that season. The squad under Sven-Göran Eriksson was ill disciplined and they lost their last game of the season 8–1. Typical City. They finally get a rich benefactor and he turns out to have frozen bank accounts. Like I said, the Midas Touch in reverse.

'This time it's different,' we were told. 'These guys are serious.' At United, I think we all still struggled to believe it was going to be any different from before. Sheikh Mansour, who was behind the Abu Dhabi United Group, was apparently keen to make an impression and City made a counter offer for Berbatov. When Berbatov's agent relayed the details of the improved offer from City to the striker, he reportedly told his agent to 'fuck off'. Which was the correct answer. Manchester United were the only team in town that any serious player would have considered. If Chelsea had come in, that might have been an issue. Arsenal were beginning their decline. But Manchester City?

In the end, City did make a signature signing later that day. Robinho, once a young Brazilian prodigy and now a player Real Madrid were desperate to move on, was signed for £32m. That did create some ripples around the world, though not entirely in the way City intended. It was a huge shock, as Robinho only three years previously had signed from Santos as one of the best twenty-one-year-olds in the world. But after three years Real Madrid had seen enough. They didn't have the new Ronaldo or Ronaldinho.

City took the bait. I think their intention was to announce to the world that they had arrived. In reality, most of the football world raised their eyebrows and agents began gathering excitedly in that way only they can when they realise there is a new sucker in town and there is some easy money to be made. The message it conveyed was the exact opposite of what they intended. Real Madrid needed Robinho off the wage bill. City obliged. All around Europe everyone realised there was a new club where they could palm off their overpaid failed rejects. The Germans have an acronym for Premier League team's judgement when it comes to buying their players: S.E.M. It stands for 'Stupid English Money'. City were, it seemed, the epitome of S.E.M.

Robinho himself thought he would be joining Chelsea. It was only at the last minute that he discovered his new club would actually be Manchester City. To be fair, Robinho scored fourteen goals in his thirty-six starts at City, which isn't nearly as bad as I remember him being. I recall him being in and out and never quite settling. He left to join AC Milan in 2010.

In that first week of the takeover, a Dubai TV personality, Dr Sulaiman Al-Fahim, seemed to be the spokesperson for Sheikh Mansour. He liked to talk big, did Al-Fahim. He was friends with Piers Morgan and hosted a TV show in the style of *The Apprentice* in Dubai. Cristiano Ronaldo was in his last season at Manchester United and, even that summer, Real Madrid had been trying to sign him. Sir Alex had convinced him to stay, but we all suspected he would be gone the following summer to Real Madrid, the club of his dreams. Not according to Al-Fahim. 'Ronaldo has said he wants to play for the biggest club in the world, so we will see in January if he is serious,' he said, announcing City's intention to join the race to buy him. We couldn't stop laughing at United when he said that.

It was a case of: 'Don't worry about them. We've got Sir Alex Ferguson, we're Man United, we win trophies and City always shoot themselves in the foot.' Some journalists were mentioning human rights issues in Abu Dhabi, and *Red Issue*, a United fanzine, wrote about it on a monthly basis. There were people who did mention the fact that homosexuality was illegal over there. But Dubai, Abu Dhabi's neighbouring emirate state, was becoming a go-to destination for footballers for holidays. Qatar was a year away from winning the right to host the 2022 World Cup. No one really seemed too concerned. We did the double over them that season (2009–10), knocked them out in the League Cup semi-final, and they finished fifth, missing out on the Champions League. They didn't seem that much of a threat.

Abu Dhabi was a place we knew little about. Over time we would learn it is the largest and richest emirate of seven sheikdoms known as the United Arab Emirates. The only time it had come up in conversation in the dressing room would have been when players were investing in their holiday villas in Dubai for use in those international breaks if you're not selected for the national team. Had it not been for Manchester City, most of us would never have investigated the Emirates history. But these separate states were once known as the Trucial States and had made a treaty with Great Britain in 1820, becoming British protectorates at the height of Empire. Back then, diving for pearls was the closest they came to riches, but they were strategically vital in the trade route to India.

By the 1950s, Britain had less need of a sea trade route to India, and Empire was in retreat. Abu Dhabi remained a poor but fortified fishing village. Even its pearl trade had withered due to new industrial methods of production. It was now an outpost of an old empire, which attracted the odd adventurer and industrialist.

However, in 1938, large reserves of oil were discovered in Saudi Arabia, so geologists began scouring the Trucial States hoping for more of the same. At first, they had little luck. Everything changed when a French diving pioneer, Jacques Cousteau, was brought in by BP and Total (then known as Compagnie Française des Pétroles) to explore the coast. In 1958, at the Umm Shaif field, which is in Abu Dhabi territorial waters but around halfway between Abu Dhabi and Qatar, they struck liquid gold, uncovering a 300km² oil field, one of the largest in the world.

Sheikh Zayed bin Sultan Al-Nahyan, a junior member of the Royal Family, was at that time in charge of the eastern administrative district of Abu Dhabi. He had helped see off Saudi Arabian attempts to grab territory and oil rights and now assisted Cousteau and his team. He quickly grasped what the discovery of oil meant for his emirate and what it might do for the wider region. But the ruler of Abu Dhabi was his older brother, Sheikh Shakhbut, and he wasn't of the same mind.

Scarred by the economic decline he had witnessed in the twentieth century, Shakhbut refused to invest the new money that had started coming into the emirate once oil started pumping in 1962 and instead hoarded it. He discouraged construction and was suspicious of banking. As Sharjah and Dubai started to thrive, opening airports, Abu Dhabi became increasingly irrelevant. No money was invested in health and education, and infrastructure and equipment for the oil industry had to be imported from Dubai. In 1966, with the support of the British, a bloodless coup took place. Sheikh Shakhbut was encouraged to leave and Sheikh Zayed became the new ruler of Abu Dhabi.

Not that it meant an awful lot in the context of the region at the time. Saudi Arabia and Kuwait, the latter of which had become independent from Britain in 1961, were the big oil producers. Even among the Trucial States, Abu Dhabi wasn't a major player, despite being the biggest and now with potentially the largest oil reserves. Sheikh Zayed was in charge of a fort, a small settlement and a swathe of desert where 36,000 people lived, pretty much an average attendance at the Etihad.

Yet if you visit Abu Dhabi now it is home to 1.5 million people, with a modern international hub airport, architecturally bold skyscrapers, and the stunning Sheikh Zayed Grand Mosque, one of the largest in the world. There are sweeping eight-lane highways and grand bridges to link the network of islands. In less than sixty years they have built a super-city on the edge of the desert with an impressive social security network and healthcare for Abu Dhabi nationals with a diversified economy that eventually will not be reliant on fossil fuels. Migrant workers make up the bulk of the population, under certain conditions they bring their families to live with them, though many human rights workers say that it's not possible for the lowest paid.

Sheikh Zayed also pretty much single-handedly pulled together the nascent state of the United Arab Emirates when the British announced they were no longer prepared to keep a garrison there to protect the rulers in 1968. Prime Minister Harold Wilson's shock announcement caused consternation. It wasn't clear that Sheikh Zayed and the ruling dynasties would survive. The perceived wisdom was that they were propped up by Britain.

But Sheikh Zayed rallied the six founding members of the UAE and brought them together as a nation in 1971, becoming their first president. His image is everywhere in Abu Dhabi. On arrival at the airport, you will be greeted by his portrait and montages of just what he did for Abu Dhabi and, by extension, the region. He died in 2004, by which time he had built a secure nation, with Abu Dhabi, which produces 90 per cent of the oil in the UAE, the richest and most dominant emirate within it. He encouraged women to work, he established the Red Crescent, the Islamic version of the Red Cross, in the region, and he saw the arrival of this new money as a gift to build the infrastructure of a new nation.

'You would have to say he was one of the most successful Arab heads of state of the twentieth century,' says Dr Chris Davidson, author of *Abu Dhabi: Oil and Beyond*.

> He pulled together the only really successful example of an Arab federation, navigated Britain's withdrawal at a time when Iran was occupying part of their territory and managed the oil booms. I lived in Abu Dhabi when he was alive and it was a lovely place. You never had a feeling of it being an authoritarian state.

That's some act to follow. And Sheikh Zayed's most famous son in the UK is Sheikh Mansour, or Mansour bin Zayed Al-Nahyan to give him his full name, the owner of Manchester City. But Sheikh Zayed had another son, who is even more powerful and actually much better known globally: Mohammed bin Zayed, known in diplomatic circles as MBZ.

'MBZ is the boss,' says Dr Davidson.

> Basically he sidelined his half-brother, Sheikh Khalifa, the eldest son of Sheikh Zayed. Though Khalifa became ruler of Abu Dhabi and president of the UAE, he did not get to choose one of his two sons as Crown Prince. Before Sheikh Zayed died in 2004, he was already persuaded by MBZ to make MBZ Deputy Crown Prince and thus the next man in line.
>
> Sheikh Khalifa was president until May 2022, when he died, but it was effectively a nominal position. Shiekh Khalifa was a non-entity in effect. The sons of Sheika Fatima, the third wife of Sheikh Zayed, have long ruled Abu Dhabi and so effectively the

UAE. They all have a piece of the pie and they know who is in charge. The minister of foreign affairs is Sheikh Abdullah, and the national security advisors have been Sheikh Hazza and then Sheikh Tahnoun. Sheikh Mansour's responsibilities have been in sovereign wealth and he is Deputy Prime Minister of the UAE. He also has this role as Minister of Presidential Affairs, giving him control over access to the president and the president's assets.

The new president, replacing Sheikh Khalifa in March 2022, is MBZ. He now has the power in name and in reality.

There are some who will say it was MBZ who saw what Man City might be for Abu Dhabi. When the deal to buy the club was finally secured on 22 September 2010, the loudmouth Dubai TV star Al-Fahim had quietly been removed. It seemed that his bragging wasn't to the taste of the Abu Dhabi royal family. 'I think once the value of being identified with Manchester City was properly understood, the club was then essentially put in the hands of the people who knew what they were doing. Another man, whose name was about to become familiar to us all, was in place: Khaldoon Al Mubarak.

'He's basically the prime minister of Abu Dhabi and controls its executive affairs authority,' says Dr Davidson. 'He is chief executive of Mubadala, the £243 billion sovereign wealth fund run by MBZ. He is essentially MBZ's top representative.'

At the first City game after the takeover had been completed, a 6–0 win over Portsmouth, it was Al Mubarak who was introduced to the fans. He was thirty-three. In terms of communication from Sheikh Mansour, City fans had to make do with a letter, which promised to honour the spirit and history of City and sensibly indicated it would take time to turn the club into what they wanted. There had been a screeching handbrake turn in terms of tone of voice from the club compared to the boasts of overnight success from Al-Fahim. Sheikh Mansour's motives, though, remained as unclear then as they do now.

'I think ultimately it's a public relations ploy,' says Dr Davidson.

I always felt the City purchase was a foreign policy exercise. It cultivates good relations with Britain but it also taps into that global brand the Premier League has in other Arab countries, as well as kids in India, Pakistan, Africa, all wearing the shirt. They know full well who owns it. They know it's an Abu Dhabi Sheikh and therefore Abu Dhabi must be the good guy.

City would wait two years for Sheikh Mansour actually to attend a game. He did so in August 2010, a 3–0 win against Liverpool. And he hasn't been back in twelve years, which maybe tells you where his priorities lie. In his book *Richer Than God*, which tells the story of the takeover, journalist David Conn asked Al Mubarak why the sheikh doesn't attend games. 'His Highness is very discreet,' said Al Mubarak. 'He enjoyed the Liverpool game when he came but it was a lot of fuss for him to be in the public eye; he isn't going to be left alone when he does [come to a game].'

Al Mubarak is more approachable, often at matches, and is a smart and impressive figure. When Chinese President Xi Jinping visited Manchester in 2015, there was a function for business leaders, to which I was invited. I spent some time talking to Al Mubarak and at the same event chatted to Ed Woodward. I came away utterly clear which individual I would rather run my club. Needless to say, it wasn't the man who oversaw zero Premier League trophies in his nine years in charge.

Al Mubarak was educated at Tufts University in Boston, so is very much the Western face of Abu Dhabi. He is a trustee of New York University, due to the fact that NYU has a campus in Abu Dhabi and that from 2012 to 2018 Abu Dhabi donated $78m to

NYU. Al Mubarak was born into this. His grandfather was an advisor of Sheikh Zayed when oil was first discovered in 1958, helped to found the judicial system of Abu Dhabi and so is revered as a kind of founding father of the nation. His father, Khalifa Al Mubarak, is honoured as a martyr of the nation. He was serving as a UAE ambassador to France when he was assassinated in the streets of Paris in 1984, shot in the back of the head by a terrorist from the Arab Revolutionary Brigade because they disagreed with the UAE's friendly policy at the time to the USA and its attitude towards Palestinian refugees. Al Mubarak was nine when it happened. He knows the cost of the UAE's Western alliances and dangers of radicalism. It is hard to over-estimate his importance to the UAE.

He's a man who is used to the best and as such he wasn't overly impressed when he was handed City to run in 2008 and was taken on a tour of the training facilities. 'I must say I was extremely surprised,' he told Conn. 'I couldn't believe what I saw. It was not the level of infrastructure that is the minimum for a top-level club. Immediately I remember leaving that trip and going back to Sheikh Mansour and showing him some pictures of the facility and he was very straight to say this was unacceptable.'

Manchester City may only have been a tiny speck on the horizon of the business Al Mubarak deals with, but he pretty much confirmed to Conn that no one in Abu Dhabi quite realised what exposure they were buying when they became a Premier League member. 'We have done some amazing deals yet the exposure I got from being associated with this club [City] far exceeds anything that happens with the business side,' said Al Mubarak. 'To be honest, I completely underestimated it. I knew it was going to be high profile to a certain extent but nowhere near what it has transpired to be . . . when you buy an English Premier League side it is a totally different ball game – the public persona, the image, the public relations side of the deal was very much bigger than the investment.'

Alongside Al Mubarak, there was another man who was co-opted on to the City board in 2008: Simon Pearce, a public relations executive who was special advisor to the Abu Dhabi's Executive Affairs Authority. Many call him the chief spin doctor for Abu Dhabi. Pearce is the man who features in the leaked emails published by German magazine *Der Spiegel*, which shed some light on how City have built their empire. In those early days, City didn't have anything like the revenue to justify their spending, but luckily a raft of Abu Dhabi companies decided to sponsor the club to make up the shortfall.

And, in football terms, those sponsorships were beginning to pay dividends. There was the awful – from United's point of view – Sergio Aguero moment in 2012, when they wrestled the league title from United in the final seconds of the season. I had left the season before, but I still felt it as though I were a player and I was a fan. They had already broken their trophy drought of thirty-five years in 2011, winning the FA Cup, knocking United out in the semi. They were beginning to be a bit more than noisy neighbours. They were neighbours who were building a massive extension, buying a flash car and putting your house in the shade.

You wanted to ask where all the money was coming from. Or rather – because we knew where it was coming from – how it met the relevant rules. When Roberto Mancini was sacked in 2013, the compensations costs, which were more than £10m, meant City would break UEFA's Financial Fair Play (FFP) rules. We know this because City admitted it in internal emails. 'We will have a short-fall of £9.9m in order to comply with UEFA FFP this season,' wrote Jorge Chumillas, Man City's then Chief Financial Officer. 'The deficit is due to RM [Robert Mancini]. I think that the only solution left would be an additional amount of AD [Abu Dhabi] sponsorship revenues that covers this gap.'

Leaked emails suggested that sponsors could pay the win bonus that would have been due for the FA Cup Final in 2013 – had City not lost that match 1–0 to Wigan! Eventually, Chumillas explained that the Abu Dhabi sponsors would fill the gap. Aabar would pay £0.5m extra, Etihad £1.5m and the Abu Dhabi Tourism Authority an extra £5.5m. Chumillas asked if it was possible to backdate the contracts to make it look as though this had been planned all along. 'Of course, we can do what we want,' Pearce replied.

But in 2011, Etihad executives wrote to Man City explaining that there appeared to be 'some confusion' about the fees they were due to pay. 'Etihad's commitment is for £4m and the remaining balance (£8m) is handled separately by the Executive Affairs Authority.' That's the Executive Affairs Authority, which is run by Al Mubarak with Pearce as the chief advisor.

By 2013, the sums involved are even greater. On 16 December 2013, Simon Pearce wrote to Peter Baumgartner, then Etihad's Chief Commercial Officer, apologising that he had underpaid Etihad relating to the City sponsorship. Traditionally, sponsorship involves the company in question paying the club, not a club director apologising for underpaying the company! 'We [City] should be receiving a total of £99m of which you will have provided £8m. I therefore should have forwarded £91m.' City have denounced the conclusions from the leaked emails saying they were 'out-of-context materials purportedly hacked or stolen' and said there was an 'organised and clear attempt to damage the club's reputation.'

Remember, all this was happening just as Sir Alex Ferguson was about to quit and David Moyes to take over at United. The fact that United won the league in 2013, a year after the Aguero moment, convinced us this would be like Chelsea's challenge again, wrestling over the title until we eventually saw them off. But City were intent on seizing this moment. They were about to disappear into the distance.

In 2022, Manchester City topped the Deloitte Rankings as the richest club in the world with £570m income, bigger it seems than Manchester United, Real Madrid and Barcelona. Their commercial team must have done extraordinarily well battling it out to win those sponsorship deals to achieve that. For example, City's shirt-sleeve sponsor, Nexen, was announced in 2017. The amount wasn't released, but that in itself might be worth around £15m a year. Coincidentally, at the same time, Mubadala, that MBZ wealth fund run by Al Mubarak, announced an equity investment in Nexen. Even better for City, in November 2019, the US private-equity firm Silver Lake announced a $500 million investment in City Football Group, the network of clubs now owned by City around the world. In September 2020, Mubadala announced a £2bn twenty-five-year investment in Silver Lake. Blue-chip sponsors like this ensure City stay within the Financial Fair Play rules.

To be clear, I don't have a problem with owner funding as long as they can afford it, as Sheikh Mansour clearly can. But it does raise questions about exactly how a state interacts with the Premier League. And what rules need to apply to regulate owner funding. But there are probably bigger questions of a graver nature to ask when we're considering whether Abu Dhabi and now Saudi Arabia should be part of a Premier League club.

I've always been in favour of foreign investment into this country. That's why I was fiercely against Brexit because I feel it was making us more insular, shutting down our opportunity to work abroad and making it more difficult for people to work here. I want to be able to travel and learn and I want different cultures and businesses here. It's partly inspired by what I experienced in football, a team of different nationalities and cultures coming together to form a unit across national boundaries. Our capacity to achieve and thrive is greatly enhanced when we allow others in and embrace different ideas. Manchester United were better under Sir Alex because we welcomed people from outside our immediate city and culture and learned from them. The Premier League has thrived because of that openness. My city has revived itself due to international investment. I welcome that and always say to sceptics that if the money wasn't coming to Manchester it would be going to another city in this country or abroad.

I live in the city centre and during lockdown, when daily walks became the habit of the nation, I would sometimes walk through the Northern Quarter, across Ancoats and towards east Manchester, where the Etihad is based. What Abu Dhabi have done there in association with the city council is exceptional. It's not just the stadium and the Etihad Campus, where I trained with England when I was Roy Hodgson's assistant and which is an extraordinary facility. The entire area has been transformed and we're a better city thanks to Abu Dhabi investment. The criticism has been that they got the land on the cheap. But, trust me, no other property developer in Manchester would have wanted to take on that land and invest £1bn to built homes. It was too risky. And they have also provided land and money to build a leisure centre, sixth-form college and a health centre for the community. There is no doubt residents have benefited from Abu Dhabi and that in turn has encouraged money from the USA and Asia to come in and enrich the city, create more jobs, better working conditions, better pay; to improve lives and improve our region. Abu Dhabi's investment in City has been a trailblazer. I know there are some criticisms over whether enough social housing and affordable homes are being made available. However, you cannot argue with the overall momentum they have generated in an area of the city that was among the poorest districts but is now a thriving place to live. You imagine Sheikh Zayed, Sheikh Mansour's father, would approve. His outward-looking view of Islam was that it is a religion that should help others. 'Since God bestows His graces on us, providing us with wealth, it is our role to use this wealth for the benefit and prosperity of our people, as an expression of gratitude to our Lord,' he said. What has happened in east Manchester might be seen as an outworking of that.

Compare that to the Glazers at Manchester United. I spoke to Tracey Crouch, who headed the fans-led review into football, and she made this point. 'I've seen the City facilities because I'm now on the board of British Cycling as well,' she said. 'They're amazing. I met the leader of the council the other day, Bev Craig. The plans that have already been enabled because of the investment by Abu Dhabi are incredible but the plans they still have are amazing. The Glazers can look with envy as to what City have done with their football team, but they should also, I think, be looking rather enviously, but also shamefacedly, at what they as Manchester United owners haven't done. Not just on the football pitch, but also what they haven't done in their community or indeed their own stadium. Any owner of a football club, it's not just about the club. It is about the wider community.'

But I know there is more to the United Arab Emirates and specifically Abu Dhabi than those shiny developments. To understand more, it's helpful to speak to Nicholas McGeehan, director of FairSquare, who has spent years researching human rights there for organisations such as Amnesty International. In January 2014, he was returning from a trip via Dubai International Airport. 'I had been investigating worker abuses in the UAE, going on to labour sites and speaking to workers about what was happening,' he explains. 'I was going through passport control and there was problem. They told me to wait a minute and they made a call. Five guys in plain clothes came and took me to a basement in the bottom of airport. You knew exactly what was happening. I was on my own and my son had been born a month before so I was frantically calling my partner to let her know. I've spoken to people who have been tortured in the UAE and you're pretty sure it's not going happen to you, but you don't know. Will the protection your British passport affords come after a few hours or a week? Some people might be cool in that situation, but I wasn't. I was terrified because you know what happens to people. I was there for two hours and eventually I had a retina scan, they took fingerprints, gave me my tickets, told me to get on my plane and never come back. I was blacklisted and no longer welcome. I think they believe I'm a national security threat. So in the end it was nothing and certainly nothing compared to what others go through.'

Take the case of African workers in Abu Dhabi. According to Amnesty International, in June 2021 the authorities arbitrarily detained at least 375 African migrant workers and jailed them at Al-Wathba prison. Many were held without representation, or the means to contact people, for up to six weeks in over-crowded cells without proper sanitation. Many were deported without due process or legal representation and other detainees reported that they were racially abused and sexually assaulted.*

The UAE Ministry of Interior when asked about the cases began their statement by calling 'upon the media not to circulate or disseminate any information not published by the relevant authorities' and explaining that the deportation 'was carried out in accordance with legal procedures'. It claimed 'these organizations, which are prostitution networks, were involved in human trafficking offences, indecent acts, and extortion and assault cases that threaten the security of society'.

It then complained that 'international organizations following the issue should have communicated with the relevant authorities, as these allegations [of psychological torture, abuse, racism] were inconsistent with the legal foundations of the UAE's criminal justice system, and UAE legislation is based on justice, equality

* Amnesty International. (n.d.). UAE: Mass Arbitrary Detention and Deportation of Africans. [online] Available at: https://www.amnesty.org/en/documents/mde25/4896/2021/en/

and the preservation of human dignity'. The ministry categorically denied the report's racist suggestions, stressing that the UAE adopts strict laws and practices with regards to non-discrimination in all cases.

We all marvel at Pep Guardiola's Manchester City, but should more questions be asked about the money that pays for it? I mean, on one hand this isn't Al Mubarak. On the other hand, Sheikh Mansour is the deputy prime minister of the country. It's hard to believe he's not aware of the reports from international oganisations.

Equidem, a human rights organisation, recently investigated the plight of workers at Dubai's Expo 2020, which took place in 2022 due to Covid delays and was visited by Prince William, Lionel Messi, Cristiano Ronaldo and was extensively advertised on City's billboards at the Etihad and on their training tops. Jack Grealish and Ruben Dias made promotional videos there. Dubai is part of the UAE and subject to their labour laws. Equidem spoke to sixty-nine workers and found only one was in possession of their own passport. Interviewees stated that it was common practice for companies to retain their employees' travel documents, despite it being illegal in the UAE. Racism and bullying was reported by 37 per cent and two-thirds said they were not always paid on time or in full, with overtime and holidays particular issues. The report concluded: 'None of the companies employing the thirty migrant workers interviewed at length for this research were fully complying with their contractual obligations as set out in the Worker Welfare Policy and accompanying Assurance Standards or the UAE's labour laws.' Expo 2020 said that it employed a twelve-strong worker-welfare team to ensure all employees were receiving the correct protection under UAE law and that contractors were bound by International Labour Organisation guidelines. It did add: 'A number of issues of non-compliance have been identified, as is typical of a project of this vast scale and complexity' and that 'the two most regularly raised topics of concern are around wage payments and food, and we've worked directly with contractors to remedy both immediately.'

McGeehan is unsurprised. 'On workers' rights, it's hard to separate the states in the region. Can a worker in Qatar or a worker in Abu Dhabi say they are better treated or better paid? Not really. The UAE have always been more progressive states on reforms. You can put something on paper, though, which looks good, but can you enforce it? You're entitled to develop your economy but not by using a system of labour that puts people into slavery in the most extreme cases. And I use that term precisely, not hyperbolically.'

He's referring to the 2017 conviction of eight princesses from the Al-Nahyan family, the royal family of Abu Dhabi who, despite despite denying the charges, were convicted of human trafficking and degrading treatment of their servants by a Brussels court. Sheikha Hamda Al-Nahyan and her seven daughters did not attend the trial and it was thought unlikely they would be extradited if they had been jailed. Despite denying the charges, they were given fifteen-month suspended jail terms and ordered to pay £145,000 each.

They had brought twenty servants with them on a 2008 visit to a luxury hotel and were accused of keeping them in near slavery. One worker escaped from the luxury hotel suite the princesses had hired and told how they were forced to be available twenty-four hours a day, had to sleep on the floor, were never given a day off, were prevented from leaving the hotel and ate the princesses' leftovers.

In the wake of the scandal the UAE introduced a law specifically to protect domestic workers, guaranteeing time off, minimum wages and giving workers contract rights that are overseen by the Ministry of Human Resources and Emiratisation. However, it is difficult to document just how effectively that law is being applied.

'There are literally no activists in the UAE now that you could speak to, and there are only three or four countries in the world you could say that about,' says McGeehan.

Some Emiratis have tried speaking up. At the time of the Arab Spring in 2011, rulers in the region were worried that revolts in Tunisia, Egypt, Libya and Syria would be contagious. A group of Emiratis petitioned the government for democratic reform. They were arrested, charged with insulting the head of state and imprisoned for between two to three years. However, they were pardoned a day after sentencing by then President, Sheikh Khalifa.

One of the five, Ahmed Mansoor, continued to press for reform despite his earlier scare. He raised concerns on arbitrary detention, torture, and claimed the UAE failed to meet international standards for fair trials and the independence of the judiciary. In 2015, he won the prestigious Martin Ennals Award for Human Rights Defenders. In March 2017, he was rearrested and charged with disseminating false information to promote sedition, hatred and damage to national unity, and subsequently convicted and sentenced to ten years in prison.

In a May 2019 report, UN human rights experts said that Mansoor had been kept in solitary confinement 'in conditions of detention that violate basic international human rights standards and which risk taking an irrevocable toll on Mr Mansoor's health'.

An Amnesty International report in 2021 said:

Since his arrest on 20 March 2017, he has only been permitted to leave his small cell for a handful of family visits, and only once allowed outside for fresh air in the prison's exercise yard. In protest, he has been on two separate hunger strikes, which have seriously damaged his health. By detaining Mansoor in such appalling conditions, the UAE authorities are in violation of their obligations under the Convention Against Torture . . . as well as Article 2 of the UAE's Code of Criminal Procedure.

The UAE authorities denied claims of poor treatment, saying in 2022 that such reports were spread 'to distort and fabricate facts based on their particular agenda'. But McGeehan says Mansoor's treatment has had a chilling effect on the country. 'There is not a single person who would go on the record and speak to a journalist or a human rights group. Human rights groups and academics can't travel into the country for security concerns. There is a significant possibility you could be arrested, detained and disappeared.

'They have the most expensive and sophisticated electronic surveillance system in the world thanks to their relationships with Israel and the use of Pegasus software and they have a close strategic relationship with China. They are a key player in shifting the manner in which the world is governed away from American hegemony and towards this far more authoritarian surveillance-driven model that China wants.'

Pegasus is software developed by Israeli firm NSO Group and licensed to governments, which can then infect mobile phones simply by sending a message. It doesn't require the recipient to click on a link to work and turns your phone into a listening device. In April 2022, the Citizen Lab at the University of Toronto said the United Arab Emirates was suspected of orchestrating spyware attacks on No. 10 Downing Street in 2020 and 2021. There has been no response from the UAE.

A spokesperson for NSO Group said the allegations were 'false and could not be related to NSO products for technological and contractual reasons. NSO continues to be targeted by a number of politically motivated advocacy organizations, like Citizens Labs and Amnesty, to produce inaccurate and unsubstantiated reports based on vague and incomplete information.'

'As it stands, it would be difficult to call the UAE allies or security partners to Britain,' says Dr Davidson.

I wouldn't even say they're particularly friendly to the west any more. But, the bottom line is, the USA and UK are still their ultimate security guarantee. They don't see Russia or China or anyone else being capable of protecting them if they are attacked by Iran.

What the future holds for Abu Dhabi and Britain remains unclear. 'There has to be engagement with Abu Dhabi and the UAE,' says McGeehan. 'But engagement has to be critical at times. It's not acceptable to lock up these brave Emiratis who think they should have freedom of speech. That's dangerous for the UAE and dangerous for everybody if you're spreading this form of governance. If you're not a white Westerner, you can expect to be tortured if you break the deal. And the deal is that you don't talk about politics. And [the state] is trying to spread that version of government through the region, the idea being that authoritarian stability is the model of governance.'

The more I learned about Abu Dhabi, beyond the City team and beyond east Manchester, the harder it is to just turn away and say these aren't our concerns. We can't really be passionate about getting things right in our own country regarding our failures over human rights and ignore what is happening in Abu Dhabi just because they also give us Phil Foden and Kevin De Bruyne. And yet clearly we can't change Abu Dhabi in a way we can affect change in the UK. Sheikh Mansour isn't going anywhere and his model of investment has revolutionised our game. If our understanding of Abu Dhabi was better it would have pricked our conscience about what goes on there.

And yet when the former president, Sheikh Khalifa, died in 2022, the Duke of Cambridge, Prince William, travelled to the

UAE to meet with MBZ and pay his condolences. 'The bond between the UK and the UAE is deep,' said a statement on Prince William's behalf. That's how important the UAE and its oil is to this country.

In this chapter I've tried to provide a balance of the great positives that Manchester Ciry's ownership have achieved on and off the pitch, and some of the major human and workers rights abuses that occur in the UAE. Should the two issues be separated? Should state related ownership be allowed? All these questions need to be answered satisfactorily by a new regulator for football. My personal position has always been to work with other nations and not expel them. Being round the table means you have more chance to change and alter behaviours than you do on opposite sides of the fence. Football is powerful and can influence political and societal issues. One thing I am clear on is that entry into football ownership in this country must be done through an independently created licensing system with transparency. This license should be regularly reviewed by the regulator to assess owners external activity away from the game. We've seen with Chelsea and Abramovich that we can't just turn a blind eye.

9

THE UGLY GAME

The monkey chants started in earnest in the forty-fourth minute. We were being taken apart by Spain. This was 2004 and we were up against the makings of a Spain team that would go on to win the Euros in 2008 and 2012 and the 2010 World Cup. We were meant to be England's golden generation but, to be honest, we were miles off. They were stroking the ball around and we couldn't get near them. Frustrated, we pretty much resorted to kicking them.

So the atmosphere was already hostile when Ashley Cole went in hard on Michel Salgado and picked up a yellow card. What came next was awful though. Among the jeers and boos came the monkey chants. It was impossible not to hear it, it was so loud. Not a handful of fans but hundreds at least, maybe thousands. In the stands, you could see what looked like respectable Madrid men and women, with kids in tow, out for a family evening, mimicking a monkey.

As the second half progressed it got worse. Every time Cole or Shaun Wright-Phillips touched the ball there was a chorus of monkey noises. I'm not sure we could quite believe what we were hearing. Anyway, we played on. Of course we did. As I've mentioned before, we didn't have the strength of personality this current generation has. I'm pretty sure they would have stopped the game, like Tyrone Mings did in Bulgaria with England. And I expect in such circumstances, they would just walk off. I'd love to say we took some kind of big stand. But history doesn't lie. We did nothing.

We didn't have the courage or intelligence that the modern player has. We played on, losing 1–0 but brutally exposed in a football sense. Looking back, though, my biggest exposure came through a lack of understanding or knowledge of the history related to racism, along with an inability to connect football and societal issues.

Then came the aftermath. I sat next to Ashley afterwards. I came off the pitch, got into the shower and didn't say a word to him. I did my interviews after the game and from memory probably ignored or semi-answered the question on racism, walked onto the bus, went back home and didn't think about it again. I just accepted it. It is appalling. Back then, I probably put racial abuse in the same category as the abuse we would receive for playing for Manchester United in England. We simply put it down as abuse. We just got on with it. I'm ashamed of the fact that I was on the Professional Footballers' Association management committee, the players' union. I fought for players' rights at nearly every level. But I didn't fight at all on this. I never went to Ashley to ask how he felt. Or spoke to the likes of Rio Ferdinand or Louis Saha at Manchester United to ask their perspective, what it feels like to be abused simply because of your race. I've been abused plenty of times, but never because of that. It's only searching back now do I think that historic issues relating to race and inequality should be taught in schools.

It would be nice to pretend that this was 2004 and things have changed since then. Or that we've been on a steady linear progression since racial abuse became so common in the 1970s. But we all know that's not true. The Euro 2020 final should have been a celebration of our team and the nation, win or lose. And yet the ugly aftermath was the racist abuse directed at Jadon Sancho, Marcus Rashford and Bukayo Saka. Those who were caught hurling such abuse weren't from abroad. They were England fans: a fifty-two year-old forklift driver from Feltham, sentenced to ten weeks in prison; a fifty year-old a father of three from Kent, sentenced to fifty days in prison suspended for a year; a forty-three year-old from Runcorn, given fourteen weeks in prison suspended for eighteen months; and a nineteen year-old from Worcester, sentenced to six weeks at a Young Offenders' Institute. Good that they got caught and punished. I'm sure there were more who got away with it. And I don't see how a suspended sentence works as a deterrent. But the message was clear. Racism is alive and thrives. It's become a completely unacceptable fact of life that if a Black player makes a mistake he can expect to be racially abused.

There was a time when maybe you could convince yourself that racism was seen as unacceptable by almost everyone. But the advent of social media and the rise of Boris Johnson and his mob has blown that apart. You can use racist language and still hold the highest office in this county. People don't see that as an issue and are happy to vote for him. Brexit has amplified the problem. Many people had good reasons for feeling the way they did on Brexit, but the debate over immigration and turning our backs on asylum seekers certainly gives encouragement and ammunition. With the Prime Minister labelling Muslim women as looking like 'letter boxes', we can hardly be surprised that racism is legitimised and abuse increases. Islamophobic incidents rose by 375 per cent in the week after the Prime Minister wrote his newspaper article in 2018 using that phrase, according to monitoring group Tell Mama, who reported that his words were repeated by racists abusing Muslims on the street and online. And, of course, that spills over into football and on to social media. Everyone has a platform now, like an unfiltered stream of consciousness showing what is really going on in their minds. And racial abuse on the pitch and from the stands is a constant stain on the game.

So we say we want to rid the game of racism. We all sign up to the campaigns, tweet the hashtag. But how much do we really care? The fans we spoke to definitely care: 71 per cent were concerned about the amount of racism directed at players. We presented fans with a range of issues and this one scored top.

I spent some time speaking to Lyle Taylor. His perspective and experiences ought to be a wake-up call to those who think racism isn't a significant issue in the game. Lyle has played at Millwall, Bournemouth, Falkirk, Wimbledon, Sheffield United and Nottingham Forest among others in his career. He's played at every level from Conference North to the Championship, including Scottish League One. I was put in touch by Troy Townsend, the veteran campaigner at Kick It Out, what used to be the go-to anti-racism body in football, and we spoke on Zoom.

'When I was in Scotland, I was playing for Falkirk and we were playing a local derby against Dunfermline,' said Taylor. 'I'd scored in front of the away fans, I'd run away and was celebrating and I've been called a c*** by some woman. A load of people were saying: "Ah, we're sorry." At that time, I was twenty-three and it just went over my head. I didn't really think much of it. I'd scored. I'd had a good game. It didn't really bother me so much. It was almost like, don't highlight it. Just leave it, kind of thing. Get on with it. Because, I mean, I've always had so much abuse from fans, away fans in particular, that it just kind of becomes water off a duck's back.

'The next time I was at Wimbledon, we played against York and there was an altercation between me and the goalkeeper at a corner. I'm marking him and I was trying to grab his shirt behind my back while I'm on him from a corner and he punched me. I said: "What the fuck you punching me for?" He went: "Well, you grabbed my balls." I went: "Someone had to, 'cause your missus don't, does she?" Just as a joke. You try and laugh it off, whatever, as we do on the football pitch. And then I'm jogging out of the box and he's run after me and he's lost it: "Well yeah, but at least she don't like *your* kind!" It was like, hang on, what? She doesn't like *my kind*? What is *my kind*? So I reported it to the ref and we ended up at Wembley a year later in front of a committee.'

In August 2016 Scott Flinders was found guilty of racial abuse by the FA commission. Fined £1,250 and ordered to pay £250 towards the costs of the hearing, he also had to attend a one-to-one FA education course and was suspended for five matches. The independent regulatory commission was unanimous in the view that Taylor was a consistent and credible witness and that his version of events was confirmed by the video evidence.

'So that was that,' says Taylor. 'But it took a year for that process to actually come to a head from start to finish. I've had to reread my witness statement because it's been so long and so much happens in a year that I can't even remember the incident, to be honest. He got his punishment, served his punishment and I'd like to think he's never done it again. But ultimately if you're big enough to say those things, you have to be big enough to own the consequences and accept them for what they are.

'Then I went to Charlton and I've scored twice in a game. I was having a good game, playing up to the crowd, as I do, and whatever, a little bit of showboating, a little bit of taking the piss. So, we're winning 3–1, when me and the full back suddenly have a little run-in because he's tried to smash me. He's missed me and I've turned round to him and called him a fucking idiot and said: "Go on, try it again. I'll nutmeg you." After the game, someone comes in to me and says: "The referee needs to speak to you." I went, "Well, why?" They said: "You've been accused of calling him an Irish cunt." I went: "You what?" Bear in mind, a week or two before I'd done a piece in the paper and it was about racism in football and the rise in abuse. I've gone: "Yeah, good one. You're having a laugh. There's no way this has happened." Because I wouldn't be stupid enough, even if I wanted to say something like that, to actually say it. Especially with what I've already been through. So, I went in to the referee. The referee said: "Yeah, it's been reported." I protested: "Well, I've not said it. Flat out. I've not said it. There's no way on this planet I've said it." The referee replied: "Okay, well it has to be put in our report and we have to go through the right channels." "Alright, cool. Do what you've gotta do, but I haven't said it." A few days later I got a shout saying that it had been dropped because the player had decided there was no way he could go ahead with something and try and ruin someone else's career. So that pissed me off because it was almost: "Well, you said it but I'll let you get away with this one."'

It would be nice to think these were rare occurrences, few and far between. But we know that's not the case. There have been many high-profile incidents in recent years. Taylor was also at Charlton when one of the more infamous contemporary cases took place, Leeds' Kiko Casilla racially abusing Charlton's Jonathan Leko in 2019. Though he denied it, the independent regulatory commission said there was no doubt over the words used. It's judgement read: 'The FA rules were satisfied to the requisite standard – and in reality, to a degree well above the requisite standard – a) that Kiko Casilla had indeed uttered the words "you fucking n*****", and b) that Jonathan Leko and [teammate] Macauley Bonne had not misheard those words, but had heard them correctly.'

Taylor takes up the story from his perspective. 'Leko came off the pitch and he was fuming, and I was like: "What's wrong?" because we just beat Leeds. And the whole conversation was relayed and Macauley came up to me and he said: "Yeah, this is what was said." I couldn't believe it, what I was hearing.'

Casilla was fined £60,000 and banned for eight matches. On his first game back, Leeds manager Marcelo Bielsa made Casilla team captain, claiming he was doing so on behalf of his teammates, who wanted it as a show of support. Like Liverpool with their T-shirts backing Luis Suarez, when he was accused of racially abusing Patrice Evra – for which he was eventually banned for eight games – everyone's good to fight racism until it's their own player accused of racism. Don't get me wrong. There is a balance to be struck here. Every report of racism should be taken seriously and yet every player deserves a defence and support to provide that. But some clubs seem to circle the wagons around a player accused of racism, even when they've been found guilty.

Troy Townsend, a former teacher and father to England international Andros, has been campaigning on this issue working for Kick It Out since 2011. In my view, his voice is one of the most important in the game. Yet he is often side-lined or silenced. He was part of our panel that sat down with Crystal Palace chairman Steve Parish and former FA chairman David Bernstein. Let's start with what's good, according to Troy.

'I think the Premier League have looked after themselves very well in this space,' he said. 'You don't predominantly go to stadiums and hear a lot of abuse. If you do, it's dealt with. Player-on-player abuse, I don't think exists any more [in the Premier League]. They've dealt with it.' That said, we were speaking before the racial abuse of Ivan Toney's and Rico Henry's families at Goodison Park at the end of the 2021–22 season. 'The Premier League has also dealt with the social media platforms very well. The clubs look after the players and their social platforms a lot better. So Manchester United, Liverpool, Manchester City, they don't wait for Twitter, they don't wait for Instagram; they've got their own filtering system now that can produce information and data that enables us to understand where these people are coming from.

'Predominantly, the abuse [on social media] is not from these shores, but that doesn't lessen the impact of the abuse that the players are receiving. It just means we monitor it better and we hand the information over to the appropriate organisations to be able to deal with it. What I don't like is that there's no joined-up approach among everyone. From maybe the bottom rung of the Premier League right through to the Football League to the non-league to grassroots, it's almost like we don't care and that abuse can continue to exist. So this weekend I supported five players who have been victimised on football pitches by fans, by opposition players, on social media. You wouldn't be aware of those cases.

'I've had more reports in the professional academy environment of racism this season than ever before. Than ever before. A lad came up to me last night and said he was suffering. Thirteen years of age. He said: "I've been abused, I've not told anyone. I don't know what to do." It's a common theme. There is a nine-year-old lad who has been sacked . . . I'm saying sacked, though he's not part of a professional [contract] deal, but at nine years of age [he's been released] for comments to a Black team-mate. The club offered education but they felt they had no choice because of the stance of the parents of the child who was abused. Nine years of age. We've got more incidents going on and they're growing, and, again, I'm asking: "What is the game doing to eliminate it? What is the game doing to hold young people, parents, to account?" It's not.'

Anita Asante played seventy-one times for England and when we spoke in May 2022 she had just retired at the end of her long and illustrious career with Aston Villa and Chelsea, which had also included spells in the USA and Sweden. She was an England teammate of Eni Aluko, many of whose family are from Nigeria. Back in 2016, when Aluko told her team manager Mark Sampson that some of her family were coming over from Nigeria to watch a game, Sampson joked: 'Nigeria? Make sure they don't bring Ebola with them.' He also made discriminatory remarks to Drew

Spence. An independent inquiry conducted by barrister Katharine Newton ruled they were 'ill-judged attempts at humour, which, as a matter of law, were discriminatory on the grounds of race', but added 'it was fundamentally important to emphasise that I have not concluded that Mark Sampson is a racist'.

Aluko was left isolated by many teammates when, at the height of the affair, in September 2017, Nikita Parris led the team in a display of solidarity with the manager, gathering around Sampson to celebrate a goal she had scored. But Asante supported Aluko's stance, which was eventually vindicated by the FA inquiry, and Parris publicly apologised to Aluko in 2020 for the celebration. 'There was an isolation,' said Asante of Aluko's treatment. 'People were not understanding about what was said or how it was said, that it would affect her or her family. To witness someone go through that . . . the whole kind of attitude was like, "Well, so what if someone said that to you? It shouldn't matter. It shouldn't hurt you." But, at the same time, we talk about being kind. Be kind matters; mental health matters. Only, in these instances, all of a sudden it doesn't matter, it's just words. Where does that come from? Where you can be dismissive of this area, whether it be homophobia, racism, whatever? Language matters all the time.'

Asante also felt let down by Sampson when she was dropped for the 2015 World Cup. What bothered her as much as the decision itself was that she felt she had been treated differently, when Sampson pulled her aside to tell her of his decision. 'There was a process where everyone gets to find out whether they're in the squad or not on a particular date,' said Asante. 'And the manager just happened to pull me aside at a particular camp, one to one, and tell me that I wasn't going to the 2015 World Cup. I spoke to teammates and asked: "Has anyone else had a meeting with the coach?" Because we had been told that on a certain date we were all going to get called or get the letter or whatever? And they were all, like: "No, I don't know what you're talking about." But that happened to me, that was my personal experience, and I couldn't say it was racism, but what I could say is that I was treated differently and I know I was treated differently.'

We hear about the high-profile incidents, like Bukayo, Marcus and Jadon. We even might see a degree of justice served in the courts. But every week, there is abuse that goes under the radar, away from the global gaze.

Kick It Out has always been the main body in football for fighting racism. But a plea from that organisation in 2019 had unintended consequences. 'Each organisation was being told by our former chair Lord Herman Ouseley that they needed to do more on racism,' said Townsend. 'What that turned into was everyone doing their own thing. So in 2019 the Premier League launched "No Room for Racism." The EFL then announced their own campaign: "Not Today Or Any Day," which has since been changed to "Together Against Discrimination."'

Kick It Out were still working, with funding from the Premier League, as were Show Racism the Red Card. So now there were four organisations or campaigns, as if to demonstrate that we were four times as determined to eradicate racism as we were before.

'There's your split straight away,' said Townsend. 'Kick It Out is the organisation that will have been in this space for thirty years next year [2023], but they announced No Room for Racism and they announced it just for twenty clubs. The EFL come out and say, well, we're going to do "Not Today Or Any Day" and we're going to announce it for our seventy-two clubs. So the organisations that have worked in this space then get pushed back down the tree almost because, obviously, the biggest stakeholder is always the Premier League, which has now said it's going to do its own thing. It's a power trip. It's a way of controlling the conversation, so you can say: "Well, look what we've done behind No

Room for Racism." It is all about power and ownership. Why is there not one common goal?'

Soon we were to get another slogan. After the murder of unarmed Black man George Floyd in the USA during the lockdown spring of 2020, there was civil unrest in the USA, protests here in the UK, including the tearing down of the statue of slave trader Edward Colston in Bristol, and an overwhelming sense that this issue should be confronted decisively. In June of that year, English footballers started to take the knee before games when the Premier League restarted after the Covid shutdown.

That gesture started when Colin Kaepernick, an NFL player, began taking the knee in September 2016 during the playing of the USA national anthem prior to games. In discussion with Nate Boyer, a former US special forces soldier, who felt that simply remaining seated during the anthem as a response to racism would have been seen as disrespectful, the pair came up with taking the knee as a prayerful, peaceful protest. Nevertheless, Kaepernick antagonised the powers that be in the NFL. He has been a free agent since March 2017 and filed a lawsuit against the NFL, alleging they were colluding to keep him out of work. The NFL settled in March 2019 for less than $10m, according to the *New York Times*.

It was a wake-up call for many institutions to do more than pay lip service to the issue of racism. The players were taking action themselves. The slogan adopted for the campaign was the most common and probably most powerful one in circulation: Black Lives Matter. However, some people had an issue with this, because it was also the name of the political organisation leading many of the protests in the USA and it had a counterpart in the UK of the same title.

Taylor was one of those concerned and declined to take the knee which some associated with BLM. While most people saw an anti-racist symbol, his take was the US Black Lives Matter group, separate to that in the UK, wanted to defund the police, was committed to disrupting the nuclear family and one of its founders had expressed sympathy with Marxism. 'The more I found out from their own website, the more I thought, hang on, this doesn't look right,' said Taylor. 'And then, over the last two years, as it seems to have panned out, people have given BLM as a company millions of dollars.' In 2020, the US branch of the BLM organisation raised $90m. Taylor didn't want to be associated with that.

As such, Black Lives Matter became controversial as a slogan. So, by the start of the 2020–21 season, we had a proliferation of campaigns and slogans that ultimately confused the message.

Within the game, there was also division about the best way forward. Taylor says his own manager at Nottingham Forest, Chris Hughton, one of the few Black managers and a trailblazer, shut him down when he talked about why he wasn't taking the knee.

'I spoke on it in the local news and then I was asked to go on LBC by Nick Ferrari one morning,' said Taylor. 'That same day the manager pulled me into the football club, into his office, and he said to me: "You're banned from doing media work." I said: "Well, why?" He said: "Well, you've gone on and spoken about Black Lives Matter." I said, "Yeah, I have. Gaffer, do you know what their mission statement is?" He went: "No, and I don't need to know what their mission statement is because the statement Black Lives Matter says it all." "Well, no, it doesn't, gaffer. That's where you're wrong. Anyone can make a statement. It's what's behind that statement that you need to look into." And he went, "No." He said, "You and your beliefs do not align with mine, so you cannot speak in the media."'

Chris Hughton, who has been at the heart of football's fight against racism, has a slightly different take. His reason for asking

Taylor to stop talking to the media was because it was confusing the club's message. 'The ruling at the club was that if players are doing media, we need to be aware. He was doing it without our knowledge. All of a sudden, I'm seeing all these quotes, which the club didn't know about. If he'd gone about it in a different way, we might have been more sympathetic. But, as a club we had decided to have a united front to take the knee and support the campaign, as we felt it was important. We felt it confused that message.' Hughton and the club had no problem with Taylor not taking the knee before games. It wasn't compulsory and was left to the individual. It's just the club wanted their stance in the media to be clear and not confused.

Lyle's view isn't shared by many people in football, and I've always associated taking the knee with being anti-racist. I think most people in the UK understand it as such. But I don't believe Lyle should have been stopped from talking about his own view. This issue, though, isn't really about how we protest or what slogan we're using. For me, it's about why isn't more happening? Why is there so little progress in the area?

Almost everyone I speak to agrees that the proliferation of different campaigns has been negative. Asante said: 'I always think collective action is far more influential than every entity working in silos because they have their own campaigns and their own objectives, maybe self-interests as well. Some entities are underfunded, so they can only do the bare minimum; the campaigning is great, the symbolic gestures are great, but in terms of real action they don't necessarily have the resources. But if you pull all those resources and expertise together, I think it has more power in it.'

Taylor is of the same mindset. 'I remember speaking to Troy when the Premier League's own campaign, whatever it's called [No Room for Racism], popped up. I said to Troy: "Why haven't they just joined forces and ploughed the funding into Kick It Out, which has a long-standing history in the game?" These things pop up so that the governing bodies are seen to be doing something. Whether they're actually doing something or not, they can turn round and say: "Well, we've got a shiny new squad of people who are combing through 4K footage sent in from Sky to see what that bloke said over there when he was doing this, that or the other monkey chants or whatever it might have been."

'Why are you just setting up another thing to plough money into? It seems to me like it's jobs for the boys [and that] if they were really genuinely interested in tackling racism, they would simply create one campaign group for the football played in this country: everything played under the English FA. They would have one campaign group, whether that involved Kick It Out or Show Racism the Red Card or Not Today Or Any Day or whatever. It's about doing what is right for the footballers playing in this country. You are a footballer. You are under our jurisdiction and we will make sure that you feel safe, supported and if anything happens or goes wrong, you will have us to fall back on and we will be there to support you. But we don't. We've got four different groups of people and everyone's going at it saying: "We're against racism." Well, okay, big whoop. But what are you *actually* doing? "Oh, well, we're doing more than that group over there . . ." Maybe, but what are *they* doing?'

A key issue, then, is representation in positions of power. But that doesn't always resonate with the public. Only 45 per cent of fans we surveyed expressed concern about the lack of racial diversity among Premier League leaders.

Professor Stefan Szymanski's report for the Black Footballers' Partnership in 2022 found that 43 per cent of the players in the Premier League are Black and 34 per cent of players in the EFL. But 4.4 per cent of managers are Black and 1.6 per cent of executives and owners. The first black man ever to be appointed to the FA board was Jobi McAnuff in May 2022. Paul Elliott is an observer to the board, a role that began in 2018, and Heather Rabbatts was the first Black person appointed to the FA board in 2011, sitting on it until 2017. In men's football, though, there is a huge proportion of Black men playing the game, but only now has the FA sought to appoint a Black man to their board. And there is a tiny percentage of Black people involved in making decisions about the game.

What football tolerates is wholly unacceptable. We've more campaigns than ever before but no joined-up approach. I believe that's the big problem faced by football. The Premier League want to deal with all the issues in the game. So do the FA, the EFL, the PFA. Yet we can't join it up and that's where you get to a regulator again. Why have we not just got one body?

When I got together with Troy, Steve Parish and David Bernstein in April 2022, this was an issue we tried to tackle. Steve raised the matter of the lack of representation among fans, even in a multi-ethnic neighbourhood like south London. 'How do we get a greater representation of diversity in the crowds? That worries me. Even in *our* club you look around and it just isn't representative of the local community, and I think that would be a start.'

Troy's answer was chilling. 'Steve, people don't see football grounds as safe. They don't see it as a safe space. Affordability has always been a massive problem, but again, until we break that mould of what crowds look like, what people experience . . . there's a lot of vile language out there as well. Not just relating to racism or discrimination, but a lot of vile language. If you take your child to a match and they repeatedly hear swearing and so forth – do you really want them to be exposed to that? Such language very quickly starts to become learned behaviour.'

Troy's point should make us all sit up. Why would you take your kids somewhere where there is even a possibility they might hear racist language? And in dealing with that, the punishment doesn't yet fit the crime. In 2012 we had the situation where Nicklas Bendtner was fined £80,000 by UEFA for displaying the name of a bookmaker that wasn't an authorised UEFA partner during a match, while Porto were fined £16,700 for their fans' racist abuse. Hungary have their stadium shut by UEFA because of racist and discriminatory language. Yet they can let in more than 30,000 children to that game – supposedly behind closed doors - and some of them boo England taking the knee. Now we have the three-step protocol if racist abuse is heard at a game: first the referee stops the game and a stadium announcement is made demanding the abuse stops; if it continues, the game is suspended for five to ten minutes; if it still continues, the game is abandoned. That still feels like you get two goes at racism before punishment kicks in.

The FA protocols set out six- to twelve-game bans for players if they racially abuse a colleague. Education is normally part of any punishment. But I have two issues with this. First, the consequences seem low to me. You get a small fine and a few games' ban. And in Lyle's case, he waited twelve months for the case to be heard. At the end of all that there was a fine and a six-game ban. It's not enough.

Second, all the education seems to be reactive, not proactive. So a club like Manchester United can sign Edinson Cavani, an investment worth several million pounds, and yet no one will sit down with him and explain what might be culturally unacceptable in this country, such as using the term 'negrito', to a friend on Instagram. The term is commonly used in South America, sometimes affectionately and Cavani said there was no racist intent. But it's not acceptable here.

'That's the club's fault,' says Townsend. 'That's the FA's fault. It's the PFA's fault. You have a player enter this country, I don't care at what stage he enters it, or whether it's the last day of a transfer window, that player should not play until he has that sort of education. Because it takes one moment, a Cavani incident, where he's respectfully responded to a fan and his story blows up.' I agree. No player should enter English football unaware of what will be expected of them. And that goes for owners and season-ticket holders, as well as junior coaches, executives, the FA chairman.

At present, the Professional Footballers' Association provides education to first-team squads, while Kick It Out does the same for academy players and club staff, as well as delivering education for fans referred to them. The FA deliver their own education courses for any player that has been found guilty of racism. Much of this, though not all, is reactive, in that it is obligatory if you commit an offence.

My view is that education should be proactive and ongoing for anyone who wants to be a stakeholder or participate in English football as an administrator, owner, player, season-ticket holder, coach or whatever. If you're an A or B licensed coach with the FA, you do the child protection course to prove that you're safe to be with children. Why wouldn't there be something similar relating to issues on inequality when you're introduced into English football? So, there's education at the beginning as you come into football, not just when things have gone wrong. Everybody has to do the course regularly.

Proactive education is better than reactive. For the likes of Cavani, who is coming from a different county and culture where certain expressions concerning people's colour aren't always perceived to be as offensive as they are here, it's a systemic failure not to have communicated that.

Is twelve games right as a suspension? We debated whether a six-month ban from playing would be better, with no wages. 'If you say someone should get a six-month ban, brilliant,' said Taylor. 'But by the same token, is a six-month ban too harsh for somebody who may have said something in jest that's been taken wrongly or is it too harsh for someone who in the heat of a moment said something they later regret? Zero tolerance has to be where we begin. That has to be the starting point. Maybe a three-month ban? But the punishment has to fit the crime. If somebody has said something racist and it can be proven, they've only themselves to blame and perhaps banning them for six months will be sufficient to teach them a lesson. But then would that fall under gross misconduct and the club could just sack them anyway, meaning their career goes down the pan?'

Taylor said: 'I have never seen anybody say something serious [racist] in their own dressing room. But if someone has said one thing then they do need to be punished. I think six months is too long. If we said two or three months, I think that would be fairer. I one hundred per cent agree with reintroduction for offenders because I believe if you do something wrong but are genuinely sorry and have suffered the consequence, there's no way you should be outlawed.'

Asante said: 'I don't think people are wholly good or wholly bad. Everyone to some degree has flaws, certain prejudices, certain things that have influenced their belief system, and so, for me, I think there could be stronger penalties for players. And that there could be bans that last more than a few months; a year to two years or something like that. But as we know as athletes, and having played the sport, when you're removed from the game even for a few months, it's painful. I do believe there is room for having mandatory education and reintroduction where those guilty of racism or using racist language also get to learn or be educated and have another opportunity to be involved in the game again. It's like any crime in society: when someone goes to prison, do we believe that just punishing them, sending them away and saying they can never be a part of something again, is the answer? I don't believe that life really works that way.'

Taylor also raises a point about bans that, for some less committed professionals, maybe aren't always the punishment we think they are. Although players are fined for racism, many will continue to receive full pay. 'I think hitting a footballer where it hurts is definitely in the pocket,' said Taylor. 'If you tell them: "Right, that's it, you're banned for six games . . ." some will go: "I'll sit my arse out. It don't bother me. I sit at home. I still get paid. I'll go and play golf." That's the way we are as people. Half of us will actually be happy that we've been left at home because you get a bit of time away from football and the stadium with your family for a little while. That's not really a punishment. Let's say they were out of the game for three months and you said: "Okay, you're going be fined two months' wages" . . . I don't think anyone could say: "Well, no, that's not fair." It's not fair that you racially abused someone. It may be the first time you've ever said it. It may be the tenth. Who knows? But you racially abused someone, so there are consequences.'

The issue of not paying someone would need industry-wide agreement. I don't see why you should be paid if you've allowed your own ignorance, stupidity or prejudice to put yourself in a position whereby you're banned and your team is suffering.

You may think owners won't go for that. What if their star player is caught racially abusing someone? The danger would be they will quit if they're not paid, get picked up by someone else for free. And there will always be a club that will take them on, almost no matter what. But if the terms of the standard punishment were imposed by a regulator, approved in law and backed up by the Professional Footballers' Association, there would no recourse to claiming a breach of contract.

Most owners, I believe, would be supportive. 'If that was the punishment, I would go along with it,' said Parish. 'Sacking the player [is difficult] . . . the player would go and play somewhere else for free and you're massively penalised. But I do think, you know, the club have got to accept that they're partly responsible for that as well if it happens, because if you've got somebody in your midst of that ilk you're not telling me you don't slightly know. So yes, the club losing the player's services, because it hasn't been capable of bringing the right people in and educating them correctly, I would go along with that. There's no punishment that's big enough for me.'

What should happen to fans? Chelsea banned a fan for life for racially abusing Raheem Sterling in September 2018. Tough, then, on fans, but not so tough on their captain when he was found guilty by the FA of saying something similar. That's often the way. We're tough until it costs us. Bans for life sound good. But the players I spoke to supported reintegration after education.

'For me it would be similar to the player's punishment,' said Taylor. 'A player misses three months of football. That means home games, away games. I think a fan should miss six months of football and should have mandatory education as a first offence. You can't get into games for this period of time. If they do it again, they get a lifetime ban from all stadia across the country.' Maybe six months doesn't sound enough. But there needs to be consistency across the board. For fans, the game is not their livelihood, it's entertainment, so taking it away doesn't take away their ability to earn. (Though they may find the publicity surrounding an offence does that if they end up losing their job.) That's why fans can legitimately be punished longer than players. A three-month ban for a player takes away a huge part of their life. For a fan, it takes away one or two entertainment events a week. But, that said, we can't just ban fans for life, throw away the key because it sounds good, and then let players back in after six games. There's a fundamental inconsistency there based on who is more valuable to the football industry.

Fans seem to be onside with three- to six-month bans: 93 per cent supported it for fans; 91 per cent agreed that players should recieve three to six month bans with a loss of wages; 88 per cent supported mandatory education on a return to the game. But while 68 per cent agreed that players and fans should be rehabilitated, 19 per cent disagreed. And 85 per cent of fans think that the consequences for fans and players found guilty of racism should be more severe.

Even with all its shiny campaigns, football is still too passive on this issue, and even today there are some who argue it shouldn't even be in the public space. As Townsend says: 'A lot of people will say, "This is not football's problem, it's a societal issue." We all walk the streets and we're all part of society, but when someone brings that into our game you cannot say to football: "Well, you don't have to deal with it. It's society's problem." I'm worried about what is going on in our game because that's where I work. Let's put this clearly now: society is influencing the game. In all other areas we talk about how football can work and influence and help society become better. But when we discuss this issue, football can't influence, it's just a sport.'

Maybe we're never going to fix the problem of racism. Maybe there will always be idiots among us. But we can surely agree that where we are at the moment isn't where we want to be? And that the game should forget its ego for a moment and join together to have one united campaign, one set of mandatory punishments that actually communicates the fact that consequences will fit the crime, and that they apply to players, fans, executives and owners. And that football could lead the way in developing education at every point in the game, so you don't just get educated when you're perceived to have done something wrong. Everyone is educated as a matter of course. Who in this world doesn't need to know more, to challenge themselves further on this issue?

Perhaps football won't change the world in an instant, but it is a massive constituent part of British society. If we do things better in football, it can have an impact on the whole country. For the millions of football fans in the UK, football is a huge part of their lives. Instead of a divided society influencing football, let's take football and use it to unite and become one team.

10

THE FORLORN FOURTEEN

'I feel sometimes that as far as the Premier League executives are concerned there are six clubs and fourteen
others, and the six don't much care who the fourteen
others are really.'
Steve Parish, Crystal Palace chairman

The 2021–22 season is drawing to an end. Manchester City are on
course to retain the Premier League, Liverpool are heading to a
Champions League final, which they will lose. Norwich are down
and Watford and Burnley will soon join them. And Crystal Palace?

Well, Crystal Palace are safe and relaxed. They might even be
dreaming that next season they could make a Europa Conference
League place or go better than reaching an FA Cup semi-final, as
they did this year, and compete for a domestic trophy. Crystal
Palace, who have been in administration twice in the last twenty-
five years, and so on the brink of extinction, are going along quite
nicely. There is no fear of relegation. They're almost an established part of the exalted Premier League, having been there for
nine years.

Except it never quite feels like that for Steve Parish. 'My team
are in the Premier League but I don't really think of myself as a
Premier League club,' says Parish. 'I think of ourselves as a middle-
class club, part of forty-three other clubs outside of the top six,
and a club that have been in the Premier League since it started.

So, I think of myself both as an insider and as an outsider. Because outside of the top six, there's Everton, West Ham and Southampton who have been in the League as long as we have. And middle-class clubs typically stay in the Premier League for six and half years.'

We're sat in his Soho office from where he runs the club on a sunny spring day in April 2022. It was Parish and a group of like-minded wealthy friends who rescued this club from their most recent financial calamity in 2010. 'I've supported this club since I was four,' he says. 'To be honest I only thought I'd [own the club] for a few months.' At Palace, they bear the scars of financial melt-downs. The season before Parish took over, the players drove down to Plymouth for a game because the team bus didn't turn up as the coach company hadn't been paid.

Twelve years on and administered thoroughly well, it is clear Steve loves running his boyhood club. He is successful and rich, but let's be clear: he's not Sheikh Mansour. He's not even John W. Henry. He's a successful British businessman who is running a club he supported all his life. This is a different class of Premier League owner: the aspiring middle classes. Tony Bloom at Brighton and Matthew Bentham at Brentford are similar: local boys, done good, who want to put something back into clubs they support and communities in which they grew up.

If there is a Big Six in the Premier League, then that means there is also a rump of fourteen. And Palace are one of the best-performing clubs among that fourteen. A smart appointment of a thoughtful manager in Patrick Vieira, building on the solidity put in place by Roy Hodgson, has brought them to this place, where next season they will be playing their tenth successive year in the Premier League.

But the strains and stresses of those owners are a little different to those of Khaldoon Al Mubarak at Manchester City or Richard Arnold at Manchester United. A story Steve relates tells you quite starkly exactly what life is like for the fourteen. He's recalling

2013–14, when Palace had just been promoted to the Premier League. It was November, winter approaching. They had played ten and lost nine. Relegation looked a certainty. Certainly I thought so. These were my early days as a pundit, but even with my mantra of not going too early on big judgements, I think we all agreed they were doomed. Steve would watch his team lose and then come back to his office in Soho. On his computer there was a number in red, which kept going up. It was the amount he needed to set aside to make sure the club didn't go bust when they went down, which seemed inevitable.

'I've got a two-screen computer over there and when I started here and it was me and my mates, I brought in people. It was a building phase. I would have a season in the Premier League with the financial numbers on it on one computer. And then a season in the Championship, if we got relegated, on the other screen. And in the bottom right-hand corner would be the cash number that I needed to fund the season in the Championship. When I started, I was constantly looking at that number, which I felt was the least we'd need to survive if we went down.'

Palace had four points from the first eleven games, which was worse than Frank de Boer's start in 2017. They really were awful. 'We were crazy odds-on to get relegated,' said Parish. 'But I got to January and I actually thought: "It's taken us ten years to get back to this, so I'm going to slightly ignore that number in the bottom right-hand corner that we need for next season because I had seen enough to believe we would stay up." Back then, you could actually buy relatively inexpensively. I bought Jason Puncheon for £400,000 – I mean, imagine that in a Premier League club now! I bought Scott Dann for £2.5m; Joe Ledley for £400,000.'

With Tony Pulis in charge, Palace finished eleventh. The gamble paid off. But – there is a big but – that figure in the bottom right-hand corner of Steve's computer is growing bigger every year. 'Just to give you the numbers – we worked them out again yesterday for this meeting – if we were to be relegated we've got to find £120m (assuming we're don't manage to sell a player), to play the first season back in the Championship. That's a factual number. We would need £80–120m of cash.

When Steve says that number, I immediately say 'that's not right and why we must change.' I then go on to tell Steve that as a football fan, and a broadcaster, that I don't want to commentate on his team knowing he has that cliff edge facing him every week. Yes, there will obviously be financial loss dropping to the Championship from the Premier League, but this number is far too great.

Steve goes on, 'Obviously what we're relying on is that we can bridge the gap from player sales, shareholder support and maybe new borrowings. But your turnover essentially goes from £160m down to below £70m in year one. And that's the first year. Second year it gets even worse. And it depends where you are in your cycle because the problem typically is that you have a lot of deferred transfer fees for players you have signed. Some of that £120m cash is your deferred transfer fees. So, when people talk about clubs that have been promoted to the Premier League and they make a profit in the first year, yes, they might make a paper profit, but if they get relegated they'll have players [still to pay for] and they'll have all the deferred transfer fees, so they must have parachute money if they won't be able to compete in the Premier League.

'The problem is that the financial growth of the Premier League has got so huge that the difference between what you get in the Championship, even with the parachute payment, the actual number you need if you go down is so big that it's scary for people to properly compete now. The way we've managed it at Crystal Palace is I have taken in different partners and shareholders so that it's not stressful for any one of us if we get relegated.' In 2015, Josh Harris and David Blitzer, Americans who own the Philadelphia 76ers, came in and bought 18 per cent of the club each, with Parish also retaining 18 per cent. In August 2021, another American, John Textor, who owns Botafogo in Brazil, bought 40 per cent.

It is one of the conundrums in English football that the success of the Premier League has made the Championship a basket case. In 2018–19 Championship clubs collectively made £785 million. Yet the amount they spent on wages was £837 million! For every £1 they earn, they spend £1.07 on wages. It's full of clubs desperately gambling to make it to the promised land. If they make it, all well and good, like Aston Villa in 2019. If they fail, like Derby in that play-off final against Villa, then their very existence is at stake.

And then there is Steve's issue. Even if you do make it, you spend the whole time terrified of falling off a financial cliff if you go down. Over time, the Premier League has developed a formula to help with this: parachute payments, designed to soften the hard landing of the relegation. Essentially, you get around £40m extra in your first year from the Premier League pot to ease the pain, which is why Steve's figure is only £120m cash to make up the shortfall, rather than £160m! If you've been a yo-yo club and gone straight back down after coming up, you only get them for two years. But in the best-case scenario you get three years' worth of money on a sliding scale of percentages, which amounts to around £32m in year two and around £15m in year three. Then you're on your own again. Sounds good. Except that the drop-off is still huge. And the extra money relegated teams receive is now so large that it completely distorts the Championship, making non-parachute-payment clubs even more likely to gamble to play catch-up.

Fulham and Bournemouth going up in 2021–22 is the perfect example. Their wage bills will have been huge compared to rivals Nottingham Forest and Luton Town, because they were beneficiaries of parachute payments. We're getting to the stage that yo-yo clubs are a fixture in the Premier League: Watford, Norwich, Fulham, Bournemouth could all be members of that group; West

Brom were. It's almost engrained in the constitution. It's one of the many problems of financial distribution through the leagues that has so skewed English football and has led to this broken model.

I wanted to understand all aspects of the game better and listen to the perspective of people in important roles as to what has gone wrong and how to put it right. So in April 2022, we gathered at Steve's office with David Bernstein, the former Manchester City and FA chairman, who led the group I was involved in that called for an independent regulator of football even before the fan-led review recommended it, which led to the government legislating for it. Troy Townsend, from Kick It Out, who is the father of Everton and England's Andros, joined us for the first half of the meeting. A week later I spoke to Tracey Crouch, who oversaw the government's fan-led review, and I have added in some of her comments to give perspective.

GARY NEVILLE: Steve, is English football working at the moment? What's good about it and what would you change if you could?

STEVE PARISH: Evidently it could work better. There's no doubt about that. But we need to be careful that we're not just looking through the lens of the period of Covid, which was extremely difficult, and make massive structural changes because of a one-off generational event. For example, pre-Covid the average finishing position of a relegated club was 8th in the first season, 13th in the second. So, parachute payments are far away from a guarantee of re-promotion, ask Sunderland, or Charlton, or Stoke. Broadly, the football family got football through that. But watching football from around the world, one of my partners [John Textor] bought a Brazilian club so I tuned in to watch a Brazilian First Division game: the quality of the football, the TV coverage that we have here, the refereeing, the overall package, everything is light years in front of most of the world. We've got this sensational, fantastic product. We're a nation that goes and supports sport, aren't we? That's why we got the Olympics because they saw just how much we go out and support, physically go and watch games. But clearly it could be better. I'm in the Premier League at the moment, my team are in the Premier League, but I don't really think of Palace as a Premier League club. The problem is that the financial growth of the Premier League has become so huge that the difference between what you get in the Championship, even with the parachute payment, and what you get in the Premier League, the actual number, is so big that it's scary for people to properly compete now. There's a chasm in the quantity of money that's been created between the Premier League and the rest of football. And I think there's also another chasm that isn't talked about, which is between the top and the bottom of the Premier League, this growing inequality of income between the top and the bottom is a bigger issue because it affects the competitiveness of the Premier League. I would like to see a game where any aspirational team can dream about getting into the Premier League and succeeding. That's the game I believe in. But some of the lenses that people are looking through in terms of how to get more money into the EFL, particularly the Championship, is basically: let's take it off the promoted clubs or reduce parachute payments while the clubs at the top get by unscathed. That can't be right.

GN: Steve, is your only chance of creating real change, then, to gamble on a regulator who would impose a more united game approach? Two things you've said stand out. First, that you're looking at that right-hand computer screen that says you lose £120m if you go down. As a football fan, I don't want you to look at your screen and think: 'I'm going to lose £120m if I go down as a Premier League club.' I want you to be able to look at your screen and think: 'If I go down this year, yeah, I'll have to cut my cost base. I'll have to reduce my players' contracts, but actually I don't have to go and sell my shares to another owner to be able to afford to stay in the Premier League.' We have to create a game where that doesn't need to happen. And the second thing is, if it *is* like that and the six are treated that way, surely we have to control them through the regulator, because they all went off into the night with the Super League? How are you going to bridge this chasm without a regulator? That's the question I'm asking. How are you going to change it?

SP: I think there's two points. Do we need somebody overseeing football somewhere? A regulator? And if we do, where do they come from and how are they constituted?

GN: So is the answer yes to the first question?

SP: I think that football has definitely fallen out on its governance. The FA, who should be the regulator of the game really . . .

GN: I think we agree with that.

SP: They should be the regulator of the game, but essentially they have had their pocket picked by the Premier League over the years. So, you know, we need to do referees, apparently, we need to organise referees . . . and the Premier League say: 'Don't worry, we'll do that for you.' And instead of the FA going: 'We'll do it and you can pay for it,' they went, 'Oh great.' And they just gave it all to the Premier League. I think that there's definitely been a loss of

216

control. I don't understand the constitution of the FA and why it's so difficult, but everybody goes in there full of enthusiasm that they can change it and they just get eaten alive. They come out of it absolutely having given up and they can't change it. So clearly that's an issue. But if they're going to represent themselves as a regulator then they need to change.

TROY TOWNSEND: Steve, the FA *could* change it if they really wanted to. The FA have their own council who have a certain amount of power and strength, by the way, and who have existed for far too long in the game. I don't want to tell you the age of some of those council members; those who get the perks of going to all the big games and who are allowed to have voting rights. In the past year they have diversified the council members and they now need to listen to those voices.

GN: But to try to get that change, the councils that you're talking about have to vote for that change.

TT: Exactly.

GN: That's the same with the Premier League. That's where we need someone to come in, like a policeman, to say, look, let's change. They're all stuck. Everyone's stuck, as I see it.

DAVID BERNSTEIN: We've said in our discussions that the regulator group, if there is one, won't necessarily be a permanent sort of thing. One of the things the regulator should be doing is ensuring the FA gets reform, becomes genuinely independent so that maybe power can be handed back to it and it can in the end become the regulator. Which is, as you say, as it should be, but it's not fit for purpose yet.

SP: The would perhaps work. Debbie Hewitt is excellent and I know has made more change in a short space of time than anyone has before. I've probably come to a point of deciding the FA might not be the right people. If you're organising any kind of club tournament, there's an in-built conflict for you in having an independence over anything else but that could be managed and the FA feels the right place for this to land in the end.

At times like this I do think back to 1992, when the FA handed the game to the Premier League, like an old father giving a seventeen-year-old the keys to his Ferrari, only to see the teenager speed off into the distance. The FA is a nineteenth-century organisation trying to adjust to the mid-twenty-first century. I'm sceptical that they could ever govern the game again. Tracey Crouch, who headed up the fan-led review that called for an independent regulator, studied this possibility in depth, so I wanted to bring her views in here.

GN: Tracey, how do you find the FA?

TC: I think their new chairman [Debbie Hewitt] is going to be brilliant. I think she's gonna be fantastic and that she'll bring some much-needed reform. It seems that everybody believes there is a need for reform in the structures and governance of the FA. I think the FA lacks self-awareness if they imagine they are capable of being the independent regulator. For one thing, they're not independent in their current format. [But] they genuinely think they can be the regulator. I assume they've been told this by the Premier League, which has a major power block on the FA board. They're just at odds with what the reform programme is. If they reformed enough, then at some point they could evolve into the regulator, but we're ten years away from that. The structures are not there. They're still run pretty much by the professional game and I think that until those governance structures are changed they couldn't be the regulator. They also don't have the skillset. We're not talking about passing pieces of paper around on governance, we're talking about really complex, nuanced financial regulation, and that's just not their ability. They don't have that in their capabilities.

GN: I'd agree that the FA and Premier League have had ample opportunity and time to be able to reform. The reason I've come to the conclusion I have is seeing football from all different angles. The only way it can change is through intervention. Once intervention occurs, and when the FA have modernised, they can eventually become the regulator when they've modernised.

TC: I was quite burnt, as previous Sports Ministers have been, by the promises that had been made by football authorities to reform in response to various crises that they'd had. I had been at the despatch box, at the House of Commons, as had my predecessors, and said: 'Football faces the last-chance saloon' in terms of reforming itself. Actually, you can go back and people like Richard Caborn [Sports Minister 2001–07] and Gerry Sutcliffe [2007–10] had said the same things ten years before me. So while I didn't have any preconception as to what the outcome would be, I was certainly of the view that we'd heard enough from the football authorities over the years about their intention to reform when nothing had happened.

DB: There's one word that encompasses what's so important: independence. The game is basically run by vested interests. The FA is not independent. Not really. It's overall influenced by the Premier League. The council, as you've said, is antiquated. I had huge trouble with the council when I was FA chairman. I did manage to inject some change. I got the first woman on to the board and some non-executive directors and so on. But to get real change was impossible and there's been plenty of opportunities going back to *The Burns Report* in 2005. Over the years there's been lots of moments when we think the time has come. But there are a lot of things coming together now and we're delighted that the government has endorsed Tracey Crouch's report. Hopefully, this is a chance for some valuable change while maintaining the strength that is the beauty of the Premier League.

TT: If we're talking about a regulator with twelve people on it, or whatever it may be, how do we stop undue influence from particular clubs? Do they have to almost own their allegiances, wherever they may come from, or eliminate those allegiances to whatever club they are part of so that actually we can see they are independent? That they're not influenced by anybody?

GN: They would have to be independent and have no direct employment or involvement with any football club, association, or organisation in this country. For the sceptics, who don't think regulator would be independent, you surely have to work on the theory that they're honest individuals. Among the group, even if one or two of them were influenced slightly, you'd have to influence the majority of them to get to a point where they carry a motion. The question I always ask to those who say they don't want a regulator is: how do we make the structural changes we need to create a fairer game, if we're not going to bring in a regulator? No one ever seems to be able to give me the answer.

SP: The Premier League, I think, have got a bit of time to try and respond to these challenges because I do believe there are risks in the independent regulator. We don't really know what it involves and of course, for me, an independent regulator needs to understand they have to take on the wider game, including UEFA, because they're the biggest single problem, and threat, to the domestic football. At least some of the six clubs that we've got in the Premier League have been working with the ECA and UEFA and the other big [European] clubs to try to ensure their pre-eminence and dominance continues for ever. The fourteen clubs in the Premier League, in my experience, understand their obligations and do want the right things for the whole game. They also understand where they came from. Trust me, West Ham can remember being relegated. They were promoted the year before us. Southampton were promoted the year before us. There's not a team in the bottom fourteen that doesn't consider the fact that they would like a softer landing if they ended up for three years in the Championship, and they would want that financial gap reduced, right. But that money can't just come from the bottom fourteen.

GN: You're not going to accept that, are you?

SP: Gary, a lot of the time it's just a few smaller clubs, firing people up, because other clubs are maybe new, or distracted by other issues. Maybe a looming relegation threat. We've also now have a situation where some clubs are sending lawyers to represent them at meetings, so there are legal barriers placed in the way of change. For example, we can't sign up to this because it might breach something we've agreed with UEFA. There's also the argument about competitiveness in Europe: 'Oh, if you take any money off us we won't be able to compete in Europe and that would damage the Premier League . . .'

GN: Why don't the fourteen of you come together and vote as one; you've got nothing to lose.

SP: I don't agree that we've got nothing to lose, in spite or everything compared to other companies the English game is in great health. At the end of the day, the regulator is a year or two away. We've got real present issues *now* that we should try and solve anyway. We should all just go, okay, we've got away with it.

I understand Steve's issues. There are real problems with UEFA Champions League money distribution, with unrestricted Saudi money coming in, and with the Big Six taking more and more of the overseas TV money. And that needs to be dealt with now. What I couldn't get my head around in all of our discussions and research for this book is why those fourteen clubs think the Premier League can sort this. You need fourteen votes to change rules in the Premier League on all the important issues. That's what frustrates the Big Six. And yet with Newcastle possibly becoming part of a Big Seven, you could see a complete impasse in the future, with the clubs involved in European competition totally at loggerheads with the rest and there being no way of getting anything done. I would have thought a regulator would be the best hope of sorting this. And it seems some of the Premier League clubs agree. In private at least.

TC: What's really interesting is that there were a lot of conversations being had behind the scenes that implied that they

[Premier League clubs] would welcome an independent regulator – or certainly the *threat* of an independent regulator – in order to bring some of the rogue clubs into line. And then, of course, when the independent regulator was being recommended, they were all sort of: 'Oh no, we don't want this at all.' So there was certainly people – not the Premier League executives, but other people at the Premier League – who were sitting there before the review was triggered by the European Super League, saying that Project Big Picture is definitely really damaging and this is why we need the review. And then when the Super League proposal actually triggered the review, the initial responses from people at the Premier League – as I say, *not* the senior team – were: 'Well, this might be helpful to us.'

SP: My aim inside the Premier League is to make sure the 'smaller' clubs are represented. I put together some of our ideas and I presented them to the Premier League and spent some money doing it. The larger clubs tend to have more time and resources. Man City use research to back up their views. For example, they had all this research telling them that the Super League was what every fan wanted! Because to a certain extent you can get research to say whatever you want it to say. So, what some inside the Premier League are pushing for is something even bigger than people have ever imagined. People go: 'Oh brilliant, you've been in the Premier League for nine years.' Honestly, it's meaningless to me. What do we have there? Some nice days out. We beat Arsenal every now and again? We beat Man United – it was great? There's no permanence and enduring improvements. We're still sitting in the stand from 1924. That [Steve points to a picture of the new Crystal Palace £20m academy] is the first thing that's given me any real sense of achievement. That's a lasting legacy for the next fifty years, not just for the football club but for the local community. We're lucky enough to be in a great catchment area; the club can exploit that. We're one of only ten clubs in the last forty-five years that haven't been out of the top two divisions, believe it or not, though that's mainly been in the Championship. Why is that? It's because we play all our kids as soon as we get in the Championship and we do well. And there's £1.6bn that flows down from the Premier League to the pyramid every year. I won't say *from us* because I'm not the Premier League. I'm just a football club that exists in the ecosystem. The Premier League pays £1.6bn down the pyramid. There's more money that goes down from the Premier League than in any other major league in Europe. Half of it is parachute payments, so I accept that, but it pays every players' pension. Every League One and every League Two club's players pension bill is, I believe, paid by the Premier League. The League One and League Two clubs do get a lot of money, but where does it go? It goes to owners. This is my problem. We give all this money to owners who just want to spend it on players and compete. We're not prescriptive about where any of the money goes and we should insist more of it is spent on infrastructure and to the lasting benefit of the club and supporters.

GN: We get a million pounds in total in League 2 at Salford. In League One it's £1.6m. It's a good amount of money, but it's not *huge*. Think about the fact that ultimately the Premier League's lowest club has £100m. A million quid is like . . .

SP: But my argument would be, if the Premier League gave £2m to most clubs in ten years' time what will they have to show for it? They'll likely still be in League One with the same ground, the same training ground, only probably a bit more run down.

GN: Why not increase to £2m but put controls on it. We're not asking for more money and then just to spend it on players. I'm pretty sure we would be happy to agree sustainability measures.

SP: I think I understand the reasons for discontent around the Premier League. If I'm a fan of a lower league club, and I'm not saying they've all got a rundown stadiums or training grounds, but my guess is most probably could be better, then that same fan looks at the Premier League and everything is improving for all those clubs. Understandably that League One or League Two fan would think: what does the Premier League do for me? They don't think about the money the owner received from the Premier League and spent on players. So, for me, we've got to be prescriptive about where any new money is spent. We've got to make sure it spent for the long-term benefit of the club, or at least some of it, and we've got to say, right, these are the things that you can spend the money on. This is not my idea, it's somebody else in the Premier League, so I don't want to steal this idea, but I think we should go huge on it. I think we should create a sizable infrastructure fund clubs can apply for and at the same time increase the amount of money we give to the League One and League Two clubs, so that they've got the money to pay it back and at the same time lend them money so that every single football pitch of a Football League club in the country can see an improvement to their pitch, their stand, their communal bar areas for not just matchdays but for the community to use. The same for the training grounds with 3G pitches that help young player development and community use as well as the first team. When the Government talks about levelling up, that's the kind of thing I imagine it to be and the Premier League can be at the heart of it.

DB: I agree with the principle that the money should be spent wisely and invested promptly, but the question I want to ask is: who should be controlling that? I don't think it's right that the Premier League are telling the rest of football how to spend it.

GN: During Covid days, Leagues One and Two voted for very low salary-capped wages in both these leagues and we got overruled by the PFA. So we voted for a £1.5m cap on wages in League Two and I think it was £2.5m in League One. That's for every club. So whether you're Sunderland or whether you're Accrington, whether you were Salford or whether you were Bristol Rovers, it was the same in your league. We then thought that would give us a good base to go on to the Premier League and say: if you give us double the funding for League One and Two, we're almost sustainable. If you then say to us, well, we'll give you double the funding, but say, for example, out of our eighteen players on the matchday sheet, five of those players have to be from your academy, because we want to be able to make sure you've grown your own players, we would have said: 'Yeah, maybe we'll go for that.' There's a deal to do here, right. But we were taken to court by the PFA and were overruled by the courts. The only way we can do that deal, though, is to get someone to police it and somebody to enforce change. That is where I see the regulator coming in.

In all of this discussion, I think the point needs making that I love the Premier League. First, I made all my money from it and probably have the likes of David Dein and Martin Edwards to thank for that 1992 revolution that blew the lid off TV deals and as a result saw players' wages spiral. I like disruption so I like what they did. I don't want to destroy what is good about the Premier

League. I just want it to take care of its family and not disappear off even further into the distance. Tracey Crouch and co. make a similar point.

TC: I'm at pains to say how much I admire the Premier League as a competition and how successful it is and how that success has driven wealth that does actually go back into its grassroots. I do think we should celebrate that. Owners like Steve are superb for their club and community. So it's not a case of the Premier League is bad. I just think that what we decided in the end is that this is about the bigger picture and about the long-term financial sustainability in football. When you've got the deepest pyramid in the world and you've got both the best league and the Championship being, what, the fourth-most-watched league in the world, you've just got to acknowledge that things have evolved quicker than the regulation around those things. I think that's why we came to the conclusion that we did. And if you want to continue to drive success then there are things that we can do to make that better, but also there's a lot that football can do for itself. My local team, Maidstone United, got promoted into the National League Premier this season and they had a gate of 4,175 on Saturday for their game against Hampton and Richmond, which is greater than some League Two teams. Yet, as a consequence of their promotion, they will now lose 60 per cent of their revenue because they're no longer allowed to sell beer to their fans during a match. And you just sit there and think: Saturday, these fans were able to drink beer and remain perfectly reasonable, not in any way yobbish, yet in August they won't be allowed. That's the sort of thing that drives me mad. They've got an artificial pitch [artificial pitches are not allowed in the Football League]. Now, say that they are successful next season and they get promoted to

League Two; that's a million pounds just wiped off their revenue because that pitch is actually being rented out seven days
a week. So football can do quite a bit for itself. I really hope
that the EFL does actually finally at some point talk about
artificial pitches, because you can drive revenue into your
own game and not just rely on the crumbs of the Premier
League. And I think there is a slightly lazy view that the
Premier League is rich and we should therefore have more of
it, when instead you could be thinking about the diversity of
your stadium and your club and your ground and everything
else. So, yes, it's not just let's attack the Premier League. It's
also let's look sensibly at what this amazing pyramid of
English football looks like and how can we continue to drive
wealth within it?

SP: I do think genuinely over the years, with all the outside
pressure and scrutiny the Premier League are under, it does
generally get us to the right answer without, unnecessarily,
having to have somebody unleashing a regulator that we
don't really understand. I think the Premier League and the
FA can respond to the issues raised with a package that
improves things for everyone and bakes in sustainability for
all clubs.

GN: I don't share the same faith in the Premier League to
unlock the complex issues, for the better of the game, in
the coming years. They haven't done it before so why
should we believe they can do it now? But there is also an
acceptance that they can't just hand money down and the
same problems reappear. Sustainability measures and
spending on infrastructure and academies must be a given
if lower league clubs are to gain more funding from the
Premier League.

TT: I'm lucky enough to go to most academies. You talk about academies being rundown. They are rundown. But they still produce players. I've seen a lot of those academies now and they're not always on pristine pitches. They haven't got all the rewards and benefits that Premier League academies and a lot of Championship ones enjoy. So there is a point where actually if we can support them better we're going produce more of those players, more of those talents, and help the clubs to develop their structure, which will help them potentially earn their own potential to be more as well. Take Oldham – I've been to Oldham. It's rundown. It's been run poorly from top to bottom and I feel for those young players who are part of now. But additional money, additional finance –like you said, Gary, it's not just there for transfer fees. It is there, though, to develop the whole structure within the environment, the benefits people don't see . . .

GN: If we were given more money but with controls, with financial monitoring stipulating where we invest the money to ensure that we have five or six academy players under twenty-one in the first team squad, so that these can develop, so that Crystal Palace can come and get them off us, we would likely all vote for it. I saw the conscience of Leagues One and Two during Covid. League One was a little bit messy, but League Two, they will vote for it. It's not difficult, these things. It's just having that leadership with a good heart at the top of the game that says, this is what we're going to do, and then basically everyone buys into it. If we want the chasm – that £120m on the right-hand side of your computer – to be less, there's no one in the game, apart from the top six, who would disagree. Everyone would think it's the right thing. We have to get it nearer.

SP: In the end, it's about being prepared to deal with the clubs at the top of the game to help those hoping to move up. The more we can help clubs build their infrastructure while they are in League One or League Two, the more they will be able to compete as they move through the leagues.

GN: But Steve, this is why I don't understand the position of the fourteen clubs and the FA. The EFL, the National League, the Football Supporters' Association all want a regulator because we want the situations that you described unlocked. If the FA want to be the governor of the game, the only way they're ever gonna get true governance of the game back is for a regulator to come in, reset, get rid of those councils that Troy's referred to, and give them back the power. We know that. And the new FA Chair, Debbie Hewitt, I know of her quality and strength as a leader, I don't understand why the FA board is actually backing the Premier League position around regulation. It would be a great result for the game if the FA became the regulator of English football. But, surely, they must see they don't have the capability or the independence to take it on. Personally, I feel this is years away. So why are the fourteen, the FA, not working with the EFL, the Football Supporters' Association, the National League – not to gang up on the top six (after all, there's my club at the top – one of them is my club – I love it to bits), but to basically bring football back to a point whereby it's got the greatest of the Premier League, but these other issues can be dealt with properly? I don't get it.

DB: I think the answer, Gary, is – and you've seen this outside football, you've got this issue with the Post Office – is that institutions cannot help it. They protect themselves. It's so difficult to really embrace radical change, to do it voluntarily.

There's just too much built-in defensive behaviours, loss of prestige. It's really hard or impossible. For the FA or whoever to get this, it has to be a voluntary change.

SP: The Premier League know that they've got to change.

DB: We talk about the Premier League as though it's some institution, but the Premier League really is twenty clubs. Six and the fourteen, to service the clubs . . .

SP: You say that. There's the executive [the Premier League has a chief executive in Richard Masters, acting chairman Peter McCormick and a board of directors, which includes non-executives Mai Fyfield and Dharmash Mistry].

DB: The Premier League is there to service the clubs.

GN: At this moment it is.

SP: Well, in some ways, but in other ways they service the Premier League itself. I do agree with David to a certain extent that we need to form a strategic view; since Richard Scudamore went [in 2018] and as a consequence of things such as Covid, we have become, somewhat understandably, a little bit too involved in just surviving. So we have tended to deal with every-thing too tactically and everyone is aware of that.

GN: But if the financial stress wasn't there, Steve, you'd get an alignment from the game. The problem is the financial stress is so great that you have this desperation and this sense of jeopardy, which is too much. There shouldn't just be a sporting pain if you go down. There is financial pain. But it shouldn't be to the level that you're talking about. I come back to the question: what is your answer to remove this stress and what is your chief anxiety? Is your concern that a regulator would basically make a wrong step and that this could prove a greater risk than actually not bringing them in?

SP: Well, I think the concern is the fact that you trust the regulator. The minute you put a bill before parliament about football you can have a hundred amendments. Every MP has got some little issue with their football club, some will be crazy amendments. It'll just be completely out of our control once the government has a football bill in parliament. I think we would agree, probably for different reasons, that this isn't a brilliant government. This is a crazy, populist government. The only reason it feels they want to get involved is to shore up the red-wall seats [in the north of England, which helped the Conservatives win the last general election]. I really believe Tracy's motivation comes from a good place. I fear the rest of the government are getting behind it is they think it's a vote-winner in the red-wall seats. They're not necessarily getting behind it because they want to improve football.

DB: It's a win-win for them; it's low-hanging fruit.

SP: It's incongruous for me to argue against independent regulation when I think the most ridiculous thing going on in world football is that UEFA and FIFA are trying to organise club tournaments and govern the game and have the final power over the rule and the calendar.

GN: Are you in favour of independence generally?

SP: I think that there should be somebody . . .

GN: Right, here we go. So who is it?

SP: I don't know what form it would take. I don't know how it's constituted. And I think we have to look at what exactly are its powers.

GN: But it cannot be independent if the Premier League set it up.

SP: The reality is the Premier League are going to have to fund it because the government aren't going to pay £25m a year for it.

DB: No, I think they are. I think they are. They are committed to fund it.

GN: I'm in favour of independent regulation, even if it's only for a period and then we [re]form the FA and restructure it and bring the FA back in as a regulator once it's formed. But the people who are against the regulator say to me, 'Gary, how can you be critical of this government but then want them to run football?'

TC: The people that are saying that to you haven't read the review, right? It's as simple as that, because it's not – and I've said it *ad infinitum* in my media – a prime ministerial appointment. This is not a government regulator in the way that you would normally have, like an Ofcom or something like that. This is more akin to the press regulator where a panel appoints the regulator, not the government. So the government would have to appoint the panel, but it's normally a panel [IPSO, the independent press regulator has a panel of six people to appoint the board and chair]. It's not going to be

Boris's mate or Keir's mate, then, that runs the regulator. There is a step in between and if people read the report they would see that. So, Gary, you can still be critical of government because it's not you but the government that's going to appoint the regulator.

GN: One other thing people say is: who can be this regulator? Assuming it's one person. There's more likely to be probably a chair and then a panel of multiple people with different skill-sets. Can you give us an understanding of what a regulator looks like, so we can describe what it would involve when it's implemented?

TC: Well, given that the most important part of the football regulator's role would be around financial regulation and good governance, it would be akin, in my mind, to something like the Financial Conduct Authority. It would have nothing to do with me, but if I was looking for a skillset in whoever was running the football regulator, it would actually be somebody with a deep knowledge and understanding of financial regulation, not somebody with a deep understanding of football. It's about the business of football, not what happens on a pitch, so you would want somebody who understands football, why it's important, but it's not somebody who has lived their entire life in football. I would be looking for somebody who understands what prudential regulation means, what capital and liquidity means, what a good corporate governance looks like, what the green code is. Stuff like that. All these things that actually your insurance companies and banks understand. The integrity test that I've put into the owners' test is a test from the banking, securities and insurance sector, so you want somebody who has an understanding of that, right. That's not a politician and that's not a football person.

GN: When I say multiple people, would it be a panel of six, eight, ten, up to twelve people? How many would there be, normally, on a committee of this type, a panel of this type?

TC: Well, the Financial Conduct Authority has a chair, a chief executive and then a board – I think so, anyway – and then there's people who work for them. We estimated that the football regulator would have probably about fifty staff. That was, though, a type of lick-the-finger-and-put-it-in-the-air kind of estimate, but that's what we're thinking because it is about law, it's about regulation, it's about contracts, it's about governance. It's a beefy organisation, which is, again, why the FA is not capable of doing this because I think at the moment their regulatory team consists of two. I mean, it's not in their skillset.

SP: I genuinely believe if you let the government do it you'll regret it because actually their history of regulation isn't fantastic. It'll become very politicised. The other thing you've got to remember is, once you have a regulator, they can change the remit of the regulator by statutory instruments. They don't even need to pass another law. So every government that comes along and that gets a bit of pressure from somebody can change the regulator's remit. So I can go along with the regulator, but it's got to be independent. Somehow, as a game, we've got to find the right answer, and we might need some legislation to support change. You're right about the salary cap; due to current UK competition law, we probably couldn't enforce one. If you look at American sports . . . they carved out all the competition laws in America. All of them. In order to get cost control, then, it may well be that we do need some help from the government, because I think that the PFA, for example, can possibly successfully challenge that legally. There's an answer somewhere, I just think we need to be sensible about it and I would like to think that before we get to a point of legislation and the government regulator that we come up with something that we can all agree on that can work. That would be my preference. Whatever that looks like, and I'm completely open.

GN: You're talking about the Premier League, who aren't independent, paying to set up a regulator. How on earth would that regulator panel be independent and have power if it's funded by the twenty premier league clubs? It feels to me this would be a re-badging of what we currently have.

DB: If the top 5 per cent of people represent taxpayers that produce let's say 50 per cent of the tax in this country, the most wealthy people, 5 per cent of the people don't decide what happens to the money. In a democracy they have to pay their tax and independent people, for better or worse, decide where the money's spent. If the Premier League, because of their wealth, are going to be the source of the money, they cannot make the decisions about how that money's going to be spent. It all has to be set up independently. The Premier League are driven by vested interests. I don't blame them for that. Their job is to run a fantastic league, do what they do . . .

SP: I think you have to have a balance. In the end, at some point, yes, you could put a tax on a commercial organisation to help the rest of the industry and then you can decide how that tax is spent, but I don't think that then means you decide everything that goes on in that league, if you're a commercial organisation that's trying to drive them. To drive the overall income of the league, we have to think beyond media income and work collectively on that. There's a report that says we are losing out hugely because we don't sell enough commercial deals as a collective, but obviously some of the current financially bigger clubs don't want us to do that. They would rather the whole pie was smaller as long as they continued to get a disproportionate amount.

GN: But Steve, the only way to achieve the things that you're talking about is through government. The way I see it is I don't want government running football. I'd like to think football could run itself. But the reason I've got to a position – and I think David has a similar position – is that the influence of the Glazers, John Henry's Fenway Sports Group, Daniel Levy, all these people that are at the top of these clubs, is going to take the game further away and they are more dangerous to *me* than the idea of a regulator.

By the end of our discussion I think Steve and I had moved closer together. I understood some of his concerns. He does see the need for regulation. He just doesn't want the government involved. And who can blame him, when you look at them? But I think he's being over-optimistic in thinking that the Premier League can sort this out. The issues around the game go beyond just sorting out the money. We've seen in previous chapters how the might of Abu Dhabi has transformed our league. But now there's a new player in town and they're bigger, richer and even more powerful. And I'm convinced the Premier League can't cope with them on their own. It feels to me that the fourteen clubs have this big brother in the top six that bullys and pacifies them, and is dishonest. But it's like a fatal attraction that means they know it's badly wrong, but they can't bring themselves to challenge in a way that would bring lasting and meaningful change.

11

FIT AND PROPER

'We assess that Saudi Arabia's Crown Prince Mohammed
bin Salman approved an operation in Istanbul, Turkey, to
capture or kill Saudi journalist Jamal Khashoggi.'
**USA's Director of National Intelligence
Report, released February 2021**

It wasn't my best day for Manchester United. As we trooped off St
James' Park in October 1996, you could be forgiven for thinking
there was a power shift taking place. We had been given the run-
around, beaten 5–0 by Kevin Keegan's Newcastle, our humilia-
tion summed up by Philippe Albert's outrageous chip over Peter
Schmeichel for the fifth. This was Newcastle in their pomp, with
Alan Shearer, Les Ferdinand and David Ginola, who killed me for
the second goal, turning inside me to score from twenty yards.

It was just a few months after we had pipped them to the league
title in 1996. Keegan's entertainers had been twelve points clear in
February that season. We went up to St James' Park in March and
won 1–0 against the run of play with an Eric Cantona goal to
close to within a point of them. Famously they cracked, Keegan
delivering his 'I'd love it if we beat them' rant after winning
against Leeds. He felt Sir Alex had implied that Leeds would roll
over for Newcastle because they hated Manchester United.
Whatever, we saw a manager and a team under pressure and knew
we would win the league.

So that evening at St James' Park after that 5–0 defeat probably felt like revenge for Newcastle fans, a confirmation they were now the coming team, that our day was done and this was their year. St James' Park is one of the great stadia in world football, sitting as it does slap bang in the centre of the city, towering above it like a cathedral. The atmosphere is raw, built on the back of those working-class supporters whose grandfathers would have worked on the shipyards, like Sir Alex did in Govan, and flocked to St James' Park after the Saturday morning shift. It's a club that embodies the roots of our game. That evening it was extraordinary, the noise shaking its foundations.

Sadly for them, the 5–0 was pretty much the high spot of the last thirty years. Keegan would resign three months later and we won the league again that year. Newcastle never got close again, though they enjoyed some great Champions League nights under Sir Bobby Robson. And then came Mike Ashley, who bought the club in 2007. The billionaire Sports Direct owner's idea for a football club was to use it as a giant advertising hoarding for his brand and run it like a budget airline, cutting all frills and restraining spending even though it resulted in two relegations. He sucked the life and soul out of the club.

So, you can understand why Newcastle fans were so ecstatic when the takeover to buy their club finally went through in October 2021. It wasn't just any old takeover. Led by Amanda Staveley, who would be buying 10 per cent of the club, the majority investors, with 80 per cent, were the Public Investment Fund, the sovereign wealth fund of Saudi Arabia. This really was like winning the owners' lottery.

But perhaps because we had been through this with Manchester City, the questions about the ethics of the deal were being asked a lot more vocally right from the start. And most of them centred around one man, Jamal Khashoggi.

His story was chilling and had dominated the news around Saudi Arabia in the run-up to this deal. When he entered the Saudi

Arabian consulate in Istanbul on 2 October 2018, officials from Saudi Arabia were heard having a conversation, in recordings that were later made available to the United Nations investigation of his murder. Saudi intelligence officer Maher Abdulaziz Mutreb, who had flown in from Riyadh for the occasion, wanted to check whether it will 'be possible to put the trunk in a bag?' Dr Salah Mohammed al-Tubaigy, a Saudi army forensic doctor, replied: 'No. Too heavy.' However, Dr al-Tubaigy insists it will 'be easy. Joints will be separated. It is not a problem. The body is heavy. First time I cut on the ground. If we take plastic bags and cut it into pieces, it will be finished. We will wrap each of them.' At the end of the conversation, Mutreb asked whether 'the sacrificial animal' has arrived. At 13:13, a voice said 'he has arrived'. That is the time Jamal Khashoggi entered the Saudi consulate in Istanbul so that he could collect a document to allow him to marry his fiancée, Hatice Cengiz.

Khashoggi was a Saudi journalist. The UN report says that he had a 'passionate vision for the potential of Arab press freedom'. He also had a Twitter following of 2 million and criticised the Saudi regime on that platform. He wrote occasional columns for the *Washington Post* in the USA. Prior to leaving Saudi Arabia, he had been well known to the Saudi royal family and even an advisor to them. But over time he had grown more critical of them, which led to him fearing for his life and leaving to live in exile in the USA. He had political connections in Turkey, which meant that, although he was nervous about attending the appointment at the consulate in Istanbul, he felt he was protected. And a previous meeting there had gone reassuringly well. Cengiz remained worried and so waited outside when he went to collect his paperwork on the second visit. The UN report concludes that he was most likely sedated and then dismembered. Middle East Eye, a London-based online news outlet covering events in the Middle East and North Africa, spoke to a source who said they had heard a recording extracted from Khashoggi's Apple watch. According to that source: 'As he started to dismember the body, Dr al-Tubaigy put on earphones and listened to music. He advised that other members of the squad do the same. "When I do this job, I like to listen to music. You should do [that] too."'

Agnès Callamard, the UN's special rapporteur, wrote: 'It is [my] conclusion that Mr Khashoggi has been the victim of a deliberate, premeditated execution, an extrajudicial killing for which the state of Saudi Arabia is responsible under international human rights law.'

The US intelligence report, released last year by President Joe Biden, went further:

> We assess that Saudi Arabia's Crown Prince Mohammed bin Salman approved an operation in Istanbul, Turkey to capture or kill Saudi journalist Jamal Khashoggi. We base this assessment on the Crown Prince's control of decision making in the Kingdom since 2017, the direct involvement of a key advisor and members of Mohammed bin Salman's protective detail in the operation, and the Crown Prince's support for using violent measures to silence dissidents abroad, including Khashoggi. Since 2017, the Crown Prince has had absolute control of the Kingdom's security and intelligence organizations, making it highly unlikely that Saudi officials would have carried out an operation of this nature without the Crown Prince's authorization.

But then, as Greg Norman said, when justifying his leadership of the new Saudi-backed golf tour: 'We've all made mistakes.' The Saudi Ministry of Foreign Affairs said of the CIA report:

> 'The Kingdom of Saudi Arabia completely rejects the negative, false and unacceptable assessment in the report pertaining to the

Kingdom's leadership and notes that the report contained inaccurate information and conclusions.

Mohammed bin Salman, known as MBS, is chairman of the Saudi Public Investment Fund, which owns 80 per cent of Newcastle United. The Premier League decided he wasn't required to submit himself to their owners' and directors' test and so they were able to approve PIF's takeover of Newcastle in October 2021. The chairman of Newcastle United is Yasir Al-Rumayyan, who is a governor of PIF. The Premier League have been given assurances that MBS will have nothing to do with PIF, of which he is chairman. The Premier League decided that only Al-Rumayyan had to pass the owners' and directors' test.

'The Newcastle deal was clearly signed off by MBS, he clearly wanted it and it had to go through the circuitous route of having the wealth fund do it with Yasir as front man', says Dr Chris Davidson, author of *From Sheikhs to Sultanism: Statecraft and Authority in Saudi Arabia and the UAE*. 'But MBS is actually the chairman of the PIF and to suggest they could be separated is laughable.'

It probably helped that PIF has some powerful cheerleaders in government. Back in September 2020, when it first looked like, after six months of wrangling, PIF would get to buy Newcastle, Prime Minister Boris Johnson is said to have asked Middle East expert and advisor Lord Lister, 'Any news from Saudi?' According to the *Daily Mail*, the peer told him: 'A call is being set up. The Newcastle deal will hopefully be signed this week.' The PM replied: 'Brilliant.'

When PIF bought Newcastle, I was in favour. I've benefited from the influx of money into the English game from broadcasters and from rich owners. We have a wealthy owner at Salford in Peter Lim and I've never been against this kind of investment. I was always against Financial Fair Play rules. I have always wanted the influx of money into the Premier League because I felt as though it's a free market, and that it was good to have the traditional teams of Manchester United, Arsenal and Liverpool challenged by new money. It would be a very boring game if we felt that the top three with the most revenues would stay as the top three for ever and clubs couldn't grow underneath to become bigger than them. Manchester City are the prime example of a football club who have transformed themselves from being a little brother in the city to becoming now a prominent world football club, an incredible team, with great players. And the owners are not just investing in the club but beyond that in the east side of Manchester, where they have created prosperity and economic value in that area. Manchester wouldn't be the city it is without international investment. It needs American, German, Asian, Middle Eastern money to come into it, to invest in the city, to grow the city, to make it better.

But the Chelsea situation, with Abramovich being sanctioned, has made me stop and rethink whether the limits of our openness are being tested. Should we have accepted Russian, Chinese, Saudi Arabian, Abu Dhabi money into football? Chelsea and City fans will say: 'What about the American money linked to George Bush or Donald Trump?' But that is different. For all our faults, the UK and the USA are democracies. There is much wrong in our country and in the USA, and you could link human rights abuses and civilian casualties to the Iraq War and War on Terror. But you won't be executed, poisoned or imprisoned for probing that or asking questions. There isn't a situation comparable to the Uyghurs being exploited and repressed in prison camps, as there is in China. It's playing student politics to claim the USA is comparable to Saudi Arabia.

This is clearly an issue which resonates with fans. When we listed a range of concerns around the English game, 83 per cent said that owners should commit to UK values and 83 per cent also agreed that human rights should be part of any fit and proper owner test. More than half – 51 per cent – thought that the current owners and directors test was insufficient (30 per cent thought it was sufficient and 19 per cent didn't know). And 79 per cent agreed with the statement: 'Having countries with poor human rights practices like Saudi Arabia own English football teams highlights the need to reform the ownership test.'

This is a fundamental human issue of how we treat people, who we are happy to do business with and where do human rights come into that conversation. And on that, right now, football hasn't got a clue what to do. The Premier League's leadership are out of their depth on these monumental issues. With the resources they have and the pressure they were under from the government, they have no means of realistically dealing with these issues. They tried to resist the PIF takeover for a while, but that mainly seemed to be because the Saudi state was behind a huge scam to show Premier League on pirate TV, mainly to annoy Qatar, who held the official rights. (Saudi Arabia denied it was behind pirate broadcaster beoutQ.) It was a good indicator of where we stand: steal our TV rights and we will fight you to the bitter end; chop up a journalist and we'll endeavour to see both sides of a complex issue.

The political, social and economic issues around football now are too big for football. Yet football is too important to every single person within the communities in this country, towns in this country, to ignore them and carry on as we have done. Football has grown so quickly in the last twenty years that the structures set up to control and govern it are totally obsolete. UEFA tried to take on Manchester City, but when they wrote their Financial Fair Play rules, they had no idea they would be dealing with one of the richest nation states in the world. The Premier League are pursuing City, we think for breaking financial rules, although the case is so secretive the Premier League and City tried to keep it out of the public domain even when it reached the civil court. City have declined to comment on the matter. When asked to adjudicate on the matter, Lord Justice Males, one of the most senior judges in the UK, commented: 'This is an investigation which commenced in December 2018. It is surprising, and a matter of legitimate public concern, that so little progress has been made after two and a half years, during which, it may be noted, the club has twice been crowned as Premier League champions.' Even our leading lawyers seem frustrated that the likes of City can simply string out an investigation until it becomes meaningless.

What we need is a clear statement of what is and isn't acceptable, what kind of money we're going to permit to be invested. Then we can work out whether we should regulate how it is spent. In reality, though, even after Chelsea effectively being nationalised by the government – which is something none of us could have imagined when I set out to write this book – no one expects a regulator to come in and ban sovereign wealth funds. Or to tell Abu Dhabi and Saudi Arabia they're no longer welcome in the Premier League. The government's official response to Tracey Crouch's fan-led review seems to make that clear. The government accepted that the owners' and directors' test needed to be strengthened and monitored by regulation. But on this issue of investment from countries like Saudi Arabia, it said that it would also 'consider limiting the scope of any integrity test, recognising that, while it is important for the regulator to undertake enhanced due diligence, there is a danger that the regulator could be drawn into issues that are geopolitical. We do not believe the regulator should get involved in issues of the government's foreign policy.'

I think that means pretty much a green light to Saudi investment. Let's be clear, whatever we may feel about the issues, football won't trump UK government policy. In June 2021, Kwasi Kwarteng, the business secretary, visited Saudi Arabia to try to persuade the country to invest in our renewable energy programme. PIF owns a chunk of BT, so if we are after a boycott we had better cancel those BT Sports subscriptions and pundits should stop taking money to appear on there. PIF has stakes in Uber, Facebook, Disney, Pfizer and Starbucks. Saudi money part-owns the *Independent* and the *London Evening Standard* and Snapchat. Modern life could start getting very tricky if we want to avoid all Saudi investment. Between 2015 and 2021, Department of International Trade figures reveal the UK has sold £6.7bn-worth of arms to Saudi Arabia. The Campaign Against Arms Trade (CAAT) calculated that the real value was around £20 billion, a figure not disputed by the Department for International Trade. CAAT chose that 2015 date because that is when the bombing of Yemen was begun by a UAE–Saudi coalition, a war that has seen the United Nations call for investigations into indiscriminate bombing of Yemeni civilians by the Saudi–UAE alliance. Over the last five years, the UK has sold over £75m-worth of spyware, wire-taps and telecom interception equipment to spy on dissidents, to over seventeen countries including Saudi Arabia, the UAE and Bahrain, according to Declassified UK, an investigative campaigning group.

Tracey Crouch made these points when we spoke. 'Should football have a higher bar than other businesses?' she said. 'PIF own [a stake] in Disney and nobody seems to be worried about *Pocahontas* or that they've got a significant stake in Facebook and Uber and so on. People who were out protesting against the Newcastle takeover probably got there in an Uber. There's a double standard sometimes with some of this. But, at the same time, I am a massive believer in the power of sport. I was forced to go to Saudi Arabia by [then Prime Minister] Theresa May, as Sports Minister, and met Princess Reema bint Bandar [then the Saudi vice minister of sport]. We talked about girls and sport. They were just on the cusp of starting to allow women to go into stadia. I think it was the week before women were allowed to drive. I ended up playing football with girls, which had never happened before. And now the women's Saudi team play in the national stadium, not some kind of pitch on the side. I just think that sport has the ability to change mindsets. The world is not going to end if you allow women to kick a ball. And so could the relationship between the Saudis and Newcastle change some of their attitudes towards other social issues? Potentially.'

Maybe football and sport can make a difference. That's how these projects, criticised as sportswashing, are always sold to us. But football isn't alone going to solve the world's geopolitical issues. We're all out of our depth. When I discussed the issue with Tracey, she came back to the point above. 'It's just really difficult to say that the PIF can't buy a football club when we're selling the country arms,' she said.

What has happened is that these investors have so far come in unchallenged and they've come in without any expectation. It's due to pressure and vision shown by Manchester City Council that Manchester City's purchase by ADUG has led to investment in the wider city, not down to the UK government or the Premier League. Abu Dhabi have paid what I call the Mancunian tax. They've had to invest a billion pounds into the infrastructure of the community and the area around the clubs. That's one lever a regulator could pull. Use sovereign wealth fund investment to improve UK cities. That has been promised as part of the Newcastle takeover by PIF. We'll have to wait and see what transpires.

In addition, there should be meaningful engagement with Lesbian, Gay, Bisexual and Trans groups. That may seem naïve. A few meetings aren't going to change a culture or centuries of religious belief. But we have to make a start and explain why it's so abhorrent that homosexuality is illegal. Which, it also was in the UK until 1967. So, it's not as though we're preaching from a position of moral infallibility. But the treatment of

LGBT people in Saudi Arabia, Qatar and Abu Dhabi is one of the principal reasons why we should be asking questions about this money.

Their leaders and owners ought to have to answer questions at open press conferences, where there is no censorship of the content, and that might get tricky for them. If that means Yasir Al-Rumayyan answering repeated questions about Jamal Khashoggi and then being asked his own personal views on gay rights, so be it. We should be past the stage of limiting our questions to transfer war chests – ironic, given the actual wars so many of these owners are embroiled in – and which players they're going to bring in.

If Abu Dhabi, Saudi Arabia and whoever comes next still want all of that, and they're happy to pay what we might call the Premier League tax, because they want to be part of this global brand, then so be it. But there has to be an expectation that if you want to own one of our crown jewel assets, we want something in return.

'The re-generation of east Manchester has been a local tax,' says Dr Davidson.

The infrastructure has improved a lot with Abu Dhabi money. I believe in Newcastle there is a similar understanding. The Premier League might want to think about what kind of rules we would have on this kind of investment. But I remember my favourite academic Fred Halliday at London School of Economics used to tell me: 'All this money flowing to our universities from Saudi Arabia and China . . . we should just take it and run off with it.' His point was that even if some point down the line we find someone has been backing terrorism or invading someone, we can freeze their assets and keep what they've invested in our economy. We're doing that to Russia now. Now it may be that, knowing what we know now about Uyghur persecution, he wouldn't have taken Chinese money. In fact, he protested against LSE accepting money from the foundation of Libyan dictator Colonel Gaddafi. But it's all about hindsight. If we know at the time and have hard credible evidence that money is criminally connected and there's hard evidence it's connected to drug trafficking, blood diamonds or whatever, we can block it. If not, we just take it and run.

My dad is a Geordie so I have a vested interest in this in that I would like Newcastle to win something for him. I also worked in Durham for fifteen years, so I'm an honorary North Easterner. The region doesn't have a lot going for it economically. This might be something big for a lot of people; it will revitalise the economy and bring some global recognition to one of their brands. In ten years' time, something may have happened, they could be sanctioned, but it really doesn't matter because the club will have been invested in and built up.

Tracey Crouch made a similar point earlier about the Abu Dhabi money in Manchester, contrasting the ownership of Sheikh Mansour with that of the Glazers at United.

One of the key issues though is what happens when the politics changes. We all welcomed Abramovich's cash in 2003. It would have been strange in those circumstances for the Premier League to prevent Abramovich buying Chelsea.

The government has recognised this in its response to the fan-led review, saying that it 'will consider potential consequences and the impacts on the club and its fans if an established owner failed the [owners' and directors'] test or, as with Chelsea, is no longer able to own the club'.

Newcastle fans preparing to watch their team play in Saudi national kit next season at away games might wish to be a little cautious in their celebrations. Saudi Arabia might be an ally to the UK now, but who can say that will be the case in ten years' time. Dr Davidson says: 'The scenario where you could have

Newcastle United frozen like Chelsea might be a terrorist incident with evidence directly linking it to Saudi state support.' Fifteen of the 9/11 terrorists who attacked New York and Washington were citizens of Saudi Arabia and two were from the United Arab Emirates. In 2021, US President Joe Biden released classified files surrounding the 9/11 attacks. Among them is a home video from 2000, which was seized by British police shortly after the terror attacks but which has now been seen publicly for the first time. It's a party at the San Diego apartment of Nawaf al-Hazmi and Khalid al-Mihdhar, who were two of the 9/11 terrorists. The party's host was Saudi national Omar al-Bayoumi, who was arrested by British police less than two weeks after the 9/11 attacks and the FBI concluded he was involved with Saudi intelligence. A heavily redacted FBI memo from 2017 says: 'In the late 1990s and up to September 11, 2001, Omar al-Bayoumi was paid a monthly stipend as a co-optee of the Saudi General Intelligence Presidency (GIP) via then Ambassador Prince Bandar bin Sultan.'

Dr Davidson said:

In the wake of Russia's Ukraine invasion, Saudi Arabia is again temporarily needed by the US to stabilize world energy markets, primarily on behalf of Washington's Western European allies. However, if something like 9/11 were to happen now, Riyadh would likely face far greater scrutiny and perhaps even punitive action. In 2001 the US was a net oil importer and needed Saudi Arabia as a producer. But America is now swimming in its own oil after the 2014 shale oil revolution. Long term, this means Saudi Arabia has lost its oil kingpin role. Gas is our problem now, and for the UK and Europe, much of that's having to come from Qatar.

Obviously, the other huge issue surrounding owners relates back to the chapter on Bury and the likes of Steve Dale coming into the game. That's some way removed from Saudi Arabia and world politics, but it is also important for the game. I've discussed how those rules need to change. The EFL rules at the time meant Dale could buy the club and then submit his financial plans 'no later than 10 Normal Working Days thereafter [the change of control]'. That can't be allowed to happen and a regulator, with the resources and powers to look into PIF and Steve Dale's financial affairs, should be able to block an ownership change. Equally, someone involved with multiple companies which have been liquidated shouldn't be permitted. Premier League and EFL rules need to be consolidated. Rules need to be consistent across the leagues, which a regulator can make happen. It may be some adjustments need to be made for League Two compared to the Premier League, but the principles need to be universal.

And the test should be reapplied every three years, as Tracey Crouch's review said. You can't just pass the test in 2003 and never be quizzed on your business and ethics again. 'One thing the government has accepted is the periodical review of the owners' test, which doesn't happen at the moment,' said Crouch. She cites the case of Owen Oyston, who bought Blackpool in 1988, was convicted of rape and imprisoned in 1996, and yet still retained ownership of that club, taking them into the Premier League in 2010. 'Without reviews you can have situations like Owen Oyston happen and no one bats an eyelid,' said Crouch. 'Or Roman Abramovich, whose right to work in the UK was removed in 2018 but it takes Russia invading Ukraine for something to be done about it. So I do think that there is an opportunity to review owners' tests going forward that we have never had before.'

I know some would therefore like football to apply a higher standard than the government in relation to Saudi Arabia or Abu Dhabi. I just don't see that is realistic at the moment. And with globalisation being the way it is, we have to accept certain compromises or else we would barely have any trading partners left. That's not to say there isn't a line we shouldn't cross. But it's clearly complex. The only solution I can offer is to make the best of the money that comes in and use it to leverage as much change as we can.

Dr Davidson makes the point:

> As countries like Saudi and the UAE sell us less and less oil, we need them less in terms of the energy relationships. They still need us in terms of the security guarantee. And as they invested heavily in our economies, at some point the scales tip somewhat. Back in 2018, a British academic Matthew Hedges was arrested in the UAE and accused of espionage. Our foreign secretary at the time Jeremy Hunt clearly said something to the UAE ambassador, which stopped it in its tracks. He was quietly pardoned a couple of days later. What Hunt said we'll never know, but I would imagine it was along the lines: 'We've calculated the value of UAE ruling family assets in this country in terms of houses owned, racehorses etc. Pursue this case and see what happens.' It's blackmail in a way but it does tip the scales.

To open a bank account in this country, the bank needs to do what is known as KYC or Know Your Customer due diligence to ensure you're not laundering money or involved in crime. That's the starting point for me. If you can open a British bank account and get through the KYC rules, then you will have passed first base. There may be other stipulations we then put on top of that, certainly around criminal records and human rights. As part of the conversation I had with Steve Parish and David Bernstein, we debated this point. We also took in the other key issue – the one that has so worried Bayern, Barcelona and Real Madrid and to a lesser extent Liverpool and Manchester United – that if nation states own football clubs, what should the spending limits be? We started off by discussing the rule in Germany, where clubs in the main have to be 51 per cent owned by the fans, a rule known as 50+1.

STEVE PARISH: Let's talk about the fit-and-proper persons test. I'm fascinated by that. In Germany, Bayern have now won the league for ten consecutive years. They'll carry on winning the league for another ten years because no one will invest in German football, because you can't control the club. But in Brazil, where [as in Germany] the clubs are all fan-owned sporting clubs, the government is desperate to sell the clubs off because none of them are paying their bills.

GN: We're not 50+1 people. We're not.

SP: But you have to get the balance right because you have to get investment. We've had some of the wrong people and we can argue about nation states. I don't think they should have ever been allowed, without any FFP or when we did have it, any real enforcement of it, but the fact of the matter is they were.

GN: I actually do think they should have been allowed. I've said that to you.

SP: I would say they should never have been allowed or they should always be allowed, but with rules on spending. The problem I've got now is that people want us to stop it now. That's brilliant for the current three [Manchester City, Newcastle and Paris St Germain, owned by Qatar]. If we pulled up the draw bridge now, I'm sure PSG would think that's absolutely fantastic.

DB: But does the nature of a nation state matter? Do human rights matter? North Korea?

SP: Human rights matter to everybody. It's a desperately difficult area because Amnesty International, for example, have got a problem - perhaps rightly - with so many nations. Who, or what, do you use as a benchmark?

DB: So basically we would say that any nation state should be able to invest? It doesn't really matter?

SP: Let me bring up a challenge, because we've knocked it around ourselves, because there have been some really poor owners, particularly in the Championship, who would probably qualify under any circumstances, and some extremely good ones who might not if things were altered along the lines suggested. Let me give you an example. One of the things suggested was [a ban on] any politically associated person. So, let's say Leicester, who have brilliant owners, have got a business licensed by the Thai government. Amnesty International have issues with the Thai government and have heavily criticised them in the past for their record on human rights in some areas. [The prime minister of Thailand has launched a review of Amnesty International, with the nation's deputy prime minister calling for the human rights organisation to be expelled from the country.] The nation was run by the royal family and a military junta [until the 2019 elections]. The Leicester owners, as I understand it, have a contract to run all the duty-free shops in Thailand granted by the government. So, they would probably be considered to be politically exposed. But there's not a person on the planet who would argue that they've not been brilliant owners for Leicester and the Leicester fans;

arguably they've done a lot of good for Leicester the town. It's a great story in the Premier League and most people don't question their relationship with Thailand and, in the end, Thailand, like Saudi, is a country we do business with in every other way. At the moment what we have is pretty good in my view and goes beyond what is usually required for areas outside football. The Premier League currently allows anybody to buy a football club who could buy a business in the UK, but an extra layer of scrutiny if you have a criminal record or have ever made a plea bargain to avoid a criminal record. Or, if you have done something in your own country that could reasonably deemed to have been a crime in the UK. Then you are disqualified. It seems hard to add much to that without making it very subjective. We are an open nation - one that welcomes outside investment. The Premier League is undoubtedly better because of it. I fear a few bad owners in the EFL, many of whom would not be able to do what they did now because loopholes have been closed, are driving us towards an unworkable solution.

Who gets to judge who is fit and proper? That's our problem. From Steve Dale at Bury to Mohammed bin Salman at Newcastle, there could hardly be a wider spectrum of problematic owners, from the global elite sitting at the top table of world power to a British businessman associated with multiple failed companies. It's hard to wrap up all of those concerns in one set of rules. Hard, but not impossible.

There should be one single entry point into English football. The criteria needs to be clear and the obligations of what we expect from an owner, be that of Salford or Newcastle, need to be laid out and established. We must have transparency.

If it's a nation state that Prince William and the Prime Minister are paying homage to, then it's simply unrealistic to freeze them out of English football. However, the expectations of what is required from them needs to be high and with constant monitoring. Our 92 professional clubs are crown jewels and need to be preserved and looked after by the guardians of the moment.

VANITY PROJECT

'A vanity project for a girl.'
**Senior football official on Tracey Crouch's fan-led review on
English football**

All roads lead back to Bury in the end, at least as far as I'm concerned they do. We started at Bury and that's where we end up. When I met Tracey Crouch for this book, I was intrigued as to why the government had even put a commitment to an independent regulator for football in its manifesto in the first place. After all, Crouch's obvious commitment notwithstanding, the Conservative Party hasn't exactly been a hotbed of football passion over the years. 'Bury,' she said. 'Bury took place before the 2019 general election. Downing Street were ringing me at the time and I wasn't even Sports Minister, as they weren't quite sure what to do. I was giving my view on how you could protect the stadium from development, because my fear was that you would get predatory developers in. We discussed at the time the need for a review and that it should be fan-led, and I think one of the reasons why the Premier League weren't quite prepared for it is that when it went into the manifesto I wasn't convinced the review was going to be focused on the Premier League. I genuinely felt it was to be a financial sustainability review of the Championship down.'

That's the glorious thing about the Super League idea, when you think about it. The Premier League probably could have dodged the big issues of the review and moulded it into something that didn't really affect them. But because John W. Henry, Joel Glazer, Roman Abramovich, Sheikh Mansour, Stan Kroenke and Joe Lewis tried to run off with the family silver, they've now landed themselves with potentially a powerful regulator. Their greed and stupidity gave us the leverage for reform.

Sometimes you just fail to read the room and get it wrong. You would have thought people would have learned from that since the Super League proposal. In some ways, the Big Six seemed to have at least learned a little. They haven't raised their voice since, a welcome period of silence, though they can't hide for ever. But as Rick Parry said when discussing Project Big Picture, they need to speak up now and be accountable.

But the Premier League? And by that I mean the executive, in CEO Richard Masters and Helen MacNamara, recent high-level executive appointment. MacNamara previously worked at No. 10 Downing St, where she provided a karaoke machine for one of the lockdown breach parties, for which she was fined and which finally stopped in the small hours of the morning after 'excessive alcohol consumption'. She was the government's Director General of Propriety and Ethics at the time. Last year she moved over to be Chief Policy and Corporate Affairs Officer at the Premier League. Basically, her job seems to me to be to smarm up to the new Prime Minister and get them to forget about an independent regulator. Luckily, it's not working so far, but we can't rely on that for ever. My feeling is that many power brokers didn't take the fan-led review seriously when it was announced. One very senior official with power-bases in the FA and the Premier League was overheard saying it was a 'vanity project for a girl.'

The Premier League just aren't trusted by most fans. In our fans' survey, only 29 per cent of fans said they would trust the Premier League to manage and safeguard the interests of the game. By contrast, 59 per cent would trust an independent regulator. Sixty-six per cent of fans believe there is a problem with the way the game is managed today and 78 per cent want an independent regulator.

I believe the Premier League played their hand terribly and were responsible for the least successful presentation to Tracey Crouch's fan-led review. From what I have heard, they assumed it was a knee-jerk reaction by the government and seemed bemused that they had been caught up in something they seemed to think was about Bury. As such, I'm not sure they made the best impression on the review panel members. They seem to think that those of us who want reform are anti Premier League. 'We made it very clear that you can still celebrate the success and the wealth of the Premier League and accept that it is the league that the world's talent wants to play in, but you can also recognise that the foundations of football are really crumbling and that something needs to be done to strengthen them,' said Crouch. 'We did reflect on some of their points in order to actually bolster our own recommendations.'

There are decent and talented people in the Premier League. No one should go away from this book thinking I dislike the league that has been my life and from which I made my money. And no one should come away with the idea that all Premier League executives are greedy conspirators forever plotting to seize the game from us.

I've known Paul Barber, chief executive at Brighton, for more than twenty years, when he was commercial director and director of marketing at the FA before he became executive director at Tottenham. He's seen everything in football. He played, his family works in football, he's heavily involved in grassroots football with Winchmore Hill FC and he's an FA councillor. 'So I am one of those old buggers now that you hate, Gary!' he told me when we met on Zoom to discuss these issues. Not hate, I reminded him. Frustration would be a better word to sum up my feelings on the FA Council.

'I sit in those meetings and I share that frustration,' said Barber. 'There are times when I sit there and bite my tongue, as some comments are ridiculous and self-centered. I want to shake some of those guys and say: "Lift your head up, think of your responsibility. Start thinking more widely than your personal interest." Despite that, the vast majority of FA councillors do outstanding work in the grass roots. But I definitely think reform is needed.'

Brighton's story itself is a perfect example of the turbulence of a professional club. In 1982–83 they were in the top flight, then known as the First Division, and reached the FA Cup Final, losing to Manchester United in a replay in the same year in which they were relegated. After that, there was steady decline until the 1996–97 season, when they were bottom of League Two, at that time called Division Three, and were twelve points adrift, seemingly certain to disappear into non-league football. Somehow, they made up the twelve-point deficit and on the final day of the season were playing Hereford, the bottom club in the division, needing a draw to avoid dropping out of the league for the first time since 1920. A goal down at half time, a Robbie Reinelt goal earned them the point that saw them stay up on goals scored. However, that would be the last match at their historic Goldstone Ground, which was sold by their owners to avoid bankruptcy. The same owners had recently changed the articles of association of the club, which had previously stated that any profits from a ground sale should go to the club, so that the directors could personally profit. The club had to play home games at Gillingham, seventy miles away. Homeless and playing to crowds of around a thousand at time, they were forever on the brink of extinction. Their renaissance began under new owners when they returned to the Withdean Stadium, a wholly unsuitable athletics stadium but at least in Brighton, which saw them promoted to the Championship, then known as League One. But it was really on the arrival of Tony Bloom, a poker player knowns as 'The Lizard', who took over in 2009, that the club has become what it is today. He invested £93m to build the new stadium at Falmer and helped fund their promotion to the Premier League in 2017. Last season, their fifth successive in the Premier League, they finished ninth.

'Tony is now £400m deep in this club,' said Barber: 'Four hundred million! And he has no expectation of getting any kind of return on that investment. If at some point his family decides that they don't want to be involved any more, his best hope is that he might get most or some of that money back. So he's come into it [with the attitude]: "I'm a local guy, I love this club, I love the community, I love football, I don't own yachts and stuff around the world. I just want to do something for football and for my club and for my city." That's his mindset. Tony's smart enough to have put that £400m somewhere else and multiplied it many times over to make himself even richer, but he didn't. He put it here, and thank God he did for us. But that's a very different mindset to John W. Henry or a similar investor at a bigger club. Very different. I feel like a fraud sometimes because every year I'm the chief executive of a club that loses tens of millions of pounds. I mean, what kind of businessman am I? If your business, Gary, was doing that you wouldn't be in your hotel for very long! So my job almost is to try and find ways of minimising Tony's losses and protecting him as much as I can from the downside of falling out of the Premier League.'

We spoke the day after I had sat down with Steve Parish, Troy Townsend and David Bernstein, so parachute payments were very much in my mind. Once again, we were back on the topic of that dreaded drop from Premier League to Championship. 'We've got to somehow smooth out this cliff edge between the Premier League and the Championship,' said Barber. 'We were relatively comfortable this season [2021–22], but it's the first time in five seasons that we've felt like that. I've looked over that cliff edge multiple times and it's horrible. I know that there's something that's got to be done there.'

At the end of compiling all the evidence for this book, I spoke to Rick Parry on a one-hour Zoom call, the day before the end of the season in May 2022. Parry is now the chairman of the EFL, was the chief executive of Liverpool and was the first chief executive of the Premier League back in 1992 when it was formed. As such, like Barber, he sees football from all sides. He backed Project Big Picture, as discussed earlier, when it came out, because he thought it was the only way to get a reform in the way money is distributed through the football pyramid. And he is leading the charge for the abolition of parachute payments.

'The Premier League must recognise there's a cliff edge or else you wouldn't need a parachute,' said Parry. 'You don't need a parachute to fall off a step.' Parry points out that in 2018–19, which is the last normal year of financial results pre-pandemic, Huddersfield, bottom of the Premier League, received £96m in TV revenue and Norwich, top of the Championship, received £8m. 'That is unbridgeable. You just can't cope with that.' The forlorn fourteen in the Premier League, any of whom could be in the Championship at some point, pick up collectively £1.6bn in TV revenue. The twenty-four clubs in the Championship receive £146m. 'And the Premier League's solution, which I think is really cynical, is to say: "Well, we'll just make sure it's more comfortable for our clubs when they drop out. We won't really address the problem and say, how do we bridge the gap?" You have this double whammy, because we're saying we want fundamental redistribution of the money. And the clubs in the Premier League are thinking: "Well, hang on, that means we're going to have to give money away while we're in the Premier League and we don't want to do that. And we know that if we drop into the EFL we're covered because we've got the parachute payments to help us get back up, so why would we vote for either of those?"'

There's a log-jam, as we pointed out before. When you're in the Premier League it would seem mad to vote to have less money. But if you fall out of the Premier League, you need that parachute or else financial Armageddon will ensue. No one seems able to lift their head and see that a more equitable distribution would, of course, mean more competition but it would also avoid the deadly cliff edge. And who knows? More competition all round might even see the TV revenue rise.

'In terms of value now, a parachute payment for a club dropping down is £44m in the first year,' said Parry. 'Solidarity payments from the Premier League to all the non-parachute clubs in the Championship from the Premier League is £4.8m.' So a club like Bristol City got, as a starter, 11 per cent the amount Fulham got at the start of last season. 'Sunderland have just come up to the Championship – a big club with a huge fan base – and they think their turnover next season will be around £37m. One parachute payment alone to Burnley, Watford and Norwich is £44m. How are they expected to compete?' said Parry. What he has also discovered, going back to the original agreement between the Premier League and the EFL, is that, stupidly, that gap is baked into the contract. 'The solidarity agreement that set up the parachute payments says that the solidarity payment to all the other Championship clubs will be fixed at 11 per cent of the year one parachute, which is pretty astonishing.' So that gap is never going to close. It's there as a permanent fixture, which partly explains why the Championship can be the most reckless league. 'The Premier League actually produced a chart that said over the last three years we have given £887m to the Championship,' said Parry. 'Of that, £660m was parachute payments! A £44m parachute payment is more than the forty-eight clubs in League One and League Two get collectively in solidarity. One club is getting more than the forty-eight. Now you tell me that's in any way fair?'

The answer is that it's not. It's a mess of a competition. The success of the Premier League is killing the Championship. There was some independent research done by Dr Rob Wilson at Sheffield Hallam University in 2017, which looked at ten years of parachute payments, and it showed that a team with parachute payments is twice as likely to go up than one without. Parry has asked him to update his work, because payments have increased hugely over the last five years and he wanted to see what the latest situation was. 'Within the last five years, parachute clubs are now three times as likely as all the others to get promoted,' said Parry. 'This year you have Fulham and Bournemouth going back up in the two guaranteed slots and Sheffield United were within penalties of getting to the [play-off] final. All received parachute payments last season. There will come a time when three parachute clubs get promoted back to the Premier League. Norwich and Fulham are becoming the archetypal yo-yo clubs.'

Sometimes all these figures are hard to engage with. For example, only 30 per cent of fans we surveyed could identify the amount parachute payments were worth when given four options from which to choose. And there isn't a great clamour among fans for them to be reformed: 48 per cent think they are fair and 36 per cent believe them to be unfair. But I do agree with Parry that they have served their time.

'If you outlawed parachute payments, the fourteen [in the Premier League] would be rushing to the negotiating table on redistribution because they would be terrified about what would happen. They would be saying: "Relegation will kill us! We have to have redistribution!" And if you look at what our suggested redistribution formula is, it's 25 per cent of the combined TV revenues, which would cost the Premier League about an extra £280m a year compared with what's being distributed now, because you would bring parachute payments into the pot.'

That figure might sound a lot: £280m a year. Put it in context, however. It's £14m a club. That's the transfer fee for a full back. For the Big Six, it's nothing. For the fourteen, it might seem like a stretch, but it's an insurance policy that allows them to plan ahead in confidence. 'It's not going to hurt the Premier League,' said Parry. 'These cries of "we won't be competitive in Europe" ... absolute rubbish. The Premier League is making twice as much in turnover as all the other major European leagues. If you look at what's happened to Premier League wages compared with the other major European leagues, in 2008–09, the Premier League was paying about £560m more in wages on average than the other major European leagues. In 2018–19, the Premier League is paying £1.6bn more in wages. The gap has widened by a billion. So don't tell me the Premier League is not going to be competitive or able to attract talent.'

I think the most compelling part of Parry's narrative is how unity would strengthen football. You will often hear the likes of West Ham's Karren Brady asking why they should help out Stoke City, owned by Denise Coates, whose family's net wealth is £8bn. But if you take a step back, a better competition with a strong Championship will more than repay its value. It's not charity. It's investment. 'This isn't us asking for handouts,' said Parry. 'This isn't us putting our hands in the Premier League's pocket. The value created for the Premier League comes from two things. First, it comes from our biggest clubs. We have to acknowledge that. I celebrate our big clubs succeeding in Europe and being on top of the pile because that's what drives value. That's why Sky pays so much money for the Premier League. But the other reason they pay a lot of money for the Premier League is the variety at the bottom. So when Sky enter into a three-year deal, they're not evaluating it purely on the basis of the twenty clubs who are in the Premier League at that moment in time, they're doing it in the knowledge that over a three-year period there are going to be nine different clubs coming upwards. The variety at the bottom, the need for stronger clubs to come up, is very much part of that value equation. If we have yo-yo clubs, which we're heading towards, in time that will be reflected in value. Because there are two things [according to our research] that fans want to see. One is big clubs winning. That's what drives audiences. They'll watch Liverpool, they'll watch Manchester United, however badly they're playing. That's a fact of life and it isn't going to change. But they'll watch relegation battles. Relegation battles are important, but mid-table Premier League, is that more attractive than really competitive games at the top of the Championship? No, it isn't. So we help to drive value.

'If we had the courage to say, "You know what, we're not getting anywhere. We'll just stop promotion and relegation," that would be a pretty drastic step. But see what would happen to the value of the Premier League media rights then. So, it's not a subsidy. I get really cross when I hear people suggesting we're just looking for handouts, like Oliver Twist asking for more. That's just condescending and it's just wrong. Do we value the pyramid? It's not the EFL against the Premier League. I'm not anti-Premier League. Why would I be? I'm the Premier League's biggest fan, having been there at the start, but I'm a bigger fan of the pyramid as a whole because that's vital to English football.'

Essentially jeopardy drives ratings. It's what the Super League conspirators forgot. It's part of the reason why the Premier League is a bigger global phenomenon than the NFL. Lose fair competition and you will lose jeopardy. I'm sold on Parry's argument that parachute payments have to go and I think Barber, Parish and other Premier League owners and executives will agree if we can get the new formula right. Next season Burnley will get £44m and Huddersfield will have received £4.8m plus their £2.5m equal split of EFL TV money. So £44m against £7.3m. 'You have to have a merit formula rather than parachute payments if you're going to narrow the gap. Very simplistically, I would say within the Premier

League you have a 2:1 ratio between top and bottom club in terms of the merit payments they receive. I would argue you need the same in the Championship. If you do that, the top club in the Championship is going to be earning about £30m and the bottom club in the Premier League might be £75–80m. You've still got a gap, but instead of the gap being £96m to £8m, which is £88m, you're more than halving the gap, which should make it more bridgeable. It's not perfect, but it's a lot more bridgeable. The reason why the Premier League clubs aren't going to vote for that is that instead of the parachute clubs getting £44m and everybody else getting £8m, parachute clubs will get a bit less – maybe they're only getting £30m – but everybody else is getting £30m, so it's more competitive. But how can you logically argue that that is wrong?'

Take Burnley as an example. They would miss out on their £44m parachute. But, with a decent season, they would be competing for £25–£30m of prize money, assuming they finish top half of the table. And that would be sustainable through the next six or seven years, rather than dropping off after three years, as parachute payments do. Crucially, it rewards success rather than failure.

Parry is firmly of the opinion that the Premier League won't ever vote for this, which is why we need a regulator, but Barber disagrees. 'My problem with a government regulator, or the potential of someone from government overseeing things, is just their understanding of this complexity that we've created and how all the different parts of football work together, come together, how the funding flows work,' he said. 'There are times when I have to draw it on a piece of paper so that I understand where the money comes in, where it then goes, what costs come out, who gets what. It's so complicated. If there is some kind of independent intervention, they should sit down and draw that map and redraw it so that there's a much greater transparency of where the money goes, because a lot more money actually flows down than people realise. But it's so complicated and so disguised that sometimes I can't even explain it and I sign off on some of the budgets.

'And then there's the independent bit of it. For me, if you truly understand football and you love football, it's very hard for you to be independent. You're either a Man United or a Tottenham fan, a Brentford fan or a Dagenham & Redbridge fan. So, "independent" is a strange word and I think we all have to understand what we mean by that. There are always going to be accusations of bias and self-interest. If someone says: "Well, I don't actually have any affinity to any club or any level of football," I question whether they really understand football.

'I actually think what the government could really usefully do is almost put a little bit of a fire under us and say: "Right, okay, we've heard that you want to keep it within football – whatever that looks like – and we've heard that you all accept that there's change needed. So, you've now got twelve months from this point to get your act together in all your different constituent groups, and come forward with a plan that will enable us and give us confidence that you can maintain regulation within your own sport and industry. You've had 150 years to sort this out and you still haven't done so. Go off and do it. But this is the time limit. If you haven't sorted it by then, then we will implement something that you may or may not like." It needs that kind of fire under people with a very specific timetable to make it happen. If, after that, we haven't got our act together, then frankly we probably deserve whatever's coming to us. And then at the end of that, if it isn't in place, Gary, then, as I say, I think we may have to simply accept that we can't do what you've just suggested and we may need external help.'

Coming from Barber, who I know is sincere, it's a powerful argument. But I come back to what Tracey Crouch says, something endorsed by Parry. It's never happened previously and I don't see why it would magically happen now. 'The game could've sorted it out, but the game hasn't sorted it out,' Parry told me. 'The game could've sorted this out any time over the last thirty years. I've been saying repeatedly that we need a fundamental financial reset, redistribution and better regulation. We've said it right through Project Big Picture. We're still waiting to be invited to hear the Premier League's strategy, whatever it is; . . . they promised a new strategy post-Big Picture, but that hasn't happened.'

In Barber's view, when it comes to parachute payments, football will need some government help in framing some kind of legal opt-out so that it can impose mandatory cuts in contracts for players if they go down. If turnover is going down 50 per cent, then so should wages. At the moment that's not possible as the PFA, the players' union, challenged the League One and League Two salary caps in court and secured a ruling that they represented illegal wage restraint. I can't quite believe I'm suggesting this, as I am an ardent PFA supporter, but I wonder whether now the time has come tfor mandatory relegation clauses in contracts. For this to happen the government would have to pass a law that allows this, recognising that sport is different from other businesses.

'The problem for clubs like us is that when we come up we need the protection afforded to us by parachute payments in order to convince us to invest in our squad,' said Barber. 'So, it's chicken and egg. We couldn't afford to invest in our squad unless there were parachute payments to give us a soft landing if it went wrong, but if we didn't invest in our squad, we'd have got relegated anyway because the squad wouldn't have been good enough to stay in the Premier League unless we were very lucky. There has to be either a parachute system or contract reductions; otherwise, what will happen is that clubs will get promoted, they won't invest, they'll just go straight back down again. And then you'll get what we all want to really avoid, which is that we don't get the kind of sporting meritocracy that we all love. It's about finding a way to create a mechanism that gives clubs confidence to invest, but security to go down. Even if you invest you can get it wrong and go down. It's not a guarantee against relegation. It's actually just to give you confidence that your business isn't going to go bang if you do go down.'

Brighton do have relegation clauses in all their contracts, including for Barber and all the senior executives. 'It's not as if we're asking the players to do something we're not doing ourselves, and if the players had, say, a 50 per cent cut, I would have the same,' he said. 'We know that we've lost players over the last five years to clubs that have just waived a relegation reduction and players have said: "Well, if I'm guaranteed four years' money at that level over there, I'm sorry, Paul, I'm not coming to you." We have 30 per cent reductions and it probably should be higher, to be honest, because even that only kind of takes a little bit of the pain away if we go down.'

Interestingly, Parry thinks the clubs don't need the automatic clauses. 'I'm not a great fan of mandatory negotiation,' he said. 'I think it's down to clubs to sort themselves out. They know what they're facing, so deal with it. That's the nature of the game. And it's not just at Premier League level. We've got to look downwards as well as upwards. We've got to be thinking about the gap between League Two and the National League, because under our 25 per cent formula of redistributing the money, it's going to potentially produce double or three times the revenue for League Two and League One clubs, which will eliminate their losses, make them sustainable. The only problem is, and there is no answer to this, the more money you have, the bigger the gap between divisions. That's a fact of life. We're not going to have equality. We're not going to share equally among ninety-two clubs ever.'

That seems a realistic assessment of the situation. We're not trying to make Oldham's turnover the same as Manchester United's and thereby ruin football. Nor do we want Salford voting on what Tottenham can do. There has to be competition and, as such, there have to be losers and failure. It's just that we can make it a normal sporting failure rather than a cataclysmic financial event.

A lot of the focus here is on parachute payments, because that is the most extreme element. But as Parry says, this needs to be applied down the divisions and into the National League. To do that, though, the parachute payments have to go. Get those abolished and we will take a huge step to normalising competition right down the EFL. That's the big reform that is needed. Get that right and we can sort League One and League Two and then focus on the gap between League Two and the National League.

There's an issue that I suspect will be nagging away at the reader. First, it's all well and good for Parry to be speaking like this now, but wasn't he the man who founded the Premier League thirty years ago in 1992, which in itself looked like an exercise in greed, the original Super League? Along with David Dein at Arsenal, Martin Edwards at Manchester United, Irving Scholar at Spurs and Rupert Murdoch at Sky, he's one of the pioneers of the structure that we have. Remember, TV money used to be distributed across all ninety-two clubs. Initially, they all had an equal share, and though that changed in 1986 to allow the top-flight clubs in the old Division One slightly more say and money, essentially the split was much more equitable. Parry worked as a consultant to what was then a Big Five of Manchester United, Arsenal, Tottenham, Liverpool and Everton, to tear up that agreement and form the Premier League. I had to put that point to him.

'I'm not going to deny that I was integrally involved and believed in the Premier League,' said Parry. 'I have a number of answers to your question. The first one is that I think it was necessary at the time in order to bring about the success of the Premier League. It would never have got there if we were just wallowing in the ninety-two-club structure, which didn't work. The tail was wagging the dog. It was very difficult to bring about change. So, I think that the breakaway and focusing on the Premier League has enabled it to succeed in a way that wouldn't have been possible. But now we've got there, and it's been immensely successful, I don't think it's in any way inconsistent to suggest that it's time now to have a rethink; to say, let's have a review.

'The big clubs wanted a fifteen-minute half-time interval rather than ten, and the Fourth Division clubs were saying: "Well, we're not going to sell more pies. We're not voting in favour of that." You just couldn't get anything voted through. It's not unlike the tensions you've got even within the Premier League at the moment, ironically. It was going nowhere. The clubs were massively concerned about the aftermath of the Taylor Report [in response to the Hillsborough Disaster], the need to go all-seater, the fact that we were losing players like Gazza and David Platt to Italy, which seems a bit ironic today.

'The second thing I would say is that when you look back at the 1993 accounts, the EFL was still making almost as much money as the Premier League. We had never envisaged that the Premier League would race away. We knew it would be successful, but the objective was never to kill off the rest. It was in order for English football to thrive, to make it more efficient. We needed a better structure.

'The other thing, though, I would say, Gary – and I'm not trying to justify my own position in any way, shape or form – but it is a matter of fact that in 1995, we did actually go to the EFL and say, "We're concerned that the gap is going to become too big. We suggest that we could pool the TV rights. The Premier League will sell them on your behalf. That'll generate more money and we will guarantee that you will receive a minimum of 20 per cent of the total pot," which is not unlike the 25 per cent formula that we're looking for today. So, the Premier League did actually propose it. Seventy-one out of the seventy-two football league clubs thought this was a good idea, but the EFL board ignored the clubs and went off and signed a deal at £25m a year with Sky. The TV deal we secured in 1992 was around £40m a year. The one we brokered in 1997 was around £170m a year.'

Essentially, the EFL rejected a deal that would have been a minimum £34m a year in favour of a £25m deal. In reality, they would have probably got closer to £50m a year, once you bundled the EFL rights into the Premier League package. 'We actually did give them the opportunity to have a coming together back in '95 and they, for whatever reason, rejected it,' said Parry.

That is it. Maybe 1995 was a sliding-doors moment for reform. If so, let's not miss this one. Let's bring the leagues back together once and for all. We must take this unique opportunity to make the changes we need.

FINAL WHISTLE

There is hope. As I write, a team of Bury Legends has just played at Gigg Lane, something I wasn't sure we would ever see again. A group of fans and businesspeople managed to raise the money to buy the stadium from administrators and then refurbish it after three years of neglect.

Bury AFC, a new club formed by another group of fans when Bury went bust, is preparing for a first season in the North West Counties Premier Division, the ninth tier of the football pyramid, after winning promotion last season.

And an initial agreement between the two groups – stadium owners and football club – means that Bury AFC could be playing at Gigg Lane in 2022–23. Fans were voting on merging the two groups at the time of publication.

Once again it is the resilience of fans that has saved the day. It was the fans who formed a club to keep the name of Bury going. It was the fans who prised Gigg Lane from the administrators with a grant from the Community Ownership Fund. Like AFC Wimbledon before them, Bury look like they are on their way back. It may take a while, but it could also be that this club is in a better position than ever before. It will be controlled by fans and run for the community.

No other business that went bust would inspire this level of action and commitment. So, let's say it again, as Tracey Crouch's fan-led review made clear, football isn't just another business. It can't be treated like any other business. Football clubs are constituent parts of our communities. There is such a thing as society and the national game is a vital part of what makes it up. We discovered during lockdown that we need our regular meeting points, our communities, our places to gather. Those institutions are the glue that binds us together.

So let's put aside all talk of football being left to find its own way in an unregulated free market. To deal in the new football market, you will have to respect the new rules that will set it apart from supermarkets or other such businesses. I believe you can be a capitalist and have compassion. I also believe you can be a socialist and believe in business. And I think football is a good vehicle to demonstrate what a regulated, fair and rule-based free market might look like.

Having spoken to all the people I did for this book, my core principles remain the same. That said, on this journey there are some areas where I have changed my mind, and I have reached seven key conclusions.

1. An Independent Regulator for Football
- Truly independent of the game.
- Empowered to reform and modernise the FA.
- Equipped with financial and regulatory expertise.
- Work closely with the game's stakeholders but empowered to broker and or step in to impose solutions where necessary.
- Tasked with handing back football governance to the FA in the future once it has been modernised, reformed, equipped and is sufficiently independent.

This is what the *Saving Our Beautiful Game* report, which I put my name to, called for back in 2020. It's what Tracey Crouch's fan-led review says should happen. It's what the government and the opposition wants. It's supported by fans' groups and the EFL. In our survey, 66 per cent of fans said the game needs reform and 59 per cent trusted an independent regulator to do that rather than the Premier League. It is only the FA and the Premier League that are holding out and hopefully soon enough they will have to get into line.

It's clear to me that football can't regulate itself, particularly in moments of stress. The game is so riven by conflicts of interest, and it's also clear that the FA are in no position to be that referee in its current form. The new regulator is coming and the government says it will provide details in autumn 2022.

Football's regulator should be wholly independent and insulated from the influence of the elite in the Premier League. However, it should work to reform and modernise the FA. It would have financial and regulatory expertise, similar to the Financial Conduct Authority. It should work closely with the game's stakeholders but should also have the power to step in and make decisions when shareholders are left paralysed by their respective self-interests. At some point in the future, if the FA was a reformed and modernised representative of the key stakeholders in football and with independent executives, I would hope it would be able to hand back the governance of football to the FA. But that time is not now. The key job now, as the government publishes its White Paper later this year in 2022, is to ensure a new regulator is not diluted in its power and has the necessary authority to make the changes in football it requires.

2. A Fairer Model of Financial Distribution

- Adopt the EFL's proposal of splitting TV money 75 per cent to the Premier League, 25 per cent to the EFL.
- Abolish parachute payments (after a suitable transition period required).
- Look at the viability of mandatory salary reductions on relegation.
- Address other financial disparity issues, from sixth to seventh in the Premier League right the way down to League Two and non-league.

We need to spread the wealth more fairly throughout the football pyramid. A free market can only thrive when there is fair competition and when it isn't rigged in favour of the few. The formula we have ended up with in English football doesn't deliver a fair market. There are some good points: the distribution of TV money in the Premier League is the most equitable in the world. The trouble is that it creates a problem for the Championship. Everything has a knock-on effect. The Premier League doesn't exist in isolation. The case for the commercial benefits of the pyramid are clear. It's one of the reasons why the Premier League is a bigger global product than the NFL. From what I've been told in writing this book, John W. Henry and Joel Glazer passionately believe in the importance of the pyramid. Fans agree. In our survey, 75 per cent said preserving the pyramid was vital to English football. If that's the case, then we need to maintain the base or else the top won't remain stable.

I back the EFL's proposal to pool the Premier League and Championship TV deals and then split the proceeds, 75 per cent to the Premier League and 25 per cent to the EFL and the rest of the game. I would abolish parachute payments, though I think there would have to be a transition period to allow everyone to adjust. We need to allow Steve Parish to stop worrying about the £120m figure on his screen if he goes down. As Rick says, if there wasn't a huge drop, you wouldn't need a parachute. Football is a sport. You have to be allowed to fail honourably and rebuild, not constantly feel like you're at the casino hoping it comes up red but fearing for your home if it comes up black. No other serious business runs that way. The fact that Huddersfield received £96m for being bottom of the Premier League in 2019 and Norwich got £8m for being top of the Championship was crazy. The EFL proposals, which would mean 25 per cent of the combined TV deal would be distributed through the leagues, would mean Huddersfield would have received less – £74m – but Norwich would have got a lot more – £32m. And the following season, Huddersfield would have benefited from those much higher Championship incomes.

This will mean that the ratio of TV money in the Premier League will look slightly less equitable, as the bottom clubs get less. So, there is another conversation we need to have in the coming months about the distribution of UEFA money and how to manage the gap between the Big Six and the rest. We need to listen to people like Steve Parish and Paul Barber when they talk about that gap in the Premier League between sixth and seventh. Success needs to be rewarded but equally there has to be opportunity for the fourteen clubs to push into the Europa League or even the Champions League. That doesn't seemed realistic at present, notwithstanding how well Leicester, West Ham and Wolves have done and the introduction of UEFA's Conference League. The Big Six should carry the bulk of the burden. It shouldn't be resolved by the fourteen getting less and the six steaming on ahead as before.

But the principle of the EFL proposals is good and makes the transition between Premier League and Championship manageable. And we need to ensure that transitions between Championship and League One, League One and League Two, League Two and the National League are manageable as well. There's no point making one cliff edge safer only to create another one. By all means, impose conditions on how the extra money is spent. There could be minimum levels of investment in infrastructure and facilities. There can be rules on playing academy players in Leagues One and Two. The financial rules we will discuss will ensure it can't just all go on wages.

Up until now, the government has let football sort this out with the threat of a regulator to intervene if they can't. But the principle is accepted. We need to have a much more equitable distribution system that works as well for the Premier League as it does for the National League. A fair market isn't Maoism. It's just a fair market.

3. A New Licencing System for Owners
- New owners to demonstrate proof of funds and be obliged to share their business plan on entry into football.
- Owners to be performance-tested on a three-year basis against key objectives.
- The regulator should be empowered to direct policy at failing clubs and, in extreme cases, step in and take ownership away if no other viable solutions appear.
- A new era of accountability with owners required to address fans and a panel of regulator experts once a year.
- Any new state owners to be obliged to commit to dialogue and local regeneration.

From Bury to Birmingham, Newcastle United to Norwich, the people who buy into our community assets – which is what football clubs are – are custodians. In our survey, 67 per cent of fans identified owners being inappropriate for their club as a key issue. The EFL has done some excellent work in this area since Bury. It's much harder today to buy a club. Unlike then, you now have to show proof of funds in advance. Of course, that has caused frustrations at Charlton, Wigan and Derby when they have turned down potential owners, but it looks like they have made the right call. The old approach seemed to be to welcome anyone with open arms. More discernment is now being applied. Anyone who has been involved in more than one insolvency event at a football club is currently disqualified. I would make this even tighter to weed out asset strippers. If you have been involved in multiple insolvency events or liquidated multiple companies, then you shouldn't be allowed to have a majority ownership of a football club. You may find that the need to show proof of funds weeds out those people anyway. But we can't be too careful.

In addition, you should have to reapply for your licence to be an owner every three years. As we have seen, politics can change, new facts come to light. It can't be a test on entry point and then you're free to do what you want. Everyone should be actively reassessed.

The regulator must have the power to step into a failing club if necessary. Ideally, this would be done in dialogue and through negotiation, as at Derby. But in an extreme case, like Bury's, there needs to be a mechanism to force through an ownership change.

It's not just the EFL clubs that need protecting. Our fans' survey shows that people are concerned about the involvement of nation states in football: 79 per cent think that the Saudi takeover of Newcastle shows that the tests to own a club need reform; 83 per cent think that preserving human rights should be part of the new test. They don't want our clubs to be the corporate public relations playthings of regimes with bad human rights records. However, that horse has bolted from the stable. I don't think there is any going back or the possibility of imposing a retrospective ban on nation states owning clubs. And in principle I'm open to foreign investment. But it seems like a one-way street at the moment. Any future investment from a nation state or a sovereign wealth fund that is clearly linked to the ruling elite should be accompanied by a regeneration plan for the local community, as Abu Dhabi has done for east Manchester.

Then there is accountability. Saudi Arabia gets a PR boost at Newcastle but no one gets to question them. And that's not just an issue for Abu Dhabi and Saudi Arabia. It is also true of the big American owners. They get the trophy, but we never hear from John W. Henry unless it's a pre-recorded apology video.

Joel Glazer has directed policy at Manchester United since 2005 and he has never once done a TV or newspaper interview in the UK or been asked questions about his multiple failures. He has started meeting with fans after the Super League fiasco but who knows how long that will last? The current lack of accountability is completely unacceptable. Whether you're from New York or Newcastle, Saudi Arabia or Southend, if you want to play our game, you should have to stick to our rules. All clubs should have an annual meeting that is open to season-ticket holders and members. The regulator should ensure that the ultimate beneficial owner of the club is there to address the fans and answer questions. If that's a head of state or a reclusive oligarch, so be it. They should be there with their chief executive. In addition, at least once a year, Premier League owners and key executives should have to come before a panel of the regulator, potentially with journalists invited to contribute as well, to answer questions in public. Not just questions about who you're going to sign in the transfer window. If the panel want to ask about Jamal Khashoggi or LGBT rights, that's totally legitimate. There should be no bars. It should be like a House of Commons Select Committee. The panel should have the right to summon EFL owners as well. If you want to enjoy the riches of English football, you should open yourself up to questions. If you don't like that, tough. It's ridiculous that Eddie Howe is the only person at Newcastle we get to ask about human rights or that Thomas Tuchel is left to answer questions on the Roman Abramovich sanctions. Owners need to be forced out of hiding. We can't change government policy in Saudi Arabia but we can scrutinise the owners of Newcastle.

4. Make Football Sustainable

- Limits on owner injections into clubs capped at the highest revenue in that division.

- No leveraged buy outs.
- No debt placed on stadiums unless secured by a personal guarantee with a sufficient convenance strength fromby the owner.
- Real time financial monitoring for all clubs.
- Secure funding in place for all obligations where costs exceed revenues.

Owners injecting money into clubs is part of our game. It always has been. It can create excitement and means clubs can challenge the established order. But it can also encourage some owners to gamble with a community asset in a bid to keep up. I want to eliminate that risk while keeping the ability of Blackburn or Leicester to create history. The rules around owner funding need to be tight. Where costs outstrip natural revenues, owners should provide sufficient guarantees or cash up front on the table for every extra pound spent. The situation Bury got themselves into or that Derby have subsequently found themselves in can't be allowed to happen again. We have a version of these rules in League Two now and I think they're good for football.

Before this book, I used to think that as long as you have the money, you should be able to spend what you like on your own club. However, listening to Steve Parish and Andy Holt, I now think there should be a limit. Otherwise, it can become distorting for the whole league. We don't want to be in a position, like France, where Paris St Germain are so wealthy compared to other clubs that they have won the league eight times in the past ten seasons. That would diminish the Premier League and its value. Our success is rooted in relative competitiveness, which sets us apart from the other major European leagues. I would propose that a formula is found to identify the largest organic turnover of a club in each division and that's the spending limit you can't go above. A plan like this will need more detail than this book can provide. For example, the Premier League's new rules on third-party transactions to ensure fair value for sponsorship deals, ought to prevent a club simply subsidising their turnover with state-sponsored deals. That would have to be part of such an assessment. I'm happy for Manchester United to be challenged. Yet I do understand that should be within football's natural limits.

I would like to think we could also change the way clubs are bought and sold, but for this we will need the government's help to create some carve-outs from the Companies Act so that football and sport is dealt with as a specific kind of business with modified rules. The European Union already recognises this, so it is a well-established principle. There are certain practices, perfectly acceptable in the business world, that are wholly inappropriate in football. I'm thinking specifically of leveraged buyouts and what the Glazers did to Manchester United. The Burnley takeover by ALK Capital shouldn't have been allowed in the form it was done. You shouldn't be able to mortgage a club's assets so that you can afford to buy it. In fact, there was an implicit acknowledgement of this when Roman Abramovich sold Chelsea to Todd Boehly. He put in an anti-Glazer clause, which meant any money borrowed had to be secured against the owners' assets and not the club's. And it's understood that the new owners have committed not to take out dividends for a set period. That should become normal. Jim O'Neill spoke to us about profit with a purpose, the genuine aim of fair capitalism. I've no problems with profit. But capitalism means taking the risk yourself and missing out on dividends when times are tough.

There should also be no debt on a club stadium unless secured by the new revenues you will generate – like at Tottenham – or secured by the owner. There should be no more cases like Derby where you mortgage the ground to live beyond your means. As my dad said, keep the ground and you will always have a club.

As Tracey Crouch's fan-led review said, real-time financial

monitoring is a must. Clubs need to file accounts every three months and the regulator needs the power to step in when it's clear there is an issue, not wait until the club is beyond saving. These are complex issues, but ones I believe that an empowered regulator can deliver.

5. A Fans' Charter for the People's Game
- A seat at the top table within the new independent regulator panel.
- Strong representation within a new modernised FA.
- Power of veto for fans on key issues at clubs.

Empower the fans to have a greater influence on the game. They are perhaps the most important constituent part of football and yet they still lack representation. The FA Council has two fan reps, but there should be representation in the boardroom at the FA, Premier League and EFL. Crucially, there should also be a fan representative as part of the new regulator. Fans' voices should be heard when decisions are being made. It's not healthy to ignore fans. And it doesn't make sense. You couldn't want a more committed and engaged audience. I broadly agree with Tracey Crouch's proposals for golden shares and shadow boards to hold clubs to account. In addition, I think a mandatory annual meeting for fans would help. The Spirit of Shankly idea of changing the articles of association for clubs to protect their heritage deserves further investigation.

The government's response to the fan-led review was to promise that its White Paper would set a minimum standard of fan engagement as a condition of the licence from the regulator. And that if the regulator was not satisfied, they could withdraw a licence. This is a good start. The government was less clear on whether this engagement will be in the form of shadow boards or whether golden shares were viable. This is something we need to keep pressing on. For now, I'll wait and see what is proposed. But fan representation must be more than just a talking shop. It needs to be able to influence the direction of football.

6. Level Up the Women's Game

- A root and branch review of the women's game.
- A fixed percentage of a club's revenue to be invested in the women's team.
- A transition period to access equal facilities to the men's teams.
- Equal exposure on social platforms and channels to the men's teams.
- Mandatory for all professional clubs to have a women's team and facilities.

We have a rich history of women's football in this country. We should be proud of that and celebrate it. And yet it's still a relatively untold story. We were pioneers before the FA ban in 1921, so let's ensure that we are again. The FA's work in this area is exemplary. But as Tracey Crouch's review said, there is now a need for a separate review of the women's game. I would urge the government to commission that as soon as possible. In the meantime, every men's Premier League club should be made to set aside a fixed percentage of its turnover to invest in the women's game. Had men's football not shut it down, women's football could be miles ahead of where it is today. And so there is some more levelling up to be done. Wage equality can't be imposed at club level. The finances don't allow it. But equal access to the best training facilities, to physio and medical care, should be standard at every leading club. Clubs need to start implementing this now and transition to full equality. Likewise social media platforms. They should be integrated so that the women's team gets similar promotion to the men's team and the popularity of the men's social media channels is leveraged to grow the women's team.

Much of this is already being done at the best clubs and Manchester City, Chelsea and Arsenal have been leaders in this space. But there should also be room for clubs such as Doncaster Rovers Belles, who drove the renaissance of the game in the 1970s. We don't want a Women's Super League just to be the preserve of the super clubs. A review will hopefully cut through the issues and provide the foundations for women's football to be world leading in England over the next fifty years.

In the summer of 2022, we witnessed the power and popularity of the women's game and what it can become given its rightful stage. If there were any sceptics left by the end of the summer, then Chloe Kelly's goal and the subsequent celebrations all over England must have felt like a punch in the face. These young women were authentic heroes who truly won over the nation. One hundred and one years after men's football banned the women's game, here they were finally ending our quest for a trophy and doing so in front of record final crowd for any Euros, men's or women's.

We have an extraordinary moment now in England and hopefully one that will reverberate around the UK. This is foundation to build on. Let's seize this opportunity.

7. Football and Society: A Team United

- One united campaign to fight racism and other equality issues.
- Mandatory education on racism and other issues of equality for all stakeholders and participants in the game, which is proactive not reactive.
- Stronger consequence for infractions and a programme of rehabilitation and reintroduction for offenders.
- Removal of pay while suspended for any players or executives within the game if found guilty.
- Football clubs to develop a world-class curriculum to deliver diversity and equality education into schools.

Unite to fight racism. I understand the good intention behind everyone doing their own thing on the fight against racism. But we should all concede it doesn't work. Too many campaigns, too many slogans, too little action. I'd like the game to come together and I think a regulator could help achieve this. One body that everyone can sign up for and one campaign across the game would be much more powerful. I want to see appropriate education at every entry point into the game, whether that's kids' football in the local park or owners and superstar players coming in from abroad. That should be true of other equality issues, such as LGBT rights. Proactive rather than reactive education is the way forward. These are our UK values and you have to sign up to them to be part of the game. And there's no excuse for ignorance. Clubs should be held responsible for their players being educated. Punishments need to be harsher for players found guilty. Three- to six-month bans are a bare minimum and there needs to be a loss of earnings too with a significant monetary consequence. Fans want this, 91 per cent agreeing with this suggestion. But there should be a way back, and rehabilitation is key, if there has been appropriate education and an understanding of the offence. I hope that a regulator can pull these strands together and restore a body like Kick It Out to lead the way. Less is more in this instance. Clubs already do excellent work with their communities but let's build on that to roll out education about equality and inclusion across the country. Let's unite together as a game to influence society for the better, rather than allow ourselves to be moulded by the worsening situation in society around us.

To conclude, there is a lot to be done but we've also come a long way in two years. And we're in a great position. It's pretty certain there will a regulator. That should be the catalyst for change and an opportunity to set the game for the next generation. Eventually, football should be able to look after itself. I hope the regulator will bring the much-needed reform of the FA, so that it becomes a modern and diverse organisation, which represents fans, players, managers, clubs and the grassroots. But one that has the independence and skill when necessary to deal with obstacles and crises that football will always have. An FA properly resourced and empowered, could govern the game. But, for now, that isn't possible. We need a referee to take control and hand the ball back to the people and a new independent regulator is a must. If this book achieves one thing, I would hope that we all recognise the future of our game, which is part of our nation's heritage and history, cannot be controlled by oil-rich nation states or American investment funds. It's our beautiful game.

ACKNOWLEDGEMENTS

This book couldn't have been written without the goodwill of scores of people willing to give up their time to talk to me. Everyone I spoke to longs for the game to be what it can, we're all hoping for something better even when we disagree. There were also those who helped to fix interviews and encouraged on the side-lines. I would especially like to thak Anita Asante, Paul Barber, Joe Blott, David Bernstein, Paul Camillin, Jamie Carragher, David Conn, Tracey Crouch, Christopher M Davidson, Nick Harris, Andy Holt, Chris Hughton, David Jones, Tim Jotischky, Kat Law, Gary Lewin, Kieran Maguire, Kevin Miles, Andy Mitten, Nicholas McGeehan, Gail Newsham, Jim O'Neill, Izzy Parish, Steve Parish, Rick Parry, Tim Peyton, Terry Robinson, Lyle Taylor, Troy Townsend, Faye White. And to my mum and brother. Also, the staff at Bury Library and Amnesty International.

Thanks to Rob Draper for helping me order my thoughts. And to Huw Armstrong, Ciara Mongey and everyone else at Hodder & Stoughton.

Finally, this game has been my life and while there will be many that disagree with the outcomes and conclusions of this book, my intention will always be to try and bring us together as a football family.

READING LIST

Unless otherwise stated, all the quotation in The Conquering Heroes chapter are from *The Bury Times*.

'The Fairer Sex' chapter draws heavily on Gail Newsham's excellent book *In a League of Their Own! The Dick, Kerr Ladies 1917-1965*

Catherine Belton: Putin's People: *How the KGB Took Back Russia and then Took on the West* provide's the background on Roman Abramovich.

'This Is How It Feels To Be City' cites Professor Christopher M Davidson's *After the Sheikhs: The Coming Collapse of the Gulf Monarchies* published by Hurst & Co. Also, David Conn's *Richer Than God; Manchester City, Modern Football and Growing Up* published by Quercus.

The Bury Review, the EFL's independent review of Bury's demise, by Jonathan Taylor is available at

https://www.efl.com/siteassets/image/201920/governance-reviews/bury-review..pdf---adobe-acrobat-pro.pdf

The full report by the United Nations Humans Rights High Commissioner cited in 'Fit and Proper' is available https://www.ohchr.org/en/special-procedures/sr-executions/inquiry-killing-mr-jamal-kashoggi. The declassified CIA report on the murder of Jamal Khashoggi is available at https://www.dni.gov/files/ODNI/documents/assessments/Assessment-Saudi-Gov-Role-in-JK-Death-20210226v2.pdf

The declassified FBI report detailing logistical support provided to two Saudi hijackers in the lead-up to the 9/11 terrorist attacks is available at https://www.dni.gov/files/ODNI/documents/assessments/Assessment-Saudi-Gov-Role-in-JK-Death-20210226v2.pdf *The Club: How The Premier League Became The Richest Most Disruptive Business in Sport* by Joshua Robinson and Jonathan Clegg was invaluable background reading for Cash Machine.

Kieran Maguire is senior teacher in accountancy finance and accounting at Liverpool University and provided stats on the Glazers. Follow him @KieranMaguire on Twitter and listen to his *Price of Football* podcast.

Likewise @SwissRamble provides invaluable and professional information on football finances.

The Fan-Led Review of Football Governance: securing the game's future, written by Tracey Crouch, MP and her panel is essential reading and available on gov.uk websites, as is the *Government Response to the Fan-Led Review of Football Governance.*

Dr Rob Wilson & Dr Daniel Plumley research from Department of Finance at Sheffield Hallam University on parachute payments is cited and worth reading in full.

The View from the Stands:
English football fans' views on key issues

June 2022

PURPOSE UNION

the BRC

the Brand & Reputation Collective and Purpose Union

June 2022

What we did

- We conducted a quantitative online survey of 1,192 football fans in England, aged 18+, who say they are interested in English football and support a club

- The survey was conducted 9 June – 15 June 2022

- The overall margin of error is plus or minus 3 percentage points at the 95% confidence interval

- Totals and or subtotals may differ from the sum of individual percentages, or may not add to 100%, due to rounding

Majorities of fans are "very" or "somewhat" concerned about racism

aimed at players (71%) and the fitness of club owners (68%)

Firstly, how concerned are you about each of the following issues related to English football?
% of fans who say they are concerned or not concerned about each statement

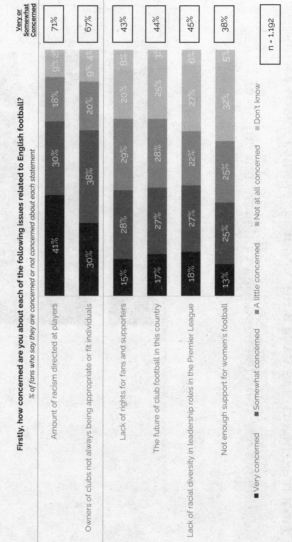

					Very or Somewhat Concerned
Amount of racism directed at players	41%	30%	18%	9% 2%	71%
Owners of clubs not always being appropriate or fit individuals	30%	38%	20%	9% 4%	67%
Lack of rights for fans and supporters	15%	28%	29%	20% 8%	43%
The future of club football in this country	17%	27%	28%	25% 3%	44%
Lack of racial diversity in leadership roles in the Premier League	18%	27%	22%	27% 6%	45%
Not enough support for women's football	13%	25%	25%	32% 5%	38%

■ Very concerned ■ Somewhat concerned ■ A little concerned ■ Not at all concerned ■ Don't know

n = 1,192

Totals and or subtotals may differ from the sum of individual percentages, or may not add to 100% due to rounding

Most have heard at least "a little" about increasing racial diversity in leadership roles and the need for an independent regulator

Those who are most likely to have heard a great deal, some/fair amount or a little about 'Increasing racial diversity in leadership and coaching roles' include:

- Younger fans (18 - 24 years old) (88%)
- Men (80%) more than Women (74%)

And how much you have seen, heard or read about each of following issues related to English football?

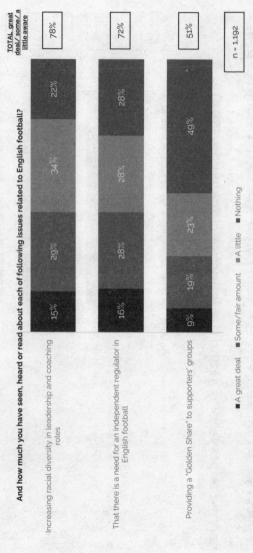

TOTAL great deal/ some/ a little aware

				TOTAL
Increasing racial diversity in leadership and coaching roles	15%	29%	34%	22%	78%
That there is a need for an independent regulator in English football	16%	28%	28%	28%	72%
Providing a "Golden Share" to supporters' groups	9%	19%	23%	49%	51%

n = 1192

■ A great deal ■ Some/fair amount ■ A little ■ Nothing

Two in three (66%) football fans believe that how football in England is run and managed is a problem and needs reform

Fans who are most likely to say how football in England is run and managed **needs reform** include:
- Older fans: Those aged 55- 64 years old (77%) and those aged 65 and older (76%)

Those who are most likely to say how football in England is run and managed is **fine and needs no reform** include:
- Younger fans: Those age 18-24 (33%) and 25-34 (29%)
- Those living in the West Midlands (36%) and London (28%)

Which of the following two views is closer to your own about English football today?

How football in England is run and managed....

- is fine and needs no reform
- is a problem and needs reform
- Don't know

June 2022

n = 1.192

5

Fans are twice as likely to say they would trust an independent regulator than the Premier League to manage English football

Fans most likely to say they trust an independent regulator to safeguard and manage the interests of English football include:
- Older fans: Those aged 55-64 years old (79%) and those aged 65+ and older (76%)

Fans who are most likely to say they trust the Premier League to safeguard and manage the interests of English football include:
- Younger fans: Those aged 18-24 years old (53%) and those aged 25-34 years old (46%)
- Those living in the West Midlands (42%) and London (41%)

Which of the following are you most likely to trust to safeguard and manage the interests of English football?

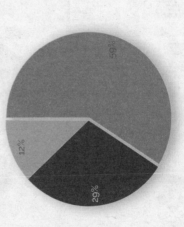

- ■ An independent regulator
- ■ The Premier League
- ■ Don't know

n = 1,192

Half (51%) of football fans in England say the current "Owners and Directors" test provides insufficient protection for English football

Fans who are most likely to say the current "Owners and Directors" test for people to be club owners in this country is **insufficient** include:

- Men (55%) more than Women (43%)
- Those aged 55- 64 years old (62%) and those 65+ years old (58%)
- Social grade ABC1 (56%) more than C2DE (44%)

Which of the following two views is closer to your own about the current "Owners and Directors" test for people to be club owners in this country?

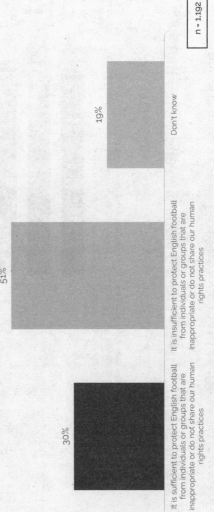

30%	It is sufficient to protect English football from individuals or groups that are inappropriate or do not share our human rights practices
51%	It is insufficient to protect English football from individuals or groups that are inappropriate or do not share our human rights practices
19%	Don't know

n = 1,192

Most fans (85%) agree there should be stronger consequences for engaging in football-related racist behaviour (48% strongly agree)

Women (88%) are more likely than men (83%) to support stronger consequences for engaging in football-related racist behaviour.

Here are some statements about the current situation with English football. Please indicate how much you agree or disagree with each statement:

% of fans who say they agree or disagree with each statement

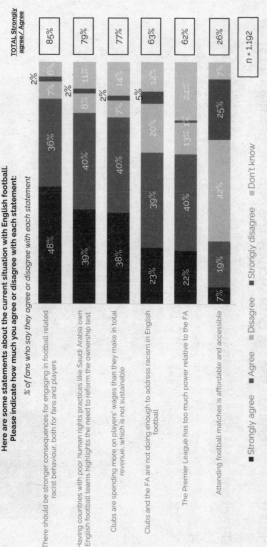

Statement		TOTAL Strongly agree / Agree
There should be stronger consequences for engaging in football related racist behaviour, both for fans and players	48% / 36% / 7% / 6% / 2%	85%
Having countries with poor human rights practices like Saudi Arabia own English football teams highlights the need to reform the ownership test	39% / 40% / 8% / 11% / 2%	79%
Clubs are spending more on players' wages than they make in total revenue, which is not sustainable	38% / 40% / 7% / 14% / 2%	77%
Clubs and the FA are not doing enough to address racism in English football	23% / 39% / 20% / 12% / 5%	63%
The Premier League has too much power relative to the FA	22% / 40% / 13% / 24%	62%
Attending football matches is affordable and accessible	7% / 19% / 42% / 25% / 7%	26%

n = 1,192

■ Strongly agree ■ Agree ■ Disagree ■ Strongly disagree ■ Don't know

Totals and or subtotals may differ from the sum of individual percentages, or may not add to 100% due to rounding

June 2022

8

Half or more strongly agree football-related racist behaviour

should incur bans for fans and bans/removal of earnings for players

Nine In ten strongly agree or agree with both these measures, with nearly as many (88%) saying they agree racist fans and players should have to participate in mandatory education and community service to help them understand the impact of their behaviour.

Here are several possible consequences for engaging in football-related racist behaviour that could be introduced to address racism in English football. Please indicate how much you agree or disagree with each:

% of fans who strongly agree or agree 'there should be stronger consequences for engaging in football-related racist behaviour, both for fans and players'

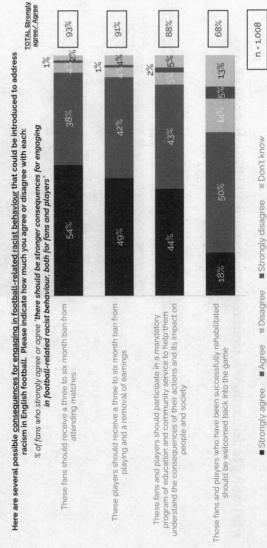

TOTAL Strongly agree / Agree

These fans should receive a three to six month ban from attending matches — 54% / 38% / 4% / 2% / 1% — **93%**

These players should receive a three to six month ban from playing and a removal of earnings — 49% / 42% / 4% / 4% / 1% — **91%**

These fans and players should participate in a mandatory program of education and community service to help them understand the consequences of their actions and its impact on people and society — 44% / 43% / 5% / 5% / 2% — **88%**

Those fans and players who have been successfully rehabilitated should be welcomed back into the game — 18% / 50% / 14% / 5% / 13% — **68%**

n = 1,008

■ Strongly agree   ■ Agree   ■ Disagree   ■ Strongly disagree   ■ Don't know

June 2022

9

Most fans agree that club owners should have to observe human rights (83%) and make a public commitment to UK values (83%)

Seven in ten or more fans also 'strongly agree' or 'agree' that the Pyramid system is vital (75%), fans should have a greater role in how English football is run (73%), and that fans should have to approve major changes in club heritage (72%)

Here are some statements about the future of English football. Please indicate how much you agree or disagree with each statement:

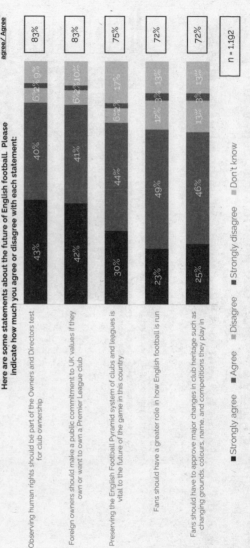

TOTAL Strongly agree/ Agree

Statement		TOTAL
Observing human rights should be part of the Owners and Directors test for club ownership	43% / 40% / 6% 2% 9%	83%
Foreign owners should make a public commitment to UK values if they own or want to own a Premier League club	42% / 41% / 6% 2% 10%	83%
Preserving the English Football Pyramid system of clubs and leagues is vital to the future of the game in this country	30% / 44% / 6% 2% 17%	75%
Fans should have a greater role in how English football is run	23% / 49% / 12% 3% 13%	72%
Fans should have to approve major changes in club heritage such as changing grounds, colours, name, and competitions they play in	25% / 46% / 13% 3% 13%	72%

n = 1,192

■ Strongly agree ■ Agree ■ Disagree ■ Strongly disagree ■ Don't know

10

June 2022

Two in three (67%) fans agree that there is a need to increase racial diversity in leadership and coaching roles in the Premier League

Those most likely to agree there is a need to increase racial diversity in leadership and coaching roles in the Premier League include:
- Women (71%) more than Men (65%)
- Those living in London (75%)

Here are some statements about the future of English football.
Please indicate how much you agree or disagree with each statement:

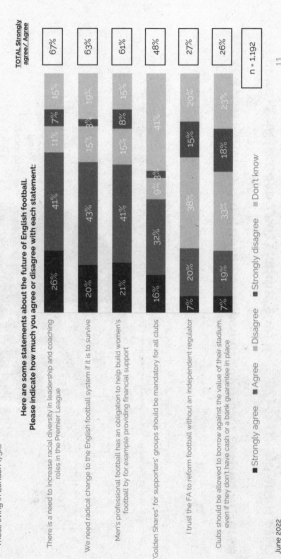

Statement	TOTAL Strongly agree / Agree
There is a need to increase racial diversity in leadership and coaching roles in the Premier League	67%
We need radical change to the English football system if it is to survive	63%
Men's professional football has an obligation to help build women's football by for example providing financial support	61%
'Golden Shares' for supporters' groups should be mandatory for all clubs	48%
I trust the FA to reform football without an independent regulator	27%
Clubs should be allowed to borrow against the value of their stadium, even if they don't have cash or a bank guarantee in place	26%

Legend: ■ Strongly agree ■ Agree ■ Disagree ■ Strongly disagree ■ Don't know

n = 1.192

Over three quarters (78%) of fans support the government creating

an independent regulator to oversee English football

Those who are most likely to **support** the creation of an independent regulator include:

- Men (80%) more than Women (72%)
- Those aged 55-64 (84%) and 65+ (81%)

Even 70% of those who think that how football is run is fine and doesn't need reform support the creation of an independent regulator.

Would you support or oppose the government creating an independent regulator to oversee English football?

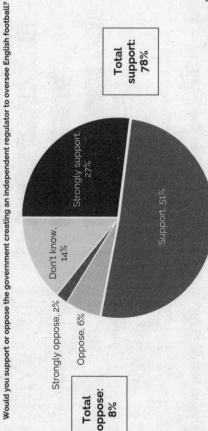

Total support: 78%

Strongly support, 27%

Support, 51%

Don't know, 14%

Strongly oppose, 2%

Oppose, 6%

Total oppose: 8%

n = 1,192

12

June 2022

Two thirds (67%) of fans say there should be a cap on what English clubs can spend on players' wages and transfers

Those who are most likely to **say that clubs should be allowed to spend what they like on players wages** include:

- Men (27%) more than Women (22%)
- Younger fans: Those age 18-24 (38%) and those age 25-34 (33%)
- Those who think that how football is run is fine and doesn't need reform (50%)
- Those who follow a Big Six club (31%)

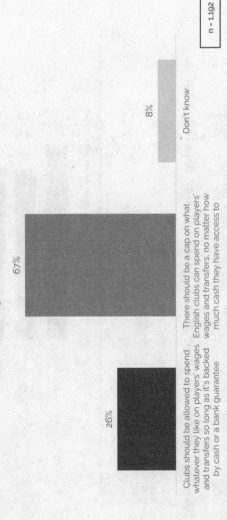

Which of the following two views is closer to your own?

26% — Clubs should be allowed to spend whatever they like on players' wages and transfers so long as it's backed by cash or a bank guarantee

67% — There should be a cap on what English clubs can spend on players' wages and transfers, no matter how much cash they have access to

8% — Don't know

n ~ 1,192

June 2022

13

Those who agree fans need a greater role in how English football is run say the best approach is to have fan reps on club boards

Fans who are most likely to **say the best approach is to have fan representatives on club boards** include:

- Men (68%) more than Women (56%)
- Those 55-64 years old (75%) and those 65+ years old (76%)

Half or more also agree that fans should be able to buy shares in a club (56%) or that there should be a fan board to work with the club board (52%)

Which of the following ways do you think are best to increase the role of fans in overseeing how English football is run?

% of fans who strongly agree or agree "Fans should have a greater role in how English football is run"

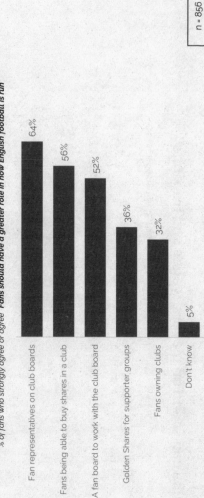

Fan representatives on club boards	64%
Fans being able to buy shares in a club	56%
A fan board to work with the club board	52%
Golden Shares for supporter groups	36%
Fans owning clubs	32%
Don't know	5%

n = 856

14

Multiple responses allowed, total adds to more than 100%

June 2022

Nearly two thirds say they know nothing about UEFA's distribution of broadcasting rights (64%) or The Dick, Kerr's ladies football team (65%)

Younger fans – those aged 18–24 years old and 25–34 years old – are more likely than older fans to be aware of The Dick, Kerr's ladies football team and UEFA's distribution of broadcasting rights.

Overall awareness is greatest for parachute payments for clubs that are regulated, with nearly two in three fans (64%) saying they have heard at least a little about them. However, less than half (43%) report substantive knowledge (i.e. great deal or some awareness).

And how much you have seen, heard or read about each of the following:

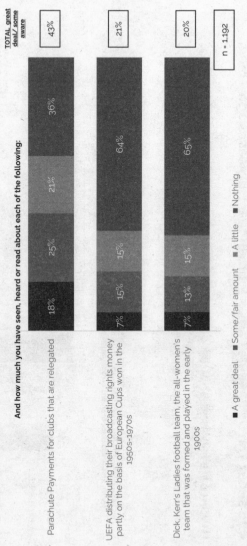

TOTAL great deal/ some aware

	A great deal	Some/fair amount	A little	Nothing	TOTAL
Parachute Payments for clubs that are relegated	18%	25%	21%	36%	43%
UEFA distributing their broadcasting rights money partly on the basis of European Cups won in the 1950s-1970s	7%	15%	15%	64%	21%
Dick, Kerr's Ladies football team, the all-women's team that was formed and played in the early 1900s	7%	13%	15%	65%	20%

n = 1,192

■ A great deal ■ Some/fair amount ■ A little ■ Nothing

June 2022

Info about The Dick, Kerr's Ladies football team increases agreement

that men's football should support women's football financially (+11%)

Fans who are most likely to **say Men's professional football has an obligation to help build women's football** include:

- Women (78%) more than Men (69%)
- Those aged 18-24 (79%)
- Supporters of Big Six clubs (75%)

Impact of information on support for women's football

Now that you've heard this information, please indicate how much you agree or disagree with the following statement:
Men's professional football has an obligation to help build women's football by for example providing financial support'

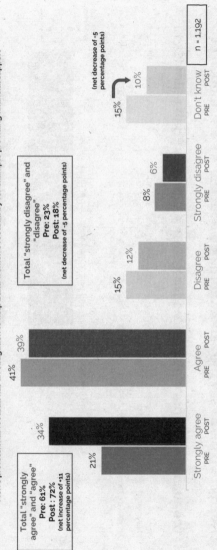

Total "strongly agree" and "agree"
Pre: 61%
Post : 72%
(net increase of +11 percentage points)

Total "strongly disagree" and "disagree"
Pre: 23%
Post: 18%
(net decrease of -5 percentage points)

Strongly agree
PRE   POST
21%   34%

Agree
PRE   POST
41%   39%

Disagree
PRE   POST
15%   12%

Strongly disagree
PRE   POST
8%   6%

Don't know
PRE   POST
15%   10%
(net decrease of -5 percentage points)

n = 1,192

June 2022

'The statement about The Dick, Kerr's Ladies football team used in this question can be found in the appendix

16

Of those fans aware of Parachute Payments, half (53%) say they are fair and should continue compared to 31% who say they are unfair

Those who are most likely to say Parachute Payments are fair and should continue include:

- Younger fans aged 18-24 (71%)
- Fans of Big Six teams (55%) and of Premier League clubs not in the Big Six (58%)

Which of the following views is closer to your own about Parachute Payments, which are funds from broadcasting rights that the Premier League gives to clubs that are relegated?

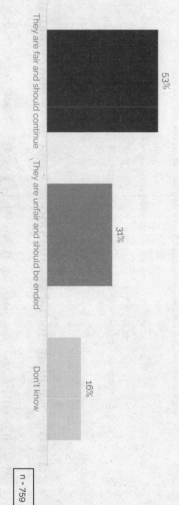

They are fair and should continue	They are unfair and should be ended	Don't know.
53%	31%	16%

n = 759

June 2022

Question only asked of fans who are aware of Parachute Payments for clubs that are relegated

Of those who are aware of Parachute Payments, only three in ten (30%) think they are worth £44m in the first year after relegation

One in five overestimate their value (19% say they are worth £75m), while another one in five (20%) underestimate their value. Another 30% say they don't know what the payments are worth.

Fans who are most likely to correctly **say Parachute Payments are worth £44m in the first year after relegation** include:

- Those 18-24 years old (47%)
- Those who think football does not need reform (37% vs. those who think football needs reform (29%)

Which of the following amounts do you think is how much Parachute Payments are worth in the first year to a club that is relegated?

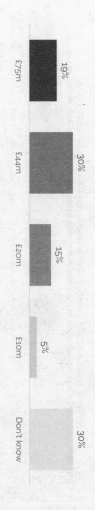

19%	30%	15%	5%	30%
£75m	£44m	£20m	£10m	Don't know

Question only asked of fans who are aware of Parachute Payments for clubs that are relegated

n = 759

Once aware of how much Parachute Payments are worth to clubs, overall support amongst football fans drops to less than half (48%)

As you may know, in the first year that a club is relegated, they get £44 million from the broadcasting rights that the Premier League receives. Now that you know this, which view is closer to your own?

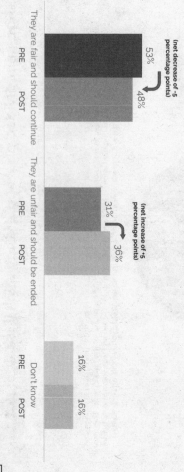

(net decrease of -5 percentage points)

53%
PRE

48%
POST

(net increase of +5 percentage points)

31%
PRE

36%
POST

16%
PRE

16%
POST

They are fair and should continue   They are unfair and should be ended   Don't know

Question only asked of fans who are aware of Parachute Payments for clubs that are relegated

n = 759

Football fans who are aware of UEFA's money distribution arrangement divided on whether they think it is fair or not

Fans who are most likely to **say UEFA's money distribution arrangement is very or somewhat fair** include:

- Those aged 18-24 years old (72%) and aged 25-34 (67%)
- Those in London (65%), the South East (63%) and the West Midlands (62%)
- Support a Big Six club (55%) rather than a non-Big Six PL club (37%)

Finally, did you know that UEFA distribute their broadcasting rights money partly on the basis of European Cups won in the 1950s-1970s. They do this because those clubs helped build the profile of the tournament. This means that clubs that are past tournament winners get more money than clubs that haven't won tournaments before. Previous winners could get €40m while newcomers could get €15m. Would you say this arrangement is:

TOTAL not so/ not at all fair: 43%

TOTAL very/ somewhat fair: 50%

Don't know: 6%

Not fair at all: 18%

Very fair: 13%

Not so fair: 26%

Somewhat fair: 37%

Asked of respondents who have heard of UEFA distributing their broadcasting rights money partly on the basis of European Cups won in the 1950s-1970s

n = 432

Gender and Age

% who say

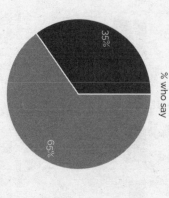

Are you ... ?

- Male
- Female

Which of the following categories includes
your age?

% who say

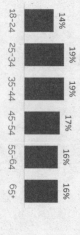

18-24	25-34	35-44	45-54	55-64	65+
14%	19%	19%	17%	16%	16%

n = 1,192

Region

% who say

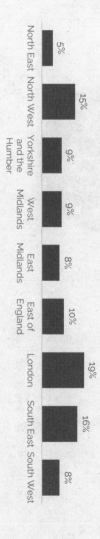

North East — 5%

North West — 15%

Yorkshire and the Humber — 9%

West Midlands — 9%

East Midlands — 8%

East of England — 10%

London — 19%

South East — 16%

South West — 8%

n = 1,192

Social Grade

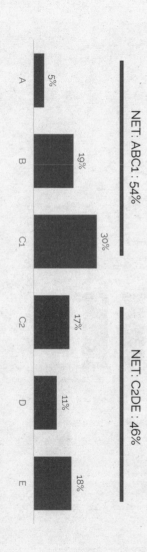

NET: ABC1 : 54%

NET: C2DE : 46%

A — 5%
B — 19%
C1 — 30%
C2 — 17%
D — 11%
E — 18%

n = 1,192

Interest in English football

n = 1192

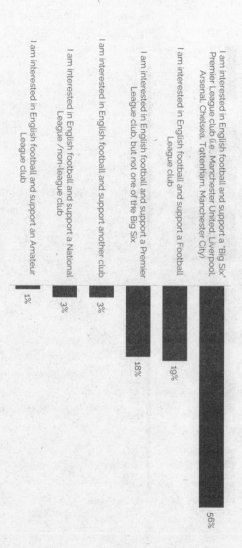

Category	Percentage
I am interested in English football and support a "Big Six" Premier League club (i.e. Manchester United, Liverpool, Arsenal, Chelsea, Tottenham, Manchester City)	56%
I am interested in English football and support a Football League club	19%
I am interested in English football and support a Premier League club, but not one of the Big Six	18%
I am interested in English football and support another club	3%
I am interested in English football and support a National League /non-league club	3%
I am interested in English football and support an Amateur League club	1%